UNDERSTANDING PHOTOSYNTHESIS

UNDERSTANDING PHOTOSYNTHESIS

By

Dr. Pooja

Deptt. of Botany
R.C.C. College
Ghaziabad (U.P.)
(India)

DPH

DISCOVERY PUBLISHING HOUSE PVT. LTD.
INDIA

Published by:
Namit Wasan

DISCOVERY PUBLISHING HOUSE PVT. LTD.
4383/4B, Ansari Road, Darya Ganj
New Delhi-110 002 (India)
Phone : +91-11-23279245; 23253475; 43596065
E-mail : discoverybooksindia@gmail.com
discoverypublishinghouse@gmail.com
namitwasan9@gmail.com
web : www.discoverypublishinggroup.com

First Edition: **2011**

ISBN: 978-81-8356-862-3

Understanding Photosynthesis

Preface

The present title *"Understanding Photosynthesis"* provides a structured approach to learning by covering all the important topics in a uniform, systematic format. The book has been comprehensively designed incorporating recent advances in this fast moving field. It is written to provide accessible information on fungi in compact form for undergraduate students in biology and related life sciences. It will be useful for both beginning students and those who are more advanced. In addition, busy lecturers who require a quick reference compendium will find it useful, particularly for tutional planning. Simple, yet hopefully clear figures and tables are provided throughout the book.

The over-riding goal of this book, and indeed of the whole *Understanding series,* is to present the essential information concering microbiology in a compact, readily accessible form which leads itself to student learning and revision. The convergence of various approaches has generated a rich panorama of detail, the significance of which we are still attempting to unraval. The present text has been written as an introduction to this rapidly growing field.

To make the work more comprehensive and informative, the author has consulted many authoritative books, research journals, abstracts, monographs etc., so there can be no claim to originality except in the manner of treatment.

The author expresses his thanks to his friends and colleagues whose continue inspirations have initiated him to bring out this book.

The author expresses his gratitude to Mr. Wasan and staff of M/s Discovery Publishing House Pvt. Ltd. for their whole hearted co-operation in the publication of this book.

In the mean time, the author will remain sincerely responsible for any shortcomings of the book and be grateful to the readers for their suggestions and constructive criticism for the continuous betterment of the book. He takes this opportunity to appeal to the readers to send their suggestions straightaway to his Publisher.

Author

CONTENTS

Chapter 1

INTRODUCTION

Of all aspects of plant metabolism, photosynthesis shows the most prominent variation under the dictates of the immediate environment. This sensitivity, and the dominance of the process in the synthetic economy of nature, has stimulated its study under more or less natural conditions during the past forty years.

Nevertheless, a majority of *physiologists* have regarded with disfavour the unstandardised and arbitrary limitations of "natural conditions"; such *experimental* conditions are generally not easily attained, even in field experiments. There appears to be no *comprehensive* and *coherent* organisation of the data now available.

The principal difficulties lie in the incomplete integration of laboratory and field observations, work on terrestrial and aquatic *vegetation*, and measurements of photosynthesis and *growth* yields. Studies on land plants developed rapidly in 1918 and the years immediately following, particularly those by BoysenJensen Henrici Lundegardh, and Stalfelt.

They benefited especially from the kinetic foundations laid by Blackman and his school in earlier decades and by Willstatter and Stoll in 1918. The unique value of *aquatic plants*, particularly zaicellular algae, was less readily appreciated for illustrating photosynthetic processes in nature than for the *laboratory* work on the *photosynthetic mechanism* that followed the pioneer experiments of Warburg. The use of these organisms developed from field experiments by marine and freshwater biologists in the 1920's and has recently shown a spectacular expansion in connection with measurements of the photosynthetic productivity of *plankton*.

The peculiar problems presented by photosynthesis in nature chiefly concern the kinetics of the process. The photosynthetic rates in any *vegetation* cover are controlled by a considerable number of internal and external factors and by *interactions* between these factors and apparently order little prospect for a unified treatment

However, light, as the energy source, can be regarded as the master factor, and shows more remarkable variation than any other environmental factor.

Much behaviour can be interpreted in relation to the rateintensity characteristic of photosynthesis, its modification in response to other factors, and its expression in the variation in space and time of photosynthetic rates under natural conditions.

This characteristic also expresses the two universal limitations of the efficiency of energy utilisation : the maximum quantum yield at low *intensities*, and *light-saturation* at high intensities.

It consequently provides a starting-point for comparing observed with potential yields. The conversion of net photosynthesis to gross photosynthesis by correcting for respiration losses is often uncertain, partly because of possible changes in respiration during illumination therefore, many field measurements of photosynthesis are expressed as net rates only.

Where possible, however, this discussion will be based upon the probable gross photosynthesis, with the consequences of respiration introduced separately.

SOURCES OF INFORMATION

In most field work small samples of plant material have

been used, exposed in some form of transparent chamber, cuvette, or bottle. Here the photosynthetic uptake of carbon dioxide or liberation of oxygen could be measured either directly or following the absorption of residual carbon dioxide from an air-stream in *alkali* solution.

Changes due to carbon dioxide uptake by both terrestrial and aquatic plants have been estimated by differences in titration, electrical *conductivity*, 1H, and-in recent years-by fixation of *radiocarbon* (^{14}C). Infrared absorption analysis, which enables the sensitive and continuous recording of carbon dioxide in air, has been much exploited recently in work on land plants.

The evolution of oxygen is readily measured only with aquatic plants, for which he Winkler method has been widely used. A brief survey of methods employed for terrestrial plants is given by Frenzel end for aquatic plants by Lund and Tailing.

Work with entire terrestrial plants or stands usually requires larger and more elaborate plant chambers; examples are described by Boysenensen Heinicke and Childers and Thomas and Hill. Any enclosure involves a danger of the development of special conditions of the *Kuvettenklima*, particularly by overheating in it and reduced mixing in water.

Various tests of these effects, and some suggested remedies such as improved circulation or cooling jackets, have been described.

These difficulties are absent, but others-especially those attributable to translocation are present in work based on the measurement of testlates formed by leaves. Field results generally fall in two main groups that are overned by the differing opportunities for exposures between terrestrial and aquatic vegetation.

With the former, the diurnal ariation of photosynthetic rate has been studied intensively y successions of short exposures, but the vertical variation of rtes in the leaf canopy is rarely investigated. For aquatic ants the variation of rate with depth has been the centre of study, with diurnal changes often obscured in long exposures besides these complementary deficiencies, the data often permit my qualitative, or semi-quantitative correlations to be made between the variation of photosynthetic rate and the more important environmental variables such as light intensity temperature, and carbon dioxide supply.

Advantages offered by a recourse to laboratory exposures are here obvious. In the first instance, such experiments allow the comparison of some photosynthetic indices using plant samples collected in different situations.

Examples are provided by studies of the variation of *photosynthetic* capacity with latitude or season and of differentiation between "*sun*" and "*shade*" material.

The application of such measurements to a reconstruction of photosynthetic activity in nature requires more extensive sampling and measurement of environmental variables than is usually made; direct comparisons of laboratory and field exposures (e.g.,) are rarely attempted.

This "*synthetic*" approach to the estimation of photosynthetic activity under natural conditions was most strikingly developed by Boysen-Jensen and his associates. Their contributions are among the most stimulating to the subject, although some oversimplification was inevitable and was criticized by others.

Some attempts have been made to avoid the limitations of small enclosed samples by estimating the total photosynthesis of a plant community from the diurnal changes produced in the gaseous composition of the ambient medium. For small water bodies the changes are often confined in horizontal and vertical directions and are relatively accessible for study.

Measurements for a representative water column of dissolved oxygen and carbon dioxide have been used; the chief uncertainties arise from the variable exchange between water and atmosphere. The diurnal changes of atmospheric composition produced by land vegetation are more susceptible to turbulent mixing and dissipation, but in favourable weather conditions can follow a regular course and affect an air-column of considerable height.

Their use in estimating photosynthetic fixation of carbon dioxide is discussed by Huber. Lastly, the carbon increase indicated by plant growth can be regarded as an integration of net photosynthesis with time.

However, there are few quantitative comparisons with gasometric data, although such are invited by one particularly successful technique of growth analysis.

POTENTIAL AND ACTUAL YIELDS

The simplest model of a photosynthetic cover of vegetat would be provided by an uniform algal suspension, absorbing all incident light and operating at the maximum quantum yield of photosynthesis.

In illustration one may assume an average of 0. 1 molecules oxygen per quantum for the latter corresponding to an average efficiency of solar energy utilisation in the spectral region of 400 to 700 mμ, of about 22 per cent.

The photosynthetically available energy in this spectral region normally accounts for a fraction, close to 0.46, of the total energy received. Consequently, a radiation total of 600 cal./ cm^2 (horizontal surface), common on very sunny days at many latitudes, would lead to a photosynthetic production of carbohydrate that was equivalent to 65 g. C/ $m.^2$ per day.

This value is a measure of the gross activity of an ideally efficient vegetation cover under conditions of radiation a little below the maximum experienced on the earth. With it, the yields of less efficient models of vegetation, as well as yields actually observed, can be usefully compared.

Two other model situations, readily visualised, may be founded on the experience of photosynthetic rates measured per unit leaf area. At lower light intensities, in which the rates increase linearly with increasing intensity, increases of 1.5 to 2.0 mg. CO_2/100 cm.^{2} per hr. in 1 kilolux increments of intensity are often observed. If a daily energy total of 600 cal./cm^2 [approximately 770 kilolux-hours] were entirely utilised in this way, in a completely absorbing leaf cover, a fixation of 31 to 42 g. C/m.^{2} per day would result.

This figure is again an upper limit of yield, as light-saturation of photosynthesis is likely to be reached during a considerable part of the supposed sunny day. One method for estimating its effects is proposed by de Wit.

Photosynthetic rates of healthy leaves at light- saturation commonly lie between 10 and 25 mg. CO_2/100 cm.^{2} per hr. in air not enriched with CO_2. If these persist during a 12-hour day with a uniform and uninter rupted vegetation cover that is one leaf in thickness, the corresponding fixation will be 3.3 to 0.2 g C/m.^{2} per day.

Values of the actual yields of vegetation can be based upon measurements for short periods (e.g., one or several days) or :h longer times (e.g., a growing season, or a year). It was noticed long ago in Europe e.g., Mayer that the annual dry weigbt yields of many dense tree and crop stands were of remarkably similar magnitude, usually 1000 to 10,000 kg./hectare.

Later experience has generally confirmed this magnitude, but has also indicated some appreciably higher yields (15,000 to 35,000 kg./hectare). If the total dry weight conmetains an average carbon content of 40 per cent (values compomonly lie between 30 and 50 per cent), the higher range quoted above corresponds to average net fixation rates of 1.6 to 3.8 g. C/m.^{2} per day in a maximum growing season of 365 days.

Owing to respiration and other losses, the corresponding gross photosynthesis is often likely to be 50 to 100 per cent higher e.g., Heinicke' and Childers Moller *et al.* The gross photosynthetic yields of dense natural populations of planktonic algae, measured by gas exchange during short periods, reach values of 3 to 4 g. C/m.^{2} per day.

These yields are clearly far below those permitted by

the maximum quantum yield of photosynthesis. The gap is equally evident in numerous other comparisons based upon percentage energy conversion over long periods.

However, recent work with both algae and terrestrial plants has shown that, in short periods under favourable field conditions, the gap between actual and maximum potential yields can be considerably reduced.

Improved growth yields in algal mass cultures under natural illumination can represent an overall energy conversion (spectral region 400 to 700 mμ) of around 6 per cent and a net carbon fixation of approximately 5 to 10 g./m.^{2} per day; and the maximum daily yields of some crops.

The preceding estimates of yields in model situations suggest that much of the difference between actual and potenmetial values originates from light-saturation of photosynthesis under natural conditions. It is also indicated by several analyses of actual yields. More specific expressions of this effect are discussed below.

THE EXPRESSION OF LIGHT-SATURATION UNDER NATURAL CONDITIONS

Rate-intensity curves of photosynthesis almost universally show a transition between a linear relation of rate and light intensity when the latter is low, and a maximum rate which ally persists over a considerable range of higher *intensities* is transition to light-saturation is often gradual, especially optically dense material but can be most precisely indicated the intensity (I_k) at which a continuation of the initial dient (θ) would reach the *lightposaturated* rate (*Pm_{ax}*).

The more common visual estimates of the intensity at which lightduration occurs are generally about twice this I_k value, The index also has the advantage of linking *Pmaz* and θ characteristics by the simple relation Pma_x=θ. I_k, and can be reintereted in terms of other mathematical formulations of the e-intensity characteristic.

A division of I_k by the ratio :ween Pm_{ax} and respiration rate (R) (i.e., Pm_{ax}/R, related to "*economic coefficient*" and "*balance quotient*" of many ropean authors), yields the value of the compensation density if this falls within the initial linear region of the rate-density characte-ristic.

The variation of I_k can be deduced from its two determinants, *Pmaa* and θ. The former is the most variable, and accounts for most of the changes in I_k. Illustrative examples provided by the sensitivity of Pm_{ax} and I_k to temperature distomatal aperture the depression of *Pmax* being associated the reduced I_k values.

It is therefore dangerous to interpret isolation the variable onset of light-saturation, as is often one in the description of supposed heliophilic or ombrophilic characteristics.

Thus Boysen-Jensen and Boysen-Jensen and uller pointed out the frequent similarity of the initial gradient (θ) in sun and shade examples of different species and in Ives of the some species: here saturation at low light intensities in the shade forms was largely imposed by correspoo-ndingly low rates at light-saturation, assessed per unit area leaf or thallus. Measurements of photosynthetic rates in the field express e consequences of light-saturation in several ways.

It is usually evident in diurnal curves of photosynthesis based upon call plant samples and in rate-intensity curves calculated there in Another illustration is given by comparative measurements of photosynthesis below artificial or natural light screens of different densities.

A pronounced light-limitation of photosynthesis is often shown only with daypolight factors (the fractional or percentage illumination relative to full day-light) of <30 per cent; such factors are often called "*tight intensities*," but represent much more complex light conditions in varying natural illumination. In the most interesting situation of this kind, best illustrated by work with planktonic algae, the light screen is provided by varying depths in the plant community under study.

Light-saturation can then be shown in a depth zone with maximum photosynthetic rates, passing below into a near-exponential decline of rates with increasing depth, and often ending above in a superficial zone with depressed rates associated with strong illumination.

Such depth-profiles can be related to basic photosynthetic character-istics by analysis, and to the overall rate under unit area of cover by integration. Thus they afford a means of connecting the integrated yields per unit area with basic photosynthetic characteristics.

The maximum rates possible in these profiles, some special problems linked with their upper and lower regions, the thickness or density of the plant cover through which they extend, their integration in relation to depth and time, and comparison with an alternative approach of growth analysis are discussed below.

VARIATION OF PHOTOSYNTHEIC RATES AT LIGHT-SATURATION

Photosynthetic rates measured at (or near) light-saturation can be used to compare the absolute capacities of plant material differing in type and origin, and to illustrate the effects of factors with ecological significance. *Ecological* consequences can be anticipated for the wellknown increase of light-saturated rates with temperature, depression and *inhibition* at very high and low *temperatures*, *sensitivity* to previous thermal history and the effects of the temperature-*dependence* of respiration rate upon net *photosynthesis*.

The abundant records of daily photosynthesis by land plants seldom indicate any strong positive influence of diurnal temperature change. *Demonstration* of such influence is also hindered by the problems of measuring true leaf temperatures and allowing for over-beating effects in small embers.

These difficulties are much reduced with water plants, for which *Gessner* describes some *probable* effects of *diurnal* temperature change. Diurnal changes of temperature usually much greater in terrestrial than aquatic environments.

In the former, high leaf temperatures, especially in afternoon, are often accompanied by depressed rates of photosynthesis. Besides the direct depression of photosynthetic rates at high temperatures several indirect consequences of temperature, affecting water deficit and respiration rate, can be involved.

Some pronounced examples of the diurnal or seasonal -depression of net photosynthesis, which could be related to the rise of respiration rate in warmer conditions, are recorded for desert plants for various mosses and lichens and for conifers.

In the algae, laboratory studies of some thermophilic strains of *Anacystis* and *Chlorella show* the utilization of high temperatures for achieving remarkably large rates of photosynthesis and growth and noticeably high rates may also be (found in tropical freshwater plankton under field conditions.

The many rates recorded for phytoplankton from other regions, assessed per unit chlorophyll content, are usually in the range ,of 3 to 15 mg. O_2/mg. hr. (or its equivalent) at light-saturation Tropical examples of terrestrial plants studied do not appear to show particularly high photosynthetic rates at light saturation.

The effects of low temperatures upon the photosynthetic activity of land plants in nature have been much investigated, particularly in relation to the performance of evergreen plants in winter. There is general agreement that significant, if reduced, photosynthesis can occur at air temperatures below 0°C.

Tranquillini describes development of the photosynthetic capacity of leaves of *Pinus cembra* still covered in alpine snow. The limitation of photosynthetic rates in nature by the carbon dioxide supply is generally agreed to be most pronoun wed in terrestrial habitats, where the *atmospheric concentration* of carbon dioxide is low and averages about 0.03 per went -or 0.59 mg./1. near sea level.

Deviations from the mean have been studied extensively. The physiological significance of the most regular form of *variation*, the decrease with altitude, is little understood. Despite the low absolute—though not relative-carbon dioxide concentrations at high altitudes, there are recurrent reports of unusually high photoposynthetic rates by alpine plants in nature. Daily changes of -concentration are also very common in and near vegetation and often are measured in rewords of the diurnal course of photosynthesis.

However, a pronounced correlation between concentrations and rates is rarely evident and the total daily variation of concentration is usually not large, though an air -column of considerable thickness may be involved.

High concentrations under a canopy near the soil have been supposed to offset the less favourable light conditions there, but direct proof is difficult and in some cases the evolution and accumulation of carbon dioxide was probably overestimated.

Wind movements have an obvious importance for such distribution patterns, and there are some quantitative data for the effects of low velocities on the supply of carbon dioxide to photosynthesizing surfaces. The stomatal control of carbon dioxide supply has been much discussed in relation to midday or afternoon depression of photosynthesis.

Variation in stomatal aperture probably also accounts for some differences in the photosynthetic activity of leaves at different levels in vegetation and possibly for some seasonal differences. There are fewer data for aquatic plants on the relation between carbon dioxide supply and photosynthetic rates in nature.

The limitations of diffusion to massive plant organs in water are well known, so that water currents and turbulence are likely to be of considerable ecological significance. Such indications are generally lacking for the dilute natural suspensions of planktoniw algae with a much greater surface to volume ratio.

The photosynthetic removal of carbon dioxide from the natural carbonate-bicarbonate buffer system is reflected in a rise in pH. Many diurnal examples have been described e.g., and some were used for the estimation of daily photosynthetic productivity.

However, a severe limitation of photosynthesis by carbon dioxide depletion is only likely at pH values higher than are commonly found. A probable example for freshwater plankton algae is described by Steemann Nielsen.

Some species, such as *Arthrospira platensis* show a remarkably dense development and active photosynthesis in very alkaline waters with pH exceeding 10.5. There is a considerable amount of evidence for the utilization of bicarbonate as carbon dioxide source by many aquatic plants.

Seasonal changes of photosynthetic capacity, which reflect the previous history of the plant material, have been described from both field exposures and from standardised laboratory measurements combined with periodic sampling of vegetation.

The first frosts of winter lead to a sharp fall in the maximum photosynthetic rates of many land plants. In evergreens relatively low photosynthetic capacities are usually found in the winter period although recovery may occur in a few days in warmer conditions.

The variation of photosynthetic activity with age of individual leaves is also a source of seasonal variation. *Seasonal rains* in hot dry regions can produce a remarkable rise in photosynthetic rates although-as in tidally exposed seaweeds the dry phase need not represent a "*resting season*" for photosynthesis.

A diurnal depression of photosynthetic capacity has been very commonly found for land plants, and is also recorded: for aquatic macrophytes. In recent years examples have been described for marine and freshwater phytoplankton, with maximum capacities usually reported near dawn and minimum near sunset.

This daily decline may be connected with the photoinhibition often-found in short exposures near the water surface; Shimada gives evidence for parallel changes in chlorophyll-a content. Behaviour in terrestrial plants is more varied, often with slight to large depressions near midday, persisting in some examples throughout the afternoon.

The occurrence of these patterns in the same species at different alotades is described by Zatensky. No single explanation can fit all the examples described; there is evidence for the effects of stomatal control [e.g., Nutman] the direct inhibition of photosynthesis at high temperatures and light intensities [cf. Stalfelt], accumulation of assimilates [e.g., Guttenberg and Bubr Kurzanov water deficit and for net assimilation-increased respiration rates at higher temperatures.

As almost all the data are derived from diurnal exposures in natural illumination, it is difficult to separate the effects of depressed rates at light-saturation (attributable to the previous history of the material) from the unfavourable influence of the immediate environment.

Kostychev and his co-workers stressed the importance of internal factors in determining large diurnal fluctuations of photoposynthetic rate, but these views were not supported by much other work. Several comparisons have been made of the maximum photosynthetic rates shown by plants from various terrestrial habitats or climatic zones.

The first field survey of this type on a large scale was undertaken by Kostychev and his associates. The high rates described for various alpine plants and the comparatively modest rates for some tropical plants have already been mentioned.

It appears that high rates of photosynthesis are often

achieved in apparently unfavourable habitats with a short growing season the brevity of which is thereby partly compensated; there are examples of this for alpine, arctic and desert plants.

Continuous photosynthesis under arctic summer conditions is describe by Kostychev *et al.* and Kisliakova considered that the variation of photosynthetic capacities of species in continental climates, as in Central Asia, was greater than in the floras of more oceanic or tropical climates.

Succulent halophytes do not appear to show marked peculiarities of gross photosynthetic behaviour, although rates expressed on a fresh weight basis are naturally low and the ratio of rates of respiration to photosynthesis on a unit area basis may be unusually high.

Work on one halophyte, *Aster tripolium* provides one of the few clear examples of different photosynthetic responses between ecologically distinct forms of the same species.

SOME LIMITATIONS OF PHOTOSYNTHESIS IN EXPOSED AND SHADED SITUATIONS

These limitations are shown most diagrammatically in many of the depthprofiles of photosynthetic activity reported for planktonic algae, and have been noted briefly. The depression: of photosynthetic rates near the water surface is common at light intensities exceeding 100 kiloerg (400 to 700 mμ)/cm.2 per sec. and a depth corresponding to 1 per cent of the surface intensity is usually taken as the lower limit of the zone in which appreciable photosynthesis can occur.

The overall= significance of the surface depression is very uncertain in relation to algal populations circulating over a greater depth range; it may affect subsequent rates of photosynthesis at light-saturation. There is also some evidence for a damaging influence of radiation, such as the ultra-violet, rapidly absorbed by the water.

The reduced photosynthesis often shown near the water

surface, when the algae were sampled from the depths at which they were later exposed may often be caused by decreased population density rather than specific rates of photosynthesis.

The decline of photosynthetic rate at greater depths reflects the exponential decline of light intensity. It bears no constant relation to the relative or percentage light values, but is also determined by the logarithmic interval between the surface light intensity (I.) and the intensity that measures the onset of light-saturation (Ik).

The greater this interval, the deeper the depth-profiles are likely to extend. This source of variation is dwarfed, however, by the enormous range of light penetration in natural waters which leads to a, variation of photosynthetic zones from 100 m. or more in the clearer oceans to 1 m. or less in highly coloured and turbid waters.

The comparative photosynthetic rates of aquatic macrobytes at different depths have been studied less, but similar restrictions at shallow and great depths are known in fresh aters and in the sea. Attached algae and mosses have been found growing at depths which probably correspond to about per cent or less of the effective surface radiation although;w adequate measurements of light penetration are available.

The significance here of adaptation to the colour or intensity of light has been much discussed. The light field is usually more heterogeneous in a terrestrial habitat than under water, and the consequences of a vertical gradient for photosynthesis are less easily demonstrated.

Measurements of such gradients are discussed by different scientists but most light data apply to a single stratum in the plant cover, such as a forest floor. As under water, the 1 per cent light level often marks the lower limit of appreciable photosynthetic activity, and values of this order are common at the soil surface beneath dense vegetation.

The light level is also likely to represent the region of

the compensation point during short exposures, as intensities of 20 to 80 kilolux are typical of average daily illumination with 0.2 to 0.8 kilolux for the compensation intensity. Some extreme shade plants can grow at lower relative intensities, some measured as below 0. 1 per cent.

Biebl describes a particularly interesting example for the moss *Mnium serratum* inhabiting rock-cavities, where the deepest shade tolerated was given as 0.024 per cent, with a midday maximum of light intensity at about 26 lux.

On exposure to full sunlight, death occurred within a few hours. Under a vegetation cover the assessment of the effective light climate is rendered more difficult by spectral modifications due to the leaf canopy the short-period fluctuations due to sun-flecks and long-period changes connected with leaf development and fall.

Botanists studied in detail the depression of photosynthetic activity that followed development of the tree canopy. Some species, such as *Anemone nemorosa* showed a change from a positive to a persistent negative balance of net photosynthesis, and in others e.g., the positive balance was regained after a shift in the compensation point. Various factors that can reduce the light-saturated photosynthetic capacity are often most pronounced at the upper exposed level of a vegetation cover.

A detailed exploration of the distribution of photosynthetic activity in the tree-crowns of *Picea excelsa* and *Fagus sylvatica* was made by Pisek and Tranquillini. Here reduced photosynthesis could be found associated with water deficit and stomatal closure in exposed shoots subjected to greater insolation.

Photosynthetic activity extended most deeply on the more illuminated side, particularly at low solar elevations. Earlier, Filzer showed differences of photosynthesis between north and south aspects of trees that were connected particularly with light intensity, and others between east and west aspects with diurnal timing.

The significance to photosynthesis of the angular distribution of light has been little studied in either aquatic or terrestrial habitats, although the ecological application of photometers recording spherical illumination have been described for both habitat types.

Stocker has emphasized the probable importance for photosynthesis of the diffused reflection by leaves in some tropical vegetation. The differentiation of photosynthetic and other characteristics between plant individuals, or their parts, in exposed and shaded situations is very common, but there is less agreement on its adaptive significance. "*Shade plants*" and "*shade leaves*" are discussed by Boysen-Jensen and Lundegardh.

They often show relatively low rates of respiration and maximum photosynthesis, with light-saturation and the compensation point found at low intensities. The last two features have elicited the most comment, but can usually be interpreted in terms of the first two in *conjunction* with a less variable initial gradient of the photosynthesis-intensity curve.

Examples of woodland plants have been particularly studied in this connection. The differentiation between sun and shade leaves on the same plant is most fully described for the beech. *Fagus sylvatica.* Differentiation between species was well illustrated in a survey of eight "sun" and five "shade" plants by Bohning and Burnside although the authors emphasized that the ecological significance is not simple, except in habitats with very low light intensities.

The differentiation of "*sun*" and "*shade*" *characteristics* of photosynthesis has been described recently in relation to depth in *phytoplankton communities* the samples of deeper origin showed light saturation at lower intensities and a greater susceptibility to photo-inhibition at higher intensities.

Ontogenetic adaptation or lability in relation to light ntensity, leading to a differentiation of "sun" and "shade" characteristics, is known for both algae and for higher errestrial plants. These modifications were studied by

Wassink *et. al.* in leaves of *Acer pseudoplatanus* that were exposed to various intensities of artificial illumination and fractions of full natural illumination.

Changes in the two series were qualitatively similar, with an increase in the light-saturated rate of photosynthesis and the onset of light-saturation with rising light intensity during adaptation, and a corresponding decrease in the chlorophyll content per unit area.

Ontogenetic differentiation of photosynthetic characteristics has also been described by Burnside and Bohning and by Bordeau and Laverick for several species of conifer seedlings. The latter emphasize that exceptions to the typical differentiation of "sun" and "shade" behaviour occur. Shade leaves usually show a high chlorophyll content per unit weight, thoughowing to their frequent thinness—not always per unit area.

THE DENSITY OF PHOTOSYNTHETIC COVER IN NATURE

The density of photosynthetic material in the unit area of a natural habitat is an essential link between data on the photosynthetic behaviour of plant samples and the overall photosynthesis of the plant cover.

However, systematic and comparative measurements in relation to photosynthesis under natural conditions are comparatively few. In some respects the simplest situation is found in natural populations of planktonic algae, whose chlorophyll content (particularly chlorophyll-a) has been much studied in recent years.

Most measurements relate to the content per unit volume of water; and although any limits are arbitrary, values of < 1 mg./m.^{3} are common in the unproductive open oceans I to 30 mg./m.^{3} in moderately productive waters and > 30 mg./m.^{3} in very productive regions.

A few calculations have been made of the content below unit area in a complete water column. Gessner estimated that in productive waters the chlorophyll content could reach values of about 1 g./m.^{2}, similar to those found in closed terrestrial communities.

The more relevant content, however, is that of the illuminated part of the water column (euphotic zone) in which appreciable photosynthesis is possible. The maximum content will depend on the extinction associated with unit density of the algal suspension.

Steemann Nielsen used absorption data of chlorophyll extracts in organic solvents to estimated roughly the maximum content as about 300 mg./m^2, which appeared compatible with actual amounts per unit area in dense natural and cultured populations.

It is also supported by observations on the increase of the light extinction during the growth of a planktonic diatom in nature. The increment of optical density (In I_o/I) associated with unit density of algae then appeared low enough (of the order of 0.02 per mg. chlorophyll-a/m.^{2}) to render unlikely any strong optical incursion by the densities of phytoplankton most commonly found in nature.

In most terrestrial vegetation the situation is obviously very different, both as regards the optical importance and the density per unit area of photosynthetic material, and its usual display in flat laminae.

Steemann Nielsen considers that the density of chlorophyll often reached per unit of ground area is significantly higher than the maximum value possible for phytoplankton in the cupbotic zone.

He connects this difference with the optical advantages offered by leaf arrangement and' structure, particularly the combination of diffusing epidermis and light channels in palisade cells.

The predominant laminar arrangement allows the density of photosynthetic cover to be conveniently expressed by a pure number, the ratio of leaf area to ground area. In recent years this measure—the leaf area index-has been widely used in analyses of crop growth light interception by vegetation comparisons of plant cover and in theoretical treatments of photosynthetic productivity. It was also involved in earlier Scandinavian work on terrestrial "Stoff produktion". Watson gives an excellent general review in relation to crop plants, and some ecological aspects are treated by Walter.

In continuous plant cover almost all values of leaf area index fall between one and eight; low values of about one are probably common in shade habitats and higher values of up to eight are illustrated by some European beech woods.

The upper limit of the index is clearly connected with the effective light extinction associated with each leaf layer. The relationship between leaf area index and vertical light extinction, indicated by Brougham, Monsi and Saeki, Nichiporovich and

Chmora appears to be less strongly influenced by the average transmission (usually near 10 per cent) of individual leaves than by the type of leaf arrangement. With the very thin leaves of mosses the leaf area index can be correspondingly high.

Light extinction is likely to be more directly related to leaf area index than to chlorophyll content per unit area, since much variation in the chlorophyll content per unit area of leaves (especially >5 mg./dm.^{2}) has a small influence on either optical density or photosynthetic efficiency in weak light.

DEPTH-INTEGRATION OF PHOTOSYNTHETIC RATES

The most complete assessment of the total photosynthetic activity below unit area of a plant cover would be provided by the summation of individual rates recorded at representative points within the cover. This approach has been applied extensively using the relatively homogenous communities of planktonic algae.

Here the area enclosed by the depth profile of photosynthesis represents the required depth integral of photosynthetic rate. It is susceptible to the depth-limitations seen in exposures of uniform samples and also to the effects of any stratification that affects population density, composition, and differentiation of photosynthetic characteristics, between cells at various levels.

The unravelling of these simultaneous variables has rarely been attempted. The effects of population density can be seen in the replotting of depth profiles with specific photosynthetic rates per unit quantity of pigments or in comparisons with crop profiles.

The separation of depth changes as due to the vertical light gradient, from the differing photosynthetic capacity of population samples from various depths, has been used in several indirect methods of estimating photosynthesis per unit area.

Photosynthetic capacity has been measured for samples exposed in illuminated constant temperature baths or near the water surface with natural illumination. Little is known of the quantitative influence of a depth-differentiation of "sun" and "shade" characteristics upon the depth-integral of photosynthesis.

The influence and interaction of individual variables also can be tested by a mathematical integration of photosynthetic rates, aimed at providing a theory that can be applied to analyse and compare actual examples. Formulations have centered upon the expression of the photosynthetic rate (P)light intensity (I) characteristic, with maximum rate (Pma_x), in relation to the varying surface intensity (I_o) and vertical light intensity gradient, the latter defined by some "average" or "effective" value of the vertical extinction coefficient (*ke*).

As a limiting case, a uniform population in the photosynthetic zone can be supposed, of density n. If the surface intensity I_o is sufficiently low so that light saturation of photosynthesis can be neglected, the formulation of the photosynthetic productivity per unit area (EP) is much simplified; examples are given by Riley Sverdrup and

Vollenweider. Berge has also used this simplification in computations for some sea areas at high latitudes.

The more usual significance of ligh-saturation for EP has been calculated graphically by Ryther and in mathematical derivation by Tailing. The central expression of Tailing using the present symbols, can be reduced to

$$\sum P = \frac{nPm_{ax}}{k_e}\left(\text{In}\frac{I_o}{0.5I_k}\right)$$

This expression was used to formulate other factors involved in the photosynthetic utilization of solar radiation by planktonic algae, and was applied to the characteristics of some specific populations in nature.

A parallel theory developed for the photosynthetic or growth kinetics of algal mass cultures has yielded expressions that can be reinterpreted in a similar form and applied over a wider range of the ratio I_o/I_k, namely

$$\sum P = \frac{nPm_{ax}}{k_e}\text{In}\left(\frac{I_o}{I_k}+1\right)$$

These equations give a formal and simplified expression to several limitations of the integral photosynthesis that have often been dis'ussed. The relation to the logarithm of the surface light intensity implies that the integral photosynthesis will be relatively insensitive to variations in I_o when this (and the I_o/I_k ratio) is high.

Such insensitivity has been commented upon by various authors who have considered the vertical displacement and enlargement of photosynthesis-depth profiles with increasing surface intensity.

Derivation of the photosynthetic productivity in nature from measure-ments on samples is clearly more difficult for a terrestrial plant cover. Some comparisons have been made between measurements of the photosynthetic behaviour of entire stands and their component leaves rate-intensity curves and diurnal changes of photosynthetic rate show less abrupt saturation at higher it tensities in the dense stands.

Transitional behaviour during stand growth is described for rice plots. Similar consequence of self-shading effects in dense leaf system have been discussed for various conifers. Several alternatives have been used in attempts to calculate indirectly the daily photosynthesis of a community in nature.

As with phytoplankton they have centered on the combination of the rate-intensity characteristic with the daily variation of incident illumination. In examples given by Boysen-Jensen Larsen and Polster the characteristics from single leaves or twigs were used, and are not suitable for dense systems of overlapping leaves.

Such a systems, utilizing the matted growth of the moss *Homalothe-cium sericlum,* was used directly by Romose in his experiments. The results were combined with data on diurnal illumination at various seasons to estimate photosynthetic activity under natural conditions, using an average gradient for rateintensity curves in relation to daily illumination-integrals (as lux-hours).

A mean gradient was used in another way by de Wit to calculate theoretically the potential daily photosynthesis of dense plant cover from daily radiation-integrals; in the latter he-distinguished two fractions, one being utilized in the calculation.

As in dense algal communities, the corresponding vertical light gradient can be related to the density of photosynthetic material. The stratification of the latter, and the associated light gradients, are illustrated for various natural communities, and discussed in relation to the transmission of individual leaves.

The depth integration of rates yields an expression that can be transformed by appropriate subsitution of symbols into a form very similar to that quoted for algal suspensions. The significance of the ratio P_{max} to *ke* (the latter now related to leaf area index), and of the logarithmic function of the ratio I_o/I_k, can then be seen.

The model is illustrated by data of loysen-Jensen on the photosyn-thesis of leaves and plant stands. Further and more direct comparisons with observed photoynthetic rates are needed to test the assumptions and simplifications involved.

Integrated yields of photosynthesis can be used for indepen comparison with growth increments if both the carbon content of the latter and the various sources of *loss* *(e g.,* aspiration) are known quantitatively. Few studies of photo inthesis under field conditions are sufficiently detailed to permit the comparison, but included among the few are those of Heinicke and Hoffman and Heinicke and Childers on *Pyrusmalus.*

Larsen on *Solanum* on *Homalothecium sericium* Thomas and Hill on several crop plants, and Tranquillini on *Pinuscembra.* In these examples, except that of *Pinus cembra,* the agreement was good considering the problems involved, particularly the one of obtaining estimates of respiration losses over long periods.

Uncertainties concerning these and other losses have generally prevented the effective comparison of growth photosynthetic rates for natural populations of planktonic or other algae. The calculation of growth increments per unit of leaf luantity (usually area) is the basis of particularly successful orm of growth analysis suitable for ecological application.

The instantaneous rate of growth, defined as the "net assimilaion rate" or "unit leaf rate" (E), can be related to the unit area productivity of the stand by the more variable factor of the leaf area index, and to the relative (specific) growth rate by he ratio of leaf area to total dry weight.

Average values of? during a growing season often show a remarkably limited ariation with species or latitude, although this is now known a be considerably broader than the "typical" range of 0.4 to .7 g./m.^{2} per week originally suggested by Heath and Gregory seasonal variation is described by Watson maxima of E may got coincide with the best development of leaf area index, thus imiting the unit area productivity. Another limitation of snit area yield, by an inverse relation between E and leaf area adex, can also develop the optimum leaf area index for yield is therefore of much interest.

The average magnitude of E corresponds roughly with that expected from the usual order of the net photosynthetic capacity of leaves at light saturation, about 0.7 to 1.7 g. carbohydrate/M.2 per hr. Although the net assimilation rate reflects factors other than the net photosynthetic rates of leaves (e.g., respiration of nonphotosynthetic organs, ash content), the relation of these quantities is sufficiently close to make their combined study in field conditions most desirable.

There is, for example, a suggestive parallel of a *modified* logarithmic relationship established between net assimilation rate and the daylight factor and a similar relationship is indicated by theory between photosynthetic productivity per unit area and light intensity in a dense homogeneous cover.

Chapter 2

CHLOROPLAST

The plastids are characteristic large cytoplasmic bodies of the cell intimately related to the metabolic processes and which impart colour to the tissues. They are found mostly in plants with possible exception of the very lowest group of plants. However, plastids are also found in few animals, especially the protozoan flagellates.

They are not found in bacteria, certain algae, myxomycetes and fungi. On the basis of presence of the plastids, the living world has been distinguished into plant and animal kingdoms. Old literature indicates that *Pringshetn* first investigated the plastids.

The terra plastid was used in 1 X85 by *A.F.W. Schimper* to include the cell organelles which are primarily involved in the formation and storage of soluble and insoluble carbohydrates. *A. Meyer* in 1883, *F. Schmitz* in 1884 and *A.F.W. Schimper* in 1885 made detailed cytological studies of these cell organelles and showed that green plastids known as chloroplasts could not be formed from cytoplasm, but only from existing chloroplasts.

The plastids vary in size, number, shape and chemical organization with the particular tissue and organism concerned. In contrast to the smaller cytoplasmic granules such as the mitochondria, important physical and chemical differences in the plastids can be easily recognized, such as changes in size or shape, the presence or absence of the

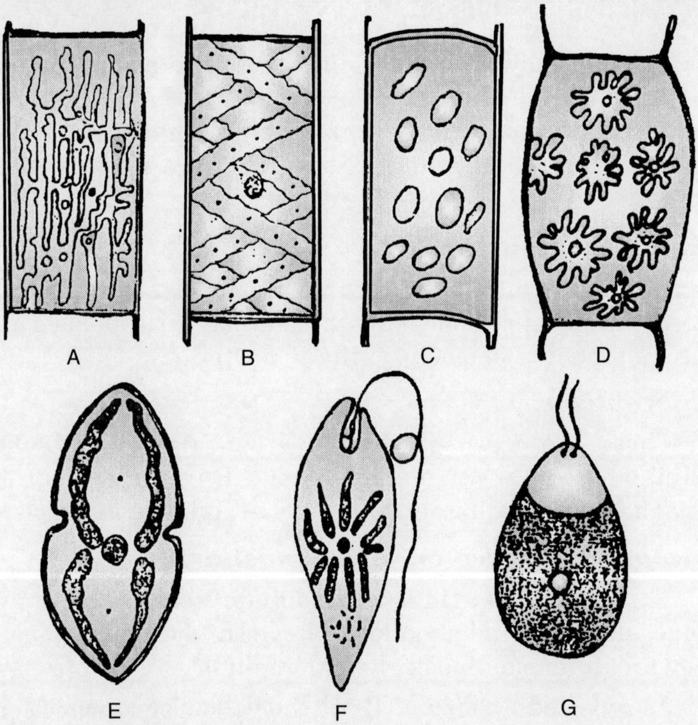

Figure 2.1: Various types of chloroplasts. A-Oedogonium, B-Spirogyra, C-Phyloiella, D-Rhodochlorton, E-Euastrun, F-Euglena, O-Chlamydomons.

chloroplastid, carotenoids and starch. Mature plastids can be shown to arise from more or less undifferen-tiated plastid primordia which occur in the meristematic cells, or hose of the developing embryo.

The plastids are self-duplicating bodies and their life history, especially of the chloroplast, may be divided into three phases. In the first phase, self duplication and enzymatic activities with some concern to RNA takes place.

The second phase is mainly concerned with differentiation to form the enzymes required for photosynthesis. In the third phase the activities of the enzymes that predominates are those concerned with photosynthesis.

VARIOUS TYPES OF PLASTIDS

Plastids may be divided into two general groups; the *chromoplasts* (coloured plastids); and the *leucoplasts* (colourless plastids). The chromoplasts may be further divided into two subgroups; those that are photosynthetically active and those that are not.

Photosynthetically Active Chromoplasts

The photosynthetically active chromoplasts are chloroplasts, phacoplasts, rhodoplasts, blue-green chromoplasts and chromatophores of photosynthetic bacteria.

Chloroplasts

These are green plastids of green algae and higher plants and contain chlorophyll A and B in the ratio of 2.3 : 1. These have different appearance and varying sizes.

Pheoplasts (Brown or yellow plastids)

This type of plastid is commonly present in the brown algae, diatoms and dinoflagellates. **In** these pheoplasts, brown carotenoids mask the chlorophyll.

As reported by *Strain* (1951) the yellow or brown colour of the pheoplasts appears to result from the physical state or condition of the pigment from their geometrical arrangement in the plastids. Brown algae contain fucoxanthin which can absorb light and transfer energy to chlorophyll.

Rhodoplasts

Various members of Rhodophyceae con tain red coloured plastids. The red colour is due to a pigment phycobilin and protein phycoerythrin. The colour of plastids may be the result of light absorption. There may be phycotcyanin too in traces. *Haxo, Blink* and *Young (1952)* found that light is absorbed by phycobilin and is transmitted to chlorophyll *a*.

Blue-green Chromatophore

Two accessory protein phycocyanin and phycoerythrin impart bluetgreen colour to algae. These pigments and chlorophyll a alongwith carotenoid form lamellar structure, the *chromatophore.*

Wilson and *Morrison* (1967) mention that all the organisms, capable of performing photosynthesis do not necessarily contain plastid structures; for example, bluetgreen algae and.

photosynthetic bacteria. In blue-greens, the light-sensitive pigments are chlorophyll and phycobilin pigments. These pigments are associated with a system of membranes and lamellae in the cytoplasm of the cell. In photosynthetic bacteria also wide diversity of structures are associated with the photosynthesis. These structures are as follows

(1) Lamellae in some purple bacteria ; for example, *Rhodomicrobium,* (2) Vesicular membrane-bound structures, known as chromatophores found in non-sulphuric and purple sulphur bacteria ; for example, *Rhodospirillium, Chromatium,* and (3) Ribosome like granules found in green sulphur bacterium, *Chlorobiumthio sultatophilum.* All these photosynthetic bacteria possess a pigment system consisting of a specialized form of ·chlorophyll, known as bacteriochlorophyll and various carotenoid pigments.

Chromoplasts Without Photosynthetic Activity

These types of chromoplasts contain carotenoids only. They are red to yellow in colour and are much more variable in shape. They impart specific colour to various plant tissues, fruits and flowers.

The new colour that arise often due to the formation of special carotenoids, for example, the *leucopene* of tomato fruits, *prolycopene* of berries, and *capsanthin* of red pepper.

Xanthophyll is also present in adequate proportions. Coloured carotenoids are also important constituents of the coloured parts of plant.

These may be found in fungi and bacteria. Acidic carotenoids of fungi are similar to astaxanthin. *Haxo (1949)* isolated a mixture of carotenoids from the *Neurospora crassa* which includes lycopene, carotene, and spiriloxanthines as the main components.

The growth of carotenoid becomes double in presence of light. These chromoplasts are supposed to develop from the leucoplasts that contain starch.

As the carotene increase in concentration the starch disappears. The older chromoplasts appear thin plates as needles with typical crystalline appearance. They are direfringen and dichroic.

Leucoplasts

The noncoloured plastids are called leucoplasts. They do not contain pigments and the membranous structures are absent. They are found mainly in the embryonic and sexual cells. They are also found in meristematic cells and in those regions of the plants which do not receive light.

They serve mainly for the storage of starch, oils and proteins. Plastids located in cotyledons and the primordium of stem are first colourless but eventually become filled with pigments and become coloured plastids. Leucoplasts are further categorized into following three types:

Amyloplasts

These are mature plastids with predominant starch contents and generally found in storage tubers, cotyldons and endosprem. Starch is characteristic of the coloured and the colourless plastids of green algae and the higher plants.

The deposition of other carbohydrates may not necessarily be with the plastids. For example, in red algae starch is formed at the surface of the plastids. In *Euglena,* paramylum grains are considered to be produced outside the plastids. The starch grains may be of two types : assimilative starch and reserve starch.

The former is characteristic of actively photosynthesizing chloroplasts and the latter is most familiar in storage organs. The starch grains are made of a series of concentric layers successively deposited about a centre, the *hilum.*

As starch continues to be deposited, the walls of the amyloplast become greatly distended. *Frey Wysslfng (1953)* observed that the formation of a new concentric layer begins as a dense region of high refractive index, then it becomes a dense layer due to more hydration.

Chemically starch contains two components : mainly a-amylose (which stain red with iodine) and minorly β-amylose (only 20-30 per cent forming helical chain structure and stains blue with iodine).

Elaioplasts

The plastids which store oils are known as elaioplasts. In most monocotyledons, the chloroplasts after losing their chlophyll start storing oil in epidermal cells (exp. Orchidaceae and Liliaceae).

The disorganised plastids fuse to form oil droplets. In brown algae, the reserve storage is oil and this oil appears to be formed in the pheoplasts.

Aleuroneplasts

These are the plastids that contain much protein and often termed as the *proteinoplasts.* Protein crystals and granules are produced in the seeds of numerous plants specially in those seeds that also form large amount of oil, *e.g. the* Brazi Neof and seeds of *Ricinus.*

Mottier (1921) referred at protein and oil formation involves the activity of permanent plastid primordia. Protein crystals may develop independently in the cytoplasm without any aid of the aleuroneplasts, for example, in peripheral layers of potato the cells are poor F starch.

Protein crystals in epidermal cells may also represent material or may be the result of virus action. Amyloplasts are the most important of all the different types of leucoplasts.

The amyloplasts resemble proplastids and differ from them only in size. They contain fewer lamellae, but in presence of light they can build up a thylacoid structure found in chloroplasts. However, chloroplasts can also synthesize starch and store it in stromal region.

The starch in chloroplasts disappears quickly and is, therefore, known as transitory starch. The starch present

Table 2.1. Showing occurrence, functions and pigments of various plastids.

Kinds of Plastids	*Occurrence*	*Functions*	*Pigment*
I. Chromoplasts			
A. Photosynthetically active chromoplasts.			
1. *Chloroplasts*	Higher plants and green algae	Photosynthesis	Chlorophyll-a and Chloro phyll-b
2. *Pheoplasts*	Brown algae, diatoms and dinoflagellates	Light absorp-tion	Fucoxanthin
3. *Rhodoplasts*	Red algae (Rho-dophyceac)	Light absorp-tion	Phycoerythrin
4. *Blue-green*	Blue-green algae	Photosynthesis	Phycocyanin Phycoerythrin Chlorophyll-a and Carote noids
5. *Chromoplasts of Photosyn-thetic bacteria*	Purple and non-Bacteria purple sulphur bacteria	Absorption of infra red por-tion of light	chlorophyll
B. Chromoplasts devoid of photosynthetic activity			
6. *Carotenoids*	Tomato, red peppar, flower parts, fungi, ornamental bacteria and fruits		Lycopene & Capsanthia
II Leucoplasts			
7. *Amyloplasts*	Storage tubers. cotyledons and endosperm	Starch-storage	None
8. *Elaioplasts*	Epidermal cells of Orchidaceae and Liliaceae	Oil-storage	None

(Table 2.1 contd.)

Kinds of Plastids	Occurrence	Functions	Pigment
9. *Aleuronplasts*	Epidermal cells of Helleborus and seeds of *Ricinus* and Brazil nut	Protein-storage	None

in leucoplasts, on the ether hand, can be stored for monger periods and is, therefore, known as reserve starch. The starch development begins with the formation of a particle in the stroma.

This particle has several tubuli and thylcoids and is surrounded by additional rings of starch. It grows till the amyloplasts is filled with starch. As a result, the tubuli are pressed against the wall and ultimately starch granule exceeds the size of amyloplast.

The wall of the plastid then ruptures and finally withers away so that only the starch granules can be seen.

Chloroplasts

Chloroplasts are the plastids that are most common and of greatest biological importance, since by *otosynthesis* they produce most of the chemical energy used living organisms. Without chloroplasts there would be no imams, because animals feed on the food stuffs produced by ants.

Distribution and Orientation

Chloroplasts are sometimes distributed homogeneously within the cytoplasm, but are frequently packed near the nucleus, or close to the cell wall.

The distribution and orientation of the chmoroplasts within the cell may vary with the amount of light energy. Chloroplasts apparently multiply by division-elongation of the plastid and constriction of the central portion.

They have a higher density than the cytoplasm and migrate to the centrifugal pole of the cell when submitted to the action of centrifugal force.

MORPHOLOGY

Shape

Higher plant chloroplasts are generally biconvex or planoconvex. However, in different plants cells, chloroplast may have various shapes, viz., *filamentous, saucer-shaped, spheroid, ovoid* or *discoid shaped.*

They are vesicular and have .a colourless centre. Some chioroplasts are *club shaped,* having a thin middle zone and bulging ends filled with chlorophyll. Algae often possess a single huge chloroplast that appears as a network, *a spiral band,* or a *stellate plate.*

Size

The size of chloroplast varies from species to species 'but is constant for a given cell type. The average size of chloroplasts in higher plants measure 4-6,u in diameter and 1

3μ in thickness. The chloroplasts of polyploid plant cells are larger than those in the corresponding diploid cells. In general, chloroplasts of plants grown in the shade are larger and contain more chlorophyll than of those plants grown in sunlight.

Number

The number of chloroplasts is relatively constant in the different plants. In higher plants there are 20 to 40 chloroplasts per cell. It has been calculated that the leaf of *Ricinus communis* contains about 400,000 chloroplasts per square millimeter of surface area.

When the number of chloroplasts is insufficient, it is increased by division; when excessive, it is reduced by degeneration.

Conformational Changes and Ion Movements

Chloroplasts undergo striking conformational changes which are dependent on the action of light. In the dark they undergo swelling and separation of the membranes of the thylakoid.

This phenomenon is reversible ; in the presence of light the membranes again return to close apposition. Mitochondira eject H+ ions during the electron transport and that the interior becomes more alkaline.

In the case of chloroplasts the opposite reactions occur. Under the action of light H^+ ions which are absorbed, the interior becomes acidified. At the same time K^+ and Mg^{++} are ejected into the medium.

In the dark, H^+ is ejected and K^+ and Mg^{++} are reabsorbed by the chloroplasts. Thus, the chloroplast membrane has a vectorial organization that is the reverse of the mitochondiral membrane.

In physical terms it is understood that dark reactions, being of a thermochemical nature, do not need an ordered structural arrangement (i.e. they are carried out by soluble enzymes).

On the contrary, photophosphorylation requires the separation of positive and negative charges into specific pathways of electron flow.

Chemical Composition

Chloroplasts of spinach leaf cells contain about 56% protein, 32% lipid and 8% chlorophyll. The lipids include xantbophylls, carotenoids, triglycerides, steroids, waxes and phospholipids. Chloroplasts of higher plants contain approximately 35-55% proteins, 20-30% lipids, 9% chlorophyll, 4-5% carotenoids and 2-3% nucleic acids. In cytoplasm the protein-lipid ratio is generally 90 : 1.

In plastids this ratio is about 40 : 30. Thus the grana have a high concentration of lipid. The nucleic acid DNA and RNA have been demonstrated in the chloroplasts of higher plants.

Chlorophyll has a tetrapyrrole structure and consists of a hydrophilic head and a hydrophobic tail. The head is made up of a magnesium atom surrounded by four pyrrolic nuclei (tetrapyrrole structure).

The long tail consists of a phytol china. Green plants

have two types of chlorophyll, *chlorophyll a* and *chlorophyll b*. In chlorophyll *b* one of the methyl (-CH=) groups of chlorophyll a is replaced by a formyl (-CHO) group.

Structure

Plastids are dynamic organelles whose structure changes in response to changes in environment. A mature plastid is having the following parts

(1) Limiting membrane

(2) Stroma

(3) Grana

Limiting Membrane

Each mature plastid is covered by a double membrane as in mitochondira, each unit is about 40 to 60A in thickness. The limiting membrane functions as a semipermeable membrane as well as a boundary.

Stroma

The inner space which is formed by a limiting membrane is filled with a proteinaceous matrix called the 'stroma'. A number of starch grains and sometimes osmiophilic droplets are embedded in the stroma. When the plastid be comes inactive or ages, the number of osmiophilic droplets may increase.

Grana or lamellar system

These are flat bodies shaped like platelets or discs, which in a lateral view appear as dense bands perpendicular to the limiting membrane of plastid. A number of grana are embedded in the stroma or matrix of plastid.

The size of the grana varies between 0.3-1.7μ depending on the species. Each granum consists of a stack of double membrane or lamellae. The lamellar membranes are composed of lipids and proteins. Protein contents are about 45% while lipids contents are 55% in amount. Each lamella is 30-35Å thick and the space between two such lamellae is of' 65-70Å. The lamellae can be placed under two groups

(*a*) Stroma lamellae

(*b*) Grana lamellae

Those lamellae, extending through the entire length of the plastids are called the stroma lamellae. These are not directly connected with the cell wall.

The grana lamellae are alwayss densely packed. Any way, the system of lamellae represents a closed unit, and thus both stroma and grana lamellae are closely related to one another, i.e., each granum lamella represents a local adhesion of two or more stroma lamellae.

Both stroma and grana lamellae may stay coupled for a long distance and then separate again from each other. Another term *thylakoid (reek ;* sac like) has been used for the double membranous lamellae already explained.

The stroma lamellae are larger thylakoids while the smaller, stacked thylakoids are the grana lamellae. One more term has been added by *Weler* and others, which is *fret* to discribe stroma lamellae as a flattened tubular channel connecting adjacent grana.

Recel studies have provided evidence that the membranes within ti chloroplasts form a continum and the cavities of the thy, lakoids (loculi) communicate via fret work connection.

The total number of grana in plastids of certain plants have been calculated. There is a considerable variation in the number of grana in a single plastid, depending upon the species. In *Euglena* only one granum is present in one plastid while in Spinach, where about 40-60 grana are present in each plastid.

In *Chlamydomonas,* the plastid envelope is sometimes continuous with elements of the endoplasmic reticulum. In *Ochromonas* as well as in *Chlamydomonas,* connection with other cytoplasmic membranes with single plastid have also been traced.

QUANTOSOME CONCEPT

The membranes of thylakoids are composed of many paracrystalline spheroid particles known as the quantosomes. The quantosomes are about 160A° by 180A° and about $100A^3$ thick. *Sauer* and *Calvin (1962)* have shown that 3 to 6 quantosomes many aggregate together to form a large particle of 500 × 100A°.

Park and *Beggins* (1964) have reported that each quantosome is composed of four subunits. According to *Honwell- and Moundrianakis* (1967) these quantosomes are the smallest units capable of carrying out the photochemical reaction and each of them contains about 200 chlorophyll molecules.

According to the size, nature and arrangement of quantosomes in the membrane of thylakoids and stromal lamellae, *Branton* and *Park* (1967) have recognised three types of membranes which are as follows

1. Membrane with quantosomes.
2. Membrane with smaller particles (110A°).
3. Membrane with rough surface and with a few or no particles.

The chloroplasts, thus, act as elaborate biochemical machines and transform the energy at the molecular level.

FUNCTIONS OF THE CHLOROPLAST

Photosynthesis

Photosynthesis involves two major sets of reactions, each set consisting of many steps. One set, the *light reactions,* transform ("transduce") energy acquired through the absorption of light into usable chemical forms, namely ATP and the reduced form (NADPH) of the coenzyme NADP.

This is accomplished via oxidation-reduction sequences that include the removal of electrons from water, releasing oxygen and protons (H+). These protons and others transferred across the thylakoid membranes during the oxidation-reduction reactions contribute to an ATP-producing proton gradient like the one described for mitochondria.

The other reactions in photosynthesis, the *dark reactions,* occur both in the light and in the dark. They use the

ATP and NADPH to build carbohydrates from CO_2. The most common pathway by which this is done is the "carbon reduction cycle" (the *Calvin cycle),* which starts with the reaction of CO_2 with the 5-carbon sugar ribulose 1,5-diphosphate. This generates two 3-carbon molecules that undergo the cycle schematized.

This initial CO_2 fixation is catalyzed by the enzyme ribulose I,5-diphosphate ("bisphosphate") carboxylase, often called RuDP carboxylase or carboxydismutase.

The Light Reactions

The green colour of chlorophyll is due to its selective

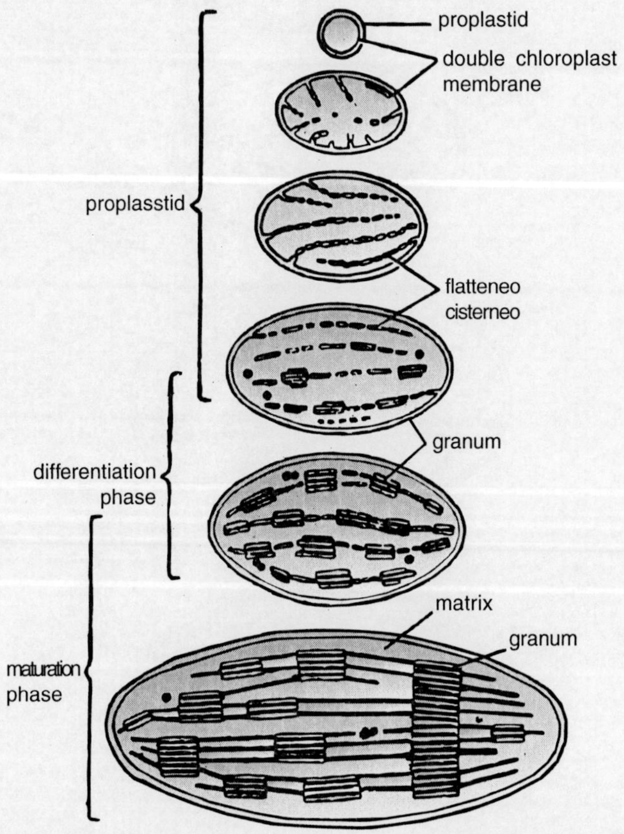

Figure 2.2: Development of a chloroplast in sun light.

absorption of light with wavelenghts of 650 to 700nm. (Light of these wave-lengths appears to the eye as red; when red light is removed from white light, as by absorption, what is left appears green.)

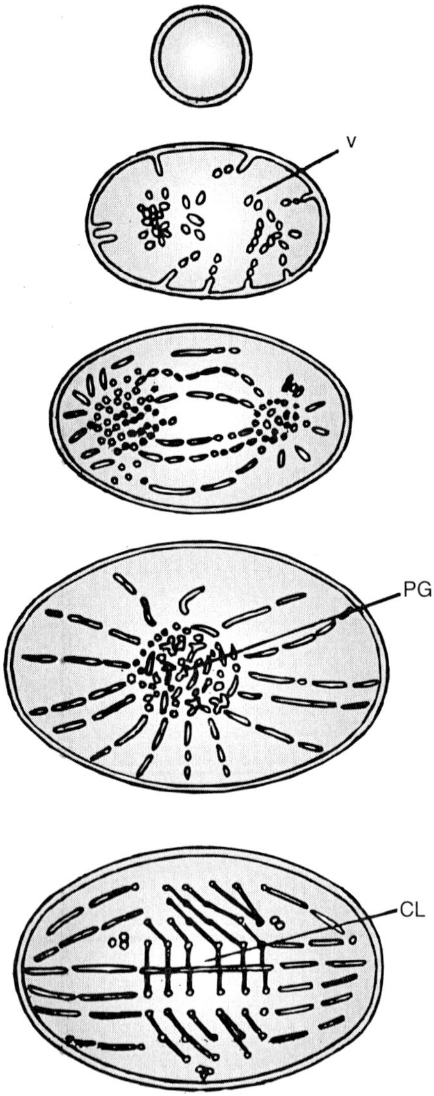

Figure 2.3: Developed of a chloroplast in dark.

Chlorophyll also absorbs light at shorter wavelenghts (4C0 to 475nm, corresponding to the violet-blue region of the spectrum). Two major chlorophyll types are present in eukaryotic plastids Chlorophyll a shows absorption maxima (peak absorption) at about 670 nm and at about 490 nm, Chlorophyll b absorbs maximally at about 650 and 470 nm.

Wavelength is an indicator of the energy carried by packets *(photons)* of light. The shorter the wavelength, the greater the energy. The absorption maxima of the chlorophylls and other photosynthetic, pigments indicate the portion of the spectrum of sunlight that can be captured for energizing photosynthesis.

When a chlorophyll molecule absorbs a photon, an electron of the chlorophyll's porphyrin ring acquires the photon's energy and thereby is excited. This is the basis of the chloroplast's ability to transduce light energy to chemical energy.

The excited electron can enter a series of electron transport reactions involving iron-containing proteins (ferrodexins, cytochromes), a copper-containing protein (plastocyanin), lipid-soluble molecules (plastoquinones) resembling coenzyme Q and other participants, some yet to be identified.

Two distinguishable "*photochemical units*", *photosystems,* cooperate in photosynthesis. This cooperation as currently envisaged by a majority of investigators. The functional heart of each unit is a reaction center (action center) that carries out the essential processes by which energy derived from light is made available to the electron transport sequences and other phenomena of the light reactions.

Each photosystem is characterized by a particular form of pigment molecule associated with the reaction center ; the pigments almost certainly are chlorophylls. In photosystem I (PSI), the reaction center pigment absorbs light maximally at 700 urn and hence, is called P 700. Excited electrons from P 700 pass from the PSI reaction center to the electron transport sequence that reduced NADP.

The electrons "lost" from P 700 in this process are replaced through electron transport from photosystern II (PSII) ; the cyclic pathway diagrammed represents an alternative replenishment mechanism, which some investigators believe is actually the predominant one, at least under some physiological circumstances.

The reaction center pigment of PSII, P 680, absorbs light preferent-ially at 680 nm. The PSII reaction center transfers electrons from this pigment to an electron transport chain that links PSII to PSI. The "loss" of electrons from P 680 is made up by the removal of electrons from water molecules; it is this PSI· mediated oxidation ("splitting") of water that generates O_2.

In net effect the two photosystems collaborate via electron transport to transfer electrons from water to NADPH. Accomnanvintt this transfer is the establishment of an electro-chemical H^+ gradient across the thylakoid membranes : The thylakoid interior is maintained at low pH relative to the stroma.

The H^+ ions freed in the "splitting" of water also contribute to this gradient. The proton gradient is used to generate ATP (photosynthetic phosphorylation).

As with mitochondira, vesicles formed from fragmented thylakoids are capable of both electron transport and phosphorylation but can no longer phosphorylate if broken open or otherwise treated to disrupt the permeability barrier inherent in the membrane.

Moreover, chloroplast vesicles can produce ATP for a brief period if simply soaked for a time in a medium of low pH, until their interior equilibrates with the medium, and then transferred into a medium of high pH, establishing a transient H+ gradient across the vesicles' membranes.

Experiments of this sort were crucial in verifying the plausibility, in general of chemiosmotic mechanisms for production of ATP.

ORIGIN OF THE PLASTIDS

Plastids are generated only by other preexisting plastids or proplastid body. They are self reproducing cell organelles like the chromosomes and the centrioles. The proplastid may be regarded as the "stem" plastid, giving rise to metabolically active leucoplasts or chloroplasts which may later develop into other types of chromoplasts through a kind of degeneration.

Plastids are transmitted directly to daughter cells during division, providing a genetic continuity in plastid lineage. Although the origin of initials that develop into proplastids is not entirely clear, some observations in fern suggest the nuclear envelope as a possible source.

In Lower Plants

In algae and lower plants, the plastids are quite large and often of different shapes and the process of their division is easy to follow. Here the division begins with an infolding of the inner membrane of the limiting chloroplast envelope. Later on the outer membrane invaginates until the plastid is divided into two. The daughter plastids thus formed, may or may not be equal in size.

In Higher or superior Plants

In higher plants the process of formation of plastids is more complicated. The process **can** be effected even by sun light, as the formation of plastids

In sun light and in dark, show vast differences in either case.

In sun light

During the development the proplastids increase in size. Protoplastids are limited by a double memo brane. In the presence of light the inner limiting boundary invaginates at several places, producing small vesicle like structures.

These vesicles later on pinch off as free units, which then aggregate in several arrangements to form the lemellae of the mature plastid.

In dark

If the proplastids are left in dark, the process of mation upto vesicle stage is the same, as in presence of light. But the arrangement of vesicles is different. In dark. the clusters of vesicles or discs constitute the lamellar system or a series of concentric rings are developed.

Formation of leucoplasts, chromoplasts and chloroplasts from proplastids. The non-lamellated proplastids can also transform themselves into leucoplasts. These, in turn, can develop into immature lamellar plastids or by a reversible process, into starch containing amyloplasts.

The mature proplastids then grow to become either mature chloroplasts or other chromoplasts or even, by storing proteins, aleurone plastids. Mature chloroplasts can become chlorophyll free chromoplasts or, by absorption of many lipids elaioplasts.

Nuclear origin

A large number of initials around the nucleus have been observed under special conditions, where the cell organelles are breaking down. This suggested that the initials originated due to evaginatin of the double nuclear membrane and gave rise to mitochondria and proplastids.

Symbiotic Origin

To much surprise, resemblance has been observed between mitocho-ndria and bacteria on the one hand and chloroplast and blue-green algae on the other hand. They are not only some what similar in shape and structure but also in function.

All possess DNA, much smaller than nuclear *DNA* and circular, not organised in chromosomes ; their ribosomes are all about the same size, smaller than the cytoplasmic matrix ribosomes of animal and plant cells. In bacteria the respiratory chain is localised in the membrane comparable to inner membrane of mitochondria.

Further comparable to cristae of mitochondria, infoldings of plasma membrane (mesosomes) have been reported in certain bacteria. In mitochondria and bacteria both, the protein synthesis is inhibited by chioramphenicol, whereas the exracellular protein synthesis of higher cells is not effected.

These similarities have led some to consider the mitochondria and chloroplasts of today as generally modified descendents of an ancestral free living bacteria and blue green-algae respectively (autotrophic microorganisms) which at one time came together with the ancestral eukaryotic cell (heterotrophic host cell) to form a symbiotic relationship.

This hypothesis is no doubt highly attractive, but still it is evident that the electron transport system in chloroplasts and the enzymes required for making the photosynthetic pigments are controlled by the nuclear genes.

Chapter 3

CHLOROPHYLL

Green is the predominant colour of the plant kingdom. With only a few exceptions all leaves are green in colour as are also many other plant organs such as herbaceous and young woody stems, young fruits, and sepals of flowers. The green colouring of plants is often termed chlorophyll, although actually a number of kinds of chlorophyll occur in plants.

Less evident is the fact that the leaves and many other organs of plants also contain yellow pigments. These are seldom apparent except in leaves in which the chlorophyll fails to develop, or in which it is destroyed as a result of senescence or other physiological changes.

Corn plants that have grown from seed in the dark, for example, do not synthesize chlorophyll, but are usually yellow in colour because of the presence of yellow pigments. In the autumn disintegration of the .chlorophyll in the leaves of many woody species results in unmasking the yellow pigments which are also present in the leaves.

The yellow chloroplast pigments of leaves belong to the group of compounds called *carotenoids.* Except in blue-green algae and the photosynthetic bacteria, chlorophylls occur only in the chloroplasts.

The carotenoids of leaves are also restricted to the. chloroplasts, and this also appears to be true of the carotenoids in the cells of most algae. All of these pigments

- appear to be present only in the grana of the chloroplasts. In certain other plant organs, such as flower petals, the yellow pigments occur in chlomoplasts.

The chlorophylls and associated carotenoids are often called the chloroplast pigments. In some kinds of algae pigments of another group, called the phycobilins, also occur in the chloroplasts.

The best known of these are the phycoerythrin of most Ted and some blue-green algae, and the phycocyanin of most blue-green and some red algae. These two pigments are -closely related chemically. Both are colloidal proteinaceous pigments and can be extracted from the cells with hot water.

The Chlorophylis

A number of different kinds of chlorophyll occur in the plant kingdom. Of these, chlorophyll a is most nearly of universal occurrence being present, as far as is known, in all photosyn-thetic organisms except the green and purple bacteria.

Chlorophyll *b* is found in all higher plants and in the green algae, but is not present in algae of most other phyla. Chlorophyll *c* is found in the brown algae and diatoms, which do not contain chlorophyll *b*.

Similarly red algae contain chlorophyll *d* but no chlorophyll *b*. In the purple bacteria still another kind of chlorophyll called *bocteriochlorophyll* is present, whereas the green bacteria contain another apparently similar pigment called *bacteriovlridln*.

All of these chlorophylls are very similar in chemical composition, and all of them are compounds which contain magnesium.

Chlorophylls *a* and *b* are the characteristic chlorophylls of the higher plants. Neither is water soluble, but both are soluble in a number of organic reagents.

Chlorophyll *a* is readily soluble in absolute-ethyl alcohol, ethyl ether, acetone, chloroform, and carbon bisulfide.

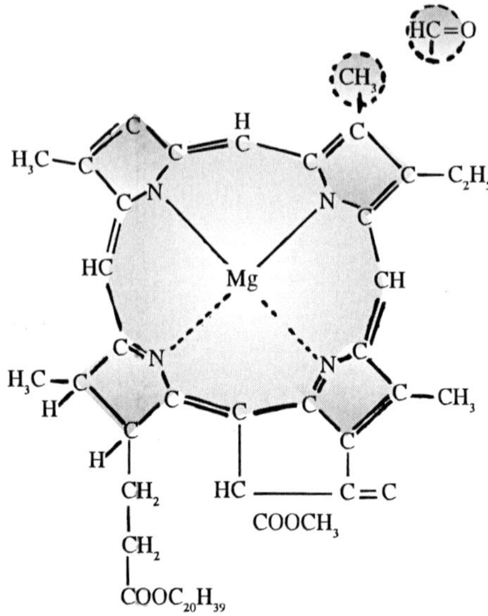

Figure 3.1: Structural formula of chlorophyll a, Another arrangement of the double bonds in this formula is possible. The formula for chlorophyll b is the same, except that a HC=O group occurs in place of the CH_3 group enclosed in the dotted circle.

Chlorophyll *b* is soluble in the same reagents, although generally less so.

Chlorophyll *a* is blue-green in solution, and blue-black in the solid state; chlorophyll *b* is almost pore green in solution, and grnenish black in the solid state.

All of the chlorophylls possess the property of *fluorescence*. This term refers to the peculiar property possessed by certain substances when illuminated of re-radiating light of wavelengths other than those absorbed by the substance.

Usually the radiated light (fluorescent light) is longer in wave length than the incident light. Chlorophyll *a* in ethyl alcoholic solution exhibits a deep blood red fluoressence, best seen by viewing the solution in reflected light.

Similar solutions of chlorophyll *b* exhibit a brownish-red fluorescence. Chlorophyll in living cells also exhibits fluorescence.

The Chemistry of the Chlorophylls

Willstatter and his associates have isolated chlorophylls *a* and *b* in pure form from over two hundred different species of higher plants and found them to be identical in chemical composition.

They also succeeded in determining the molecular formulas of these two chlorophylls. For chlorophyll *a* this is $C_{55}H_{72}O_6N_4Mg$; for chlorophyll *b* it is $C_{b6}H_{70}O_6N_4Mg$. Each chlorophyll yields a separate series of degradation products, but one of the products derived from both after mild hydrolysis is an unsaturated primary alcohol which is, called *phytol* ($C_{20}H_{39}OH$).

Splitting of the phytol group from the chlorophyll molecule can also be accomplished by the enzyme *chlorophyllase,* which occurs in leaves. Phytol makes up about one-third of the chlorophyll molecule. It has a strong affinity for oxygen and may be responsible for the reducing action of chlorophyll.

When ashed pure chlorophyll leaves a residue composed solely of magnesium oxide. Although iron and other minerals seem essential for the formation of chlorophyll in living cells magnesium' is the only metallic constituent of the chlorophyll molecule.

From the results of the intensive study of the chemistry of the degradation. products of chlorophyll the probable structural formulas of both chlorophyll *a* and chlorophyll *b* have been determined.

As shown in Figure elsewhere in this chapter the nucleus of a molecule of chlorophyll a consists of a complex ring structure composed principally of four pyrrol nuclei linked together by intermediate atomic groupings. Each such ring bears side chains, the most prominent of which is the phytyl ($C_{20}H_{29}O$—) grouping which upon hydrolysis gives rise to phytol.

Absorption Spectra of the Chlorophylls

When a coloured solution such as an ether solution of

a chlorophyll is interposed between a source of "white light" and a spectroscope, it can readily be shown that certain wave lengths of light are much more completely absorbed than others.

The regions of the spectrum in which complete or nearly complete absorption takes place appear as dark bands. Chlorophylls *a* and *b* both show a definite and characteristic absorption spectrum when in solution.

The exact appearance of such absorption spectra will vary, however, depending upon the kind of solvent and the concentration and thickness of the layer of solution which is examined.

Absorption curves for chlorophyll a and *b* in ether solution as determined by photoelectric measurements we shot in Figure elsehwhere in this chapter. Both chlorophylls exhibit maximum absorption in the blue-violet region and a secondary maximum in the short red.

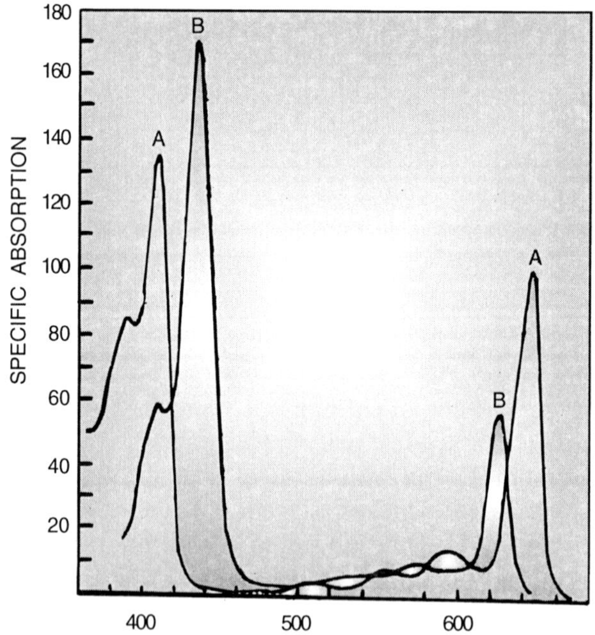

Figure 3.2: Absorption spectra of chloropbylls a and b in ether solution.

As a rule the absorption spectrum of a leaf does not correspond very closely with the spectrum of a solution of the pigments from that same leaf.

In general there is relatively more absorption of light by leaves in those spectral regions where absorption by solutions is low, and a relatively less absorption of light by leaves in those spectral regions where absorption by solutions is high. Some of the principal reasons for this are :

(1) the pigment in the leaf is not continuous, but located only in the plastids; hence some light may pass. through the leaf without traversing any pigment;

(2) actual or apparent absorption, the latter a result of scattering of light within the leaf, by the nonpigmented parts of cells affects the overall absorption of light by the leaf; and

(3) the concentrationof thepigment in the leaf is usually different from its concentration in extracts; as a result, specific absorption values of pigments in the leaf are different from those in a solution.

Physicochemical State of the Chlorophylls in the Chloroplasts

Although the extensive investigations of extracts of chlorophylls in organic solvents have advanced our knowledge of their physical and chemical properties, it should be rememberd that these are only *extracts* and the physicochemical state of the chlorophylls in them bears little or no relation to its conditions in the chloroplasts.

One necessary step in learning how the chloropbylls of living cells operate will be to discover how they are related physically and chemically to the other constituents of the chloroplasts.

Any acceptable picture of the physicochemical relationships of the chlorophylls within the chloroplasts must also be reconcilable with the known structural arrangement of the chlorophylls in the grana of the chloroplasts.

A number of investigators have shown that green, opalescent, aqueous extracts can be prepared from the leaves of many species by grinding them with sand in water or solutions and clarifying by filtration, precipitation, or centrifugation. These extracts possess many of the properties of protein sols or suspensions and the chlorophyll molecules seem to be definitely associated with the protein micelles or particles.

These results have led to the postulation of the existence of *a* chlorophyll-protein compound of constant composition in plants, analogous to the hemoglobin (hemin plus globin, a protein) of the blood.

Although results of these experiments indicate that some sort of an association of chlorophylls with proteins in the chloroplasts is highly probable, there are strong reasons for doubting that this association takes the form of a protein-chlorophyll compound in the strictly chemical sense.

Actual chemical analyses of the chloroplast substance have been made by Chibnall (1939), Menke (1940), Granick (1938), Comar (1942), and others.

The protein content of the chloroplast material from several species has been found to lie within a range of 35 to 55 per cent, and the lipid content within a range of 18 to 32 per cent on the dry weight basis (chloroplasts are probably about 50 per cent water).

In the leaf cells of g oh most of the lipids present are constituents of the chloroplasts. In such chemical analyses the chlorophylls and carotenoids constitute a part of the lipid fraction, about 5-10 per cent of which is chlorophylls and 2-4 per cent carotenoids.

The relatively large quantity of lipids in the chloroplasts suggests that the pigments commonly present in tome manner may be associated with lipids as well as with proteins. The physicochemical properties of the lipids are such that it seems more probable that any association between them and the chlorophylls or carotenoids is of a physical rather than a chemical nature.

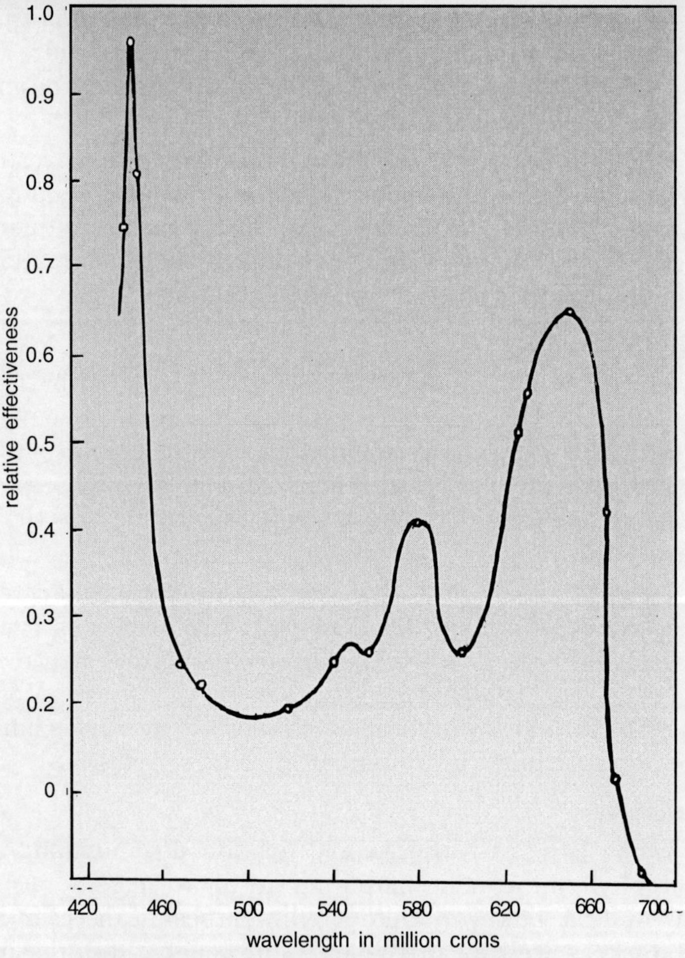

Figure 3.3: Relative effectiveness of different wave lengths in the formation of chlorophyll.

Chlorophyll Synthesis

Chlorophylls, in common with practically all the other organic substances which occur in plants, are products of the synthetic activities of the plant. A number of conditions are known to be necessary for or at least to influence greatly, the synthesis of chlorophylls in plants.

Absence of any one of these factors will inhibit chlorophyll synthesis resulting in the condition often called *chlorosis.* This term is most frequently applied when the failure of chlorophylls to develop is the result of a deficiency of one of the essential mineral elements.

Different types of chlorosis may develop in to leaves of any species depending upon the factor limiting chlorophyll formation. The following discussion of the factors influencing chlorophyll synthesis refers primarily to the formation of chlorophyll; *a* and *b* in the higher plants.

Genetic Factors

That certain genetic factors are necessary for the development of chlorophylls is shown by the behaviour of so· me varieties of maize in which a certain proportion of the seedlings produced cannot synthesize chlorophylls, even if all environmental conditions are favourable 'for their formation.

As soon as the food stored in the grain is exhausted such "albino" seedlings die. This trait is inherited in such strains of maize as a Mendelian recessive and hence is apparent only in plants homozygous for this factor. More or less similar genetic effects on chlorophyll synthesis have been demonstrated in a number of other species.

Light

Light is usually necessary for the development of chlorophyll in the angiosperms. In the algae, mosses, ferns, and conifers, however, chlorophyll synthesis can occur in the dark as well as in the light, although the quantity produced is often less in the absence of light than in its presence.

In a few angiosperms such as seedlings of the water lotus *(Nelumbo),* and in the cotyledons of citrus embryos chlorophylls can also develop in the absence of light. Relatively low intensities of light are generally effective in inducing chlorophyll synthesis in those species in which light is required for this process.

All wave lengths of the visible spectrum will, if their

energy value is adequate, cause chlorophyll development in etiolated seedlings (chlorophyll-free seedlings which have been grown in the dark) except those longer than 680 mμ.

For equal irradiances, a narrow band of wave lengths in the blue at about 445 mμ is most effective in inducing chlorophyll formation in oat seedlings, a broader wave band in the orange red (about 620-660 mμ) being next most effective. Like other complex compounds synthesized in plants, chlorophyll undoubtedly represents the terminal product of a long chain of reactions.

Cost of the steps in this sequence of 'reactions are unknown, but the evidence regarding the final step in chlorophyll synthesis seems clear. Dark-grown seedlings of higher plants are usually yellow in colour, but .actually contain traces of a green pigment, called *protochlorophyll.*

Chemically this compound is closely related to the other chlorophylls, differing from chlorophyll a only in having 'two less hydrogen atoms in the molecule. There is good evidence that protochlorophyll is the immediate precursor of chlorophyll a. Reduction of protochlorophyll to chlorophyll a appears to be the last step in the synthesis of this latter compounds.

In the higher plants, at least, this reaction occurs only in the light, and the protochlorophyll is the light-absorbing agent for its own transformation to chlorophyll *a*.

If a solution of chlorophyll in an organic solvent is exposed to bright light its colour soon fades because of a destructive effect of light upon the chlorophyll. This is in all probability a photo-oxidation process, since it is accomplished by the absorption of oxygen.

Strong light also brings about the disintegration of the chlorophylls in leaves, although at a less rapid rate than in chlorophyll solutions. In leaves exposed to intense light, therefore, synthesis and decomposition of chlorophylls are probably going on simultaneously.

In accord with this concept are the results of Shirley (1929) who found in a number of species of plants that the, chlorophyll content per unit leaf weight or per unit leaf area increased with decreasing light intensity until a relatively low intensity was reached. Further decrease in light intensity below this value caused a decrease in chlorophyll content.

Oxygen

In the absence of oxygen etrolated seedlings fail to develop chlorophylls even when illuminated underconditions otherwise favorable for chlorophyll formation. Oxygen must therefore be required in some of the steps in the sequence of reactions whereby chlorophyll is synthesized.

Carbohydrates

Etiolated leaves which have been depleted of soluble carbohydrates fail to turn green even when all of the other conditions to which they are exposed favourchlorophyll synthesis. When such leaves are floated on a sugar solution, sugar is absorbed and *chlorophyll* formation occurs rapidly. A supply of carbohydrate foods is therefore essential for the formation of chlorophyll.

Nitrogen

Since nitrogen is a part of chlorophyll molecules it is not surprising to find that a deficiency of this element in the plant retards chlorophyll formation. Failure ofchlorophylls to develop is one of the commonly recognized symptoms of nitrogen deficiency in plants.

Magnesium

Like nitrogen this element is also a part of chlorophyll molecules. Deficiency of magnesium in plants results in the development of a characteristic mottled chlorosis of the older, leaves.

Iron

In the absence of iron in an available form green. plants are unable to synthesize chlorophylls and the leaves soon become blanched or yellow in colour. While not a constituent

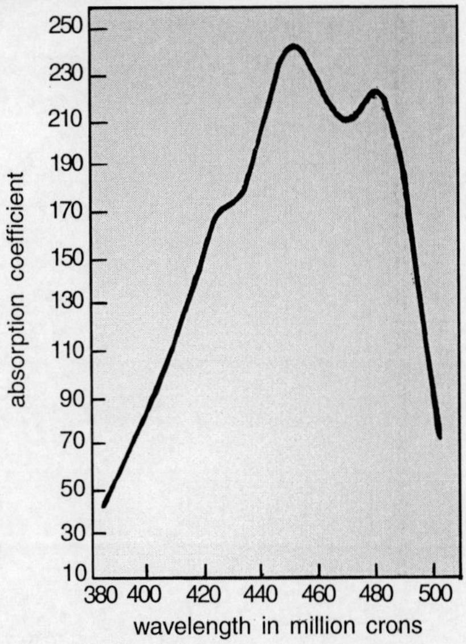

Figure 3.4: Absorption spectrum of β-carotene in ether-alcohol solution.

of chlorophyll molecules, iron is essential for its synthesis.

Other Mineral Elements

In the absence of manganese, copper, or zinc, more or less characteristic chloroses develop in plants. These substances apparently play at least indirect roles in the synthesis of chlorophyll.

Temperature

In general, chlorophyll synthesis can cur over a wide range of temperatures. In etiolated wheat plants synthesis of chlorophylls occurs at any temperature within the range 3°-48°C, but is most rapid between 26° and 30°C.

Somewhat similar results have been obtained on chlorophyll synthesis in potato tubers except that synthesis appears to be most rapid in the approximate range 11°-19°C. The range off temperatures over which chlorophyll synthesis occurs as well as the temperature of most rapid synthesis undoubtedly varies considerably from one species to another.

Table 3.1. Molecular proportions of the chioroplast pigments present in leaves at different seasons.

Species	Date	Appearance of leaves	Molecular propartions		
			Chlorophyll a Chlorophyll b	*Carotene Xmuhophylls*	*Chlorephyll a and b Carotens and Xanthophylls*
European Elder	July	Green	2.74	0.59	3.33
(Sambucusnigra)	Oct. 21	Green	2.61	0.60	3.15
Sunflower	Oct. 7	Green	2.86	0.54	3.66
Helionthus	Nov. 5	Yellow green	4.01	0.26	1.27
annuus	Nov. 5	Yellow	.95	0.17	0.32
Horse Chestnut	Oct. 24	Green	4.23	0.47	3.06
(Aesculus hlp-pocastanum)	Oct. 24	Yellow green	4.23	0.20	0.81

Water

Desiccation of leaf tissues not only inhibits synthesis of chlorophylls but seems to accelerate disintegration of the chlorophylls already present. A familiar example of this effect is the browning of grass during droughts.

The mechanism of chlorophyll synthesis is very sensitive to any type of physiological disturbance within the plant. Many other conditions besides those already discussed, such as lack of certain other mineral elements, deficient aeration of the roots, infestations of insects, or infection with bacterial fungous or viral diseases, may induce, directly or indirectly, partial or complete chlorosis of the leaves.

The failure of chlorophyll synthesis to take place normally is often one of -the first observable symptoms of almost any derangement in the metabolic conditions within a plant.

The Carotenoids

This group of orange, red, yellow, and brownish pigments includes a number of chloroplast pigments. At least sixty different carotenoids are known to be present in plants. Best known of the pigments in this group is the - orange-yellow *carotene.*

This is a hydrocarbon with the formula $C_{40}H_{54}$ and exists in three isomeric forms. β-carotene is the most abundant of these in plants, and appears to be invariably present in the chloroplasts.

This compound is the precursor of vitamin A which is formed in the animal body by a simple hydrolytic splitting of the molecules of n-carotene, as follows:

$$C_{40}H_{51}+2H_2O \rightarrow 2C_{20}H_{29}OH$$

Lycopene, a red pigment found in the fruits of tomato, red peppers, roses, and other species, is also isomeric with carotene.

The xanthophylls or carotenols are mostly yellow or brownish pigments, many, but not all, of which have molecular formula $C_{40}H_{65}O_2$. Chemically the carotenols are closely related to carotene, and undoubtedly transformations from one kind of carotenoid to another occur readily in plants.

Luteol is by far the most abundant carotenol is leaves other leaf xanthophylls include zeaxanthol, violaxanthol, cryptoxanthol, flavoxanthol, and neoxanthin.

Numerous other xanthophylls occur in the various *phyla* of *algae*. Among the most abundant of these pigments art the fucoxanthins which impart to brown algae their distinctive colour.

Several brownish carotenols are also present in the diatoms, including fucoxanthins, diatoxanthin, and diadinoxanthin. The carotenoids are not water soluble, but they can be extracted from plant tissues by use of suitable organic solvents.

Carotene, for example, is soluble in ethyl ether, chloroform, and carbon bisulfide. Leaf xanthophylls are soluble in chloroform and ethyl alcohol, but only slightly soluble in carbon, bisulfide.

All of the carotenoids are highly unsaturated compounds and hence readily oxidizable. Loss of a considerable proportion of the carotenoids present in a plant tissue may be occasioned by oxidation during extraction procedures.

As shown by its absorption spectrum, β-carotene absorbs only wave lengths in the blue-violet portion of the visible spectrum. The absorption spectra of other carotenoidse are similar to that of carotene.

Most, if not all, of the carotenoid pigments can be synthesized by plants in the absence of light.

Relative Quantities of the Chloroplast Pigments Present fn ,Green Leaves. Data regarding the molecular proportions of the chloroplast pigments in the leaves of several species are presented in Table elsewhere in this chapter.

The leaves listed in this table contain about three molecules of the chlorophylls to one molecule of 'the carotenoids, about three molecules of chlorophyll a to each molecule of chlorophyll *b*, and about two molecules of xanthophylls to each molecule of carotene.

Although these values can be taken as representative, considerable variation in the proportions of the chloroplast pigments occurs as a result of differences in genetic factors, environmental conditions, and the age of the Leaf.

As shown in Table elsewhere in this chapter, with senescence of leaves in the autumn there is a marked increase in the proportion of carotenoids to chlorophylls as a result of the disintegration of the chlorophylls.

The proportion of chlorophyll a to b in leaves may vary considerably depending upon the light intensity to which the leaves have been exposed. Will Matter and Stoll (1928) and others, for example, have shown that the proportion of chlorophyll b to a is higher in shade leaves of many species than in sun leaves of the same species.

As an example of genetic differences in the pigment content of leaves, results obtained with dark and burley varieties of tobacco may be taken as illustrative.

Although the ratio of chlorophyll *a* to *b* was virtually the same in all varieties studied the total chlorophyll content per gram of dry weight was, on the average, more than 50 per cent greater in the dark varieties than in the burley varieties. Carotene content of the dark varieties was also appreciably higher than in the burley varieties.

THE ROLE OF CHLOROPHYLL IN PHOTOSYNTHESIS

Any effort to understand the basis of life on this planet must always come back to photosynthesis : the process that enables plants to grow by utilizing carbon dioxide (CO_2), water (H_2O) and a tiny amount of minerals.

Photosynthesis is the one large-scale process that converts simple, stable, inorganic. compounds into the energy-rich combination of organic matter and oxygen and thereby makes abundant life on earth possible. photosynthesis is the source of all living matter on earth, and of all biological energy.

The overall reaction of photosynthesis can be summarized in the following equation : CO_2+H_2O+light "' (CH_2O)+O_2 → 12,000 calories of energy permole. (CH_2O) stands for a carbbhydrate ; for example, glucose : $(CH_2O)_6$. "Mole" is short !hr' "*gram molecule*": one gram multiplied by the molecular weight of the substances in question-in this case carbohydrate and oxygen.

The state of knowledge of photosynthesis was first summarized 30 years ago. The whole process was, heavily shrouded in fog.

Rabinowitch; Scientific American Offprint 34]. Later investigation had penetrated the mists sufficiently to disclose some of the main features of the process [see "Progress in, Photosynthesis," by Eugene I. Rabinowitch ; Scientific American, November, 1953].

Since then much new knowledge has been accumulated in particular the sequence of chemical ,steps that convert carbon dioxide into carbohydrate is now understood in considerable detail [see "The Path of Carbon ins Photosynthesis," by J.A. Bassham ; Scientific American .Offprint 122].

The fog has thinned out in other areas, and, the day when the entire sequence of physical and chemical events in photosynthesis will be well understood seems much, closer.

The photosynthetic process apparently consists of three main stages:

(1) the removal of hydrogen atoms from water and the production of oxygen molecules;

(2) the transfer of the hydrogen atoms from an intermediate compound in the first stage to one in the third stage, and

(3) the use of the hydrogen atoms to convert carbon dioxide into a carbohydrate.

The least understood of these three stages is the first : the removal of hydrogen atoms from water with the release of oxygen. All that is known is that it entails a series of steps probably requiring several enzymes, one of which contains manganese.

The third stage-the production of carbohydrates from carbon dioxide-is the best understood, thanks largely to the work of Melvin Calvin and his co-workers at the University of California at Berkeley. The subject of our article is the second. stage : the transfer of hydrogen atoms from the first stage to the third.

This is the energy-storing part of photosynthesis ; in it, to use the words of Robert Mayer, a discoverer of the law of the conservation of energy, "the fleeting sun rays are fixed and skillfully stored for future use."

The light energy to be converted into chemical energy by photosynthesis is first taken up by plant pigments, primarily the green pigment chlorophyll. In photosynthesis chlorophyll functions as a photocatalyst; when it is in its energized state,. which results from the absorption of light it catalyzes an energy-storing chemical reaction.

This reaction is the primary photochemical process ; it is followed by a sequence of secondary "dark"—that is, non photo-chemical-reactions in which no further energy is stored. Once it was thought that in photosynthesis the primary photochemical process is the decomposition of carbon dioxide into carbon and oxygen, followed by the combination of carbon and water.

More recently it has been suggested that the energy of light serves primarily to dissociate water, presumably into hydroxyl radicals (OH) and hydrogen atoms; the hydroxyl radicals would then react to form oxygen molecules.

It is better than either of these two formulations to say that the primary photochemical process in photosynthesis is the boosting of hydrogen atoms from a stable association with oxygen in water molecules to a much less stable one with carbon in organic matter.

The oxygen atoms "*left behind*" combine into oxygen molecules, an association also much less stable than the one between oxygen and hydrogen in water. The replacement of stable bonds (between oxygen and hydrogen) by looser bonds (between oxygen and oxygen and between hydrogen and carbon) obviously requires a supply of energy, and it explains why energy is stored in photosynthesis.

The transfer of hydrogen atoms from one *molecule* to another is called *oxidation-reduction*. The *hydrogen atom* is transferred from a donor molecule (a "*reductant*") to an acceptor molecule (an "*oxidant*"); after the reaction the donor is said to be oxidized and the acceptor to be reduced.

The transfer of an electron can often substitute for the transfer of a hydrogen atom: in an aqueous system (such as the interior of the living cell) there are always hydrogen ions (H+), and if such an ion combines with the electron acceptor, the acquisition of an electron becomes equivalent to the acquisition of a hydrogen atom (electron + H^+ ion $\rightarrow$ H^+ atom).

The chain of oxidation-reduction reactions in photosynthesis has some links that involve electron transfers and others, that involve hydrogen-atom transfers. For the sake of simplicity we shalls speak of electron transfers, with the understanding that in some cases what is actually transferred is a hydrogen atom. Indeed, the end result of the reactions undoubtedly is the transfer of hydrogen atoms.

In the oxidation-reduction reactions of photosynthesis the electrons must be pumped "*uphill*", that is why energy must be supplied to make the reaction go.

The tiny chlorophyll containing chloroplasts of the photosynthesizing plant cell act au chemical pumps; they obtain the necessary power from the absorption of light by chlorophyll (and to some extent from absorption by other pigments in the chloroplast).

It is important to realize that the energy is stored in the two products organic matter and free oxygen and not in either of them separately. To release the energy by the combustion of the organic matter (or by respiration, which is slow, enzyme-catalyzed combustion) the two products must be brought together again.

How much energy is stored in the transfer of electrons from water to carbon dioxide, converting the carbon dioxide to -carbohydrate and forming a proportionate amount of oxygen?

Oxidation-reduction energy can conveniently be measured an terms of electrochemical potential. Between a given donor of electrons and a given acceptor there is a certain difference of oxidation-reduction potentials.

This difference depends not only on the nature of the two reacting substances but also on the nature of the products of the reaction ; it is characteristic of the two oxidation-reduction "couples." For example, when oxygen is reduced to water (H_2O) its potential is +.81 volt, 'but when it is reduced to hydrogen peroxide (H_2O_2) the potential is +.27 volt.

The more positive the potential, the stronger is the oxidative power of the couple; the more negative the potential, the stronger is its reducing power.

When two oxidation-reduction couples are brought together, the one containing the stronger oxidant tends to oxidize the one containing the stronger reductant. In photosynthesis, however, a weak oxidant (CO_2) must oxidize a weak reductant (H_2O), producing a strong oxidant (O_2) and a strong reductant (a *carbohydrate*).

This calls for a massive investment of energy. The specific amount needed is given by the difference "between the oxidation-reduction potentials of the two couples involved in the reaction:oxygen-water and carbon-dioxidec-arbohydrate.

The oxygen-water potential is about -h.8 volt ; the carbon-dioxide-carbohydrate potential, about -.4 volt. The transfer of a single electron from water to carbon dioxide thus requires +.8 minus-.4, or 1.2, electron volts of energy.

For a molecule of carbon dioxide to be reduced to

CH_2O—the elementary molecular group of a carbohydrate *four* electrons (or hydrogen atoms) must be transferred ; hence the total energy needed is 4.8 electron volts.

This works out to 112,000 calories per mole of carbon dioxide reduced and of oxygen liberated. In short, the pumping of electrons in the second stage of photosynthesis entails the storage of 112,000 calories of energy per mole for each set of four electrons transferred.

We know the identity of the primary electron donor in photosynthesis (water) and of the ultimate electron acceptor (carbon dioxide), but what are the intermediates involved in the transfer of electrons from the first stage to the third?

This has become the focal problem in recent studies of the photosynthetic process. As a matter of fact, it is not yet definitely known what compound releases electrons from the first stage, and what compound receives them in the third; that is why these compounds are respectively labeled ZH and X in the illustration at the left. About the donor, ZH, we have almost no information ; the following considerations suggest the possible nature of the primary acceptor, X.

From the study of the mechanism of respiration we are familiar with an important oxidation-reduction catalyst : nicotinamide adenine dinucleotide phosphate, or NADP (formerly known as triphosphopyridine nucleotide, or TPN). NADP has an oxidation reduction potential of about-.32 volt, thus in itself it is not a strong enough reductant to provide the -.4-electron volt potential needed to reduce carbon dioxide to carbohydrate.

NADP can achieve this feat, however, if it is supplied with additional energy in the form of the high-energy compound adenosine triphosphate, or ATP. A molecule of ATP supplies about 10,000 calories per mole when its terminal phosphate group is split off, and this is enough to provide the needed boost to the reducing power of NADP.

Furthermore, we know that NADP is reduced when cell-free preparations of chloroplasts are illuminated. Put together, these two facts led to the now widely accepted hypothesis that the second stage of photosynthesis manufactures both ATP and reduced NADP and feeds them into the third stage.

At first it was assumed that NADP is identical with X, the primary acceptor in our scheme. Subsequent experiments by various workers-notably Anthony San Pietro at Johns Hopkins University and Daniel. Arnon and his colleagues at the University of California at Berkeley-suggested, however, that NADP is preceded in the "*bucket brigade*" of electron transfer by ferredoxin, a protein that contains iron.

This compound has an oxidation-reduction potential of about -.42 volt ; therefore if it is reduced in light it can bring about the reduction of NADP by a "dark" reaction requiring no additional energy supply. More recently Bessel Kok of the Research Institute for Advanced Studies in Baltimore has found evidence suggesting that compound X may be a still stronger reductant, with a potential of about -.6 volt.

If this is so, plants have the alternatives of either applying this stronger reductant directly to the reduction of carbon dioxide or letting it reduce first ferredoxin and then NADP and using reduced NADP to reduce carbon dioxide.

It seems a roundabout procedure to create a reductant sufficiently strong for the task at hand, then to sacrifice a part of its reducing power and finally to use ATP to compensate for the loss. It is not unknown, however, for nature to resort to devious ways in order to achieve its aims.

For photosynthesis to be a self-contained process the required high-energy phosphate ATP must be itself manufactured by photosynthesis. The formation of ATP has in fact been detected in illuminated fragments of bacteria by Albert W. Frenkel of the University of Minnesota and in chloroplast fragments by Arnon and his co-workers.

As a matter of fact, November, 1960. As a matter of fact, ATP is needed not only to act as a booster in the reduction of an intermediate in the carbon cycle by reduced NADP but also for another step in the third stage of photosynthesis.

According to a sequence of reactions worked out in 1951 by Andrew A. Benson and his colleagues at the University of California at Berkeley, carbon dioxide enters photosynthesis by first reacting with a "*carbon dioxide acceptor*," a special sugar phosphate called rebulose diphosphate.

It turns out that the production of this compound from its precursorribulose monophosphate-cells for a molecule of ATP. ATP is produced both in chloroplasts and in mitochondria, the tiny intracellular bodies that are the site of the energyliberating stage of respiration in animals as well as plants.

The mitochondria produce ATP as their main function, exporting it as packaged energy for many life processes. The chloroplasts, on the other band, make ATP only as an auxiliary source of energy for certain internal purposes.

The energy of the light falling on the chloroplasts is stored mostly as oxidation-reduction energy by the uphill transfer of electrons. Only a relatively small fraction is diverted to the formation of ATP, and this fraction too ultimately becomes part of the oxidation reduction energy of the final products of photosynthesis : oxygen and carbohydrate.

Let us now consider the uphill transport of electrons in greater detail. Recent investigations have yielded considerable information about this stage. Apparently the pumping of the etectrons is a two-step affair, and among the most important intermediates in it are the catalysts called cytochromes.

The idea of a two-step electron transfer process grew from a consideration of the energy economy of photosynthesis. Precise measurements, particularly those made by the late-Robert Emerson and his co-workers at the University of Illinois, showed that the reduction of one molecule of carbon· dioxide to carbohydrate, and the liberation of one molecule of' oxygen, requires a minimum of eight quanta of light energy.

The maximum quantum yield of photosynthesis, defined as,, the number of oxygen molecules that can be released for each quantum of light absorbed by the plant cell, is thus 1/8, or 12 per cent. Since the transfer of four electrons is involved in the reduction of one carbon dioxide molecule, it was suggested that it takes two light quanta to move each electron.

Emerson and his colleagues went on to determine the *quantum* yield of *photosynthesis* in *maximicronatic right* of different *wavelengths* throughout the visible spetrum. They found that the yield, although is remained constant at about 12 per cent in most of the spectrum, dropped sharply near thespectrum's far-red end.

This decline in quantum yield, called the "red drop," begins at a wavelength of 680 millimicrons in green plants and at 650 millimicrons in red algae. These are two chlorophylls present in green plants; chlorophyll *a* and chlorophyll *b*.

Only chlorophyll *a* absorbs light at wavelengths longer than 680 millimicrons; the absorptionn of chlorophyll b rises to a peak at 650 millimicrons and becomes negligible at about 680 millimicrons.

Emerson found that the quantum yield of photosynthesis at the farred end of the spectrum beyond 680 millimicrons can be brought -to the full efficiency of 12 per cent by simultaneously exposing the plant to a second beam of light with a wavelength of 650 milli microns.

In other words, when light primarily absorbed by chlorophyll a was supplemented by light primarily absorbed by chlorophyll *b*. both beams gave rise to oxygen at the full rate.

This relative excess in photosynthesis when a plant is exposed to two beams of light simultaneously, as compared with the yield produced by the same two beams separately, is known as the Emerson effect, or enhancement.

On the basis of his discovery Emerson concluded that photosynthesis involves two photochemical processes: one using energy supplied by chlorophyll a, the other using energy supplied by chlorophyll *b* or some other "*accessory*" pigment.

Experimenting with various combinations of a constant far-red beam with beams of shorter wavelength. and using four different types of algae (green, red, blue-green and brown), Emerson's group found that the strongest enhancement always occurred when the second beam was absorbed mainly by the most important accessory pigment (the green pigment chlorophyll *b* in green cells, the red pigment phycoerytbrin in red algae, the blue pigment phycocyanin in blue-green, algae and the reddish pigment fucoxanthol in brown algae).

Such results suggested that these other pigments are not mere accessories of chlorophyll a but have an important function of their own in photosynthesis.

Certain findings concerning the behaviour of pigments in living plant cells, however, seemed to make this conclusion untenable, illuminated plant cells fluoresce; that is pigment molecules energized by the absorption of light quanta reemit some of the absorbed energy as fluorescent light. The source of fluorescence can be identified, because each substance has its own characteristic fluorescence spectrum.

The main fluorescing pigment in plants always proves to be chlorophyll a, even when the light is absorbed by another pigment. This had first been shown for brown algae in a study conducted in 1943 by H. 7. Dutton, W. H. Manning and B. B. Duggar at the University of Wisconsin; later the finding was extended to other organisms by L. N. M. Duysens of the University of Leiden.

Known as sensitized fluorescence, the phenomenon indicates that the initial absorber has transferred its energy of excitation to chlorophyll *a*; the transfer is effected by a kind of resonance process.

Careful measurements have shown that pertain accessory pigments-chloropbyll *b,* phycoerythrin, phycocyanin and facoxanthol—pass on to chlorophyll a between 80 and 100 percent of the light quanta they absorb.

For some other accessory pigments-for example carotene—the transfer is less efficient. This puts accessory pigments back 'n the role of being mere adjuncts to chlorophyll a. True, they can contribute, by means of resonance transfer, light energy to photosynthesis, thereby improving the supply of energy in regions of the spectrum where chlorophyll *a* is a poor absorber.

Chlorophyll *a,* however, collects all this energy before it is used in the primary *photochemical* process. Why, then, the enhancement effect ? .Why should chlorophyll a need, in order to give rise to fullrate photosynthesis, one "*secondhand*" quantum obtained by resonance transfer from another absorber in addition to the one quantum it had absorbed itself?

A better understanding of this paradox resulted from the discovery that there apparently exist in the cell not *only* chlorophyll *a* and chlorophyll *b* but also two forms of chlorophyll *a.* These two forms have different light-absorption characteristics, and they probably also have different photochemical functions.

In the living cell chlorophyll a absorbs light most strongly in abroad band with its peak between 670 and 680 millimicrons. In our laboratory at the University of Illinois we ,undertook to plot the Emerson effect more carefully than before as a function of the wavelength of the enhancing light.

We found that for green and brown cells the resulting curve showed, in addition to peaks corresponding to strong absorption by the accessory pigments, a peak at 670 millimicrons that most be due to chlorophyll a itself. It was this finding that suggested the existence of two forms of chlorophyll *a.*

The form that absorbs light at the longer wavelengths-mainly above 680 millimicrons—seemed to belong to one pigment system, now often called System I.

The form that absorbs at 670 millimicrons seemed to belong to another pigment system ; System II. In the second system the form of chlorophyll a that absorbs at 670 millimicrons is strongly assisted by accessory pigments, probably by resonance transfer of their excitation energy.

Careful analysis of the absorption band of chlorophyll a by C. Stacy French of the Carnegie Institution of Washington's Department of Plant Biology, and also in our laboratory, confirmed that the band is double, with one peak near 670 millimicrons (at 668 millimicrons) and another band at 683 millimicrons.

If chlorophyll a is extracted from living plants, there is only one product; we must therefore assume that in the living cell the two forms differ in the way malecules of chlorophyll a are clumped together, or in the way they are associated with different chemical partners (proteins lipids or other substances).

Be this as it may, the important implication of the new finding is that photosynthesizing cells possess two light-absorbing systems, one containing a form of chlorophyll a absorbing around 683 millimicrons and the other a form , absorbing around 670.

The latter system includes chlorophyll *b* (in green-plant cells) or other accessory pigments (in brown, red and blue-green algae). Further investigation-particularly of red algae-has suggested however that the distribution of these two components in the two systems may be less clear-cut.

In red algae a large fraction of the chlorophyll a absorbing at 670 millimicrons seems to belong to System I rather than System II. In all likelihood the two systems provide energy for two different photochemical reactions, and efficiency in photosynthesis requires that the rates of the two reactions be equal.

What are these reactions? This question brings us to

another significant finding, which suggested the participation of *cytochromes* in *photosynthesis*.

Cytochromes are proteins that carry an iron atom in a& attached chemical group. They are found in all mitochondria, where they serve to catalyze the reactions of respiration. Robert Hill and his co-workers at the University of Cambridge—first found that chloroplasts also contain cytochromes-two kinds of them. One, which they named cytochrome f, has a positive oxidation-reduction potential of about 4 volt.

The other, which they named cytochrome b_6, has a potential of about 0 volt. In 1960 Hill, together with Fay Bendall, proposed an ingenious hypothesis as to how the two cytochromes. might act as intermediate carriers of electrons and connect the two photochemical systems.

They suggested that cytochrome b_6 receives an electron by a photochemical reaction from the electron donor ZH ; the electron is then passed on to cytochrome f by a "downhill" reaction requiring, no light energy. (The oxidation-reduction potential of cytochrome *f* is much more positive than that of cytochrome b_6).

A second photochemical reaction moves the electron uphill again, from cytochrome *f* to the electron-acceptor X in the third stage of photosynthesis. In this sequence the photochemical reactions store energy and the reaction between the two cytochromes releases energy.

Some of the released energy, however, can be salvaged by the formation of an ATP molecule; this occurs in, the transfer of electrons among cytochromes in respiration. In this way ATP is obtained without spending extra light quanta on its formation, which the tight energy economy of photosynthesis does not allow.

Experiments by Duysens and his associates confirmed this, hypothesis, by showing that the absorption of light by System 1 causes the oxidation of a cytochrome, whereas the absorptionn of light by System II causes its reduction.

This is exactly what we would expect. The illustration

on the opposite page shows that the light reaction of System II should flood the intermediates between the two photochemical reactions with electrons taken from ZH; the light reaction of System I should drain these electrons away, sending them up to the acceptor X and into the third stage of photosynthesis.

This, then, describes in a general way the oxidation-reduction process by which the chloroplasts store the energy of light in photosynthesis. Several other investigators havecontributed evidence for the two-step mechanism; notable among them are French, Kok, Arnon, Horst Witt of the MaxVollmer Institute in Berlin and their colleagues.

In detail the process probably is much more complex than our scheme suggests. Its "*downhill*" central part seems to include, in addition to the two cytochromes, certain compounds of the group known as quinones and also plastocyanin, a protein that contains copper. What is known of the submicroscopic structure in which the reactions of the second stage of photosynthesis take place?

There is, much evidence that the *photosynthetic* apparatus consists of "*units*" within the chloroplasts, each unit containing about 300 *chlorophyll molecules.* This picture first emerged. from experiments conducted in 1932 by Emerson and William Arnold on photosynthesis during flashes of light; it was later supported by various other observations.

The pigment molecules are packed so closely in the unit that when one of them is excited by light it readily transfers its excitation to a neighbor by resonance. The energy goes on traveling through the unit, rather as the steel ball in a pinball machine bounces around among the pins and turns on one light after another.

Eventually the migrating energy quantum arrives at the entrance to an enzymatic "conveyor belt," where it is trapped' and utilized either to load an electron onto the belt or to unload one from it. (The steel-ball analogy should not betaken litorally the migration of energy is a quantum-mechanical phenomenon, and the quantum's location can only be defined in terms of probability; its entrapment depends on the probability of finding it at the entrance to the conveyor belt).

How is the quantum trapped ? The trap must be a pigment molecule with what is called a lower excited state; the migrating quantum can stumble into such a molecule but cannot come out of it. Kok has found evidence that System I contains a small amount of a special form of chlorophyll called pigment 700 because it absorbs light at a wavelength of 700 millimicrons; this pigment could serve as a trap for the quantum bouncing around in System I.

There seems to be a proper amount of pigment 700: about one molecule per unit. Furthermore, experiments suggest that pigment 700 is oxidized by light absorbed in System I and reduced by light absorbed in System II.

It has an oxidation reduction potential of about +.4 volt. All these properties fit the role we have assigned pigment 700 in our scheme: collecting energy from a 300-molecule unit in System I, using it to transfer an electron to the acceptor X and recovering the electron from cytochrome *f*.

One suspects that there should be a counterpart of pigment 700 in System II, but so far none has been convincingly demonstrated. We believe, however, that a pigment we have tentatively named pigment 680-from the anticipated position of its absorption band-does serve as an energy trap in System II.

Its existence is supported by the discovery of a new fluorescent emission band of chlorophyll at 693 millimicrons, which is compatible with absorption at 680 millimicrons. This band is emitted by certain algae when they are exposed to strong light of the wavelengths absorbed by System II.

What is the spatial organization of the pigment systems in the electron-boosting mechanism of the second stage of photosynthesis ? It seems that the two systems may be arranged in two monomolecular layers, with a protein layer between them containing the enzymatic conveyor belt. Chloroplasts are known from electron microscope studies to consist of a set of lamellae thin alternating layers of protein and fatty material piled one atop the other. Each layer appears to consist of particles arrayed rather like cobblestones in a pavement.

The particles were first observed in electron micrographs made by E. Steinmann of the Technische Hochschule in Zurich ; subsequently Roderio B. Park and John Biggins of the University of California at Berkeley made clearer micrographs of the particles and named them quantasomes.

The units comprising Sytems I and II may operate independently or they may be sufficiently close together to exchange energy by resonance, when such exchange is needed to maintain a balanced rate of operation by the two systems.

The picture of the energy-storing second stage of photosynthesis presented in this article is, of course, still only a working hypothesis. Alternative hypotheses are possible, one of which we shall briefly describe.

For many years the late James Franck, who shared the Nobel prize in physics for 1925, tried to develop a plausible *physio-chemical* mechanism of photosynthesis. In 1963 he proposed, together with Jerome L. Rosenberg of the University of Pittsburgh, a concept according to which the two consecutive photochemical steps occur in one and the same energy trap.

In other words, according to Franck, the same *chlorophyll molecule* that takes the electron away from the initial donor ZH and transfers it to a cytochrome then supplies energy for the transfer of the electron from the cytochrome to the acceptor X. In the first transfer, Franck suggested, the chlorophyll a molecule functions in the short-lived "*singlet*" excited state (in which the valence electrons have opposite spins) ; in the second transfer it functions in the long-lived "*triplet*" state (in which the valence electrons have parallel spins).

Franck's hypothesis avoids certain difficulties of the "two trap" theory, but new difficulties arise in their place. On balance the two-trap picture seems to us the more plausible one at present.

No doubt this picture will change as more information emerges. It is merely a first effort to penetrate the inner sanctum of photosynthesis, the photocatalytic laboratory in which the energy of sunlight is converted into the chemical energy of life.

Chapter 4

MEASURING PHOTOSYNTHETIC PIGMENTS

The concentration of photosynthetic pigments is commonly used as a measure of the amount of plant material in a sample, and photosynthesis rates are frequently normalized to chlorophyll a concentration.

In addition, assessments of pigment composition provides qualitative information on the physiological condition of natural samples by providing information on the presence of breakdown products and provides information on the taxonomic composition of algal populations *via* an analysis of accessory pigments.

Estimations of pigment content and complement are also the basis of quantitative assessments of the relationship among light harvesting, photosynthesis, and growth.

Chlorophyll a is the only photosynthetic pigment found in all oxygenevolving photoautotrophs and so provides a convenient and unambiguous measure of algal abundance.

However, the ratio of chlorophyll a to algal biomass ranges from 0.1% to 5% of dry weight, and varies in response to changes in irradiance, nutrient availability, and temperature.

In addition to chlorophyll a, algae contain accessory pigments that often account for most of the *in vivo* absorption. These pigments include chlorophylls *b* and c, carotenoids, and phycobiliproteins.

EXTRACTION OF CHLOROPHYLLS AND CAROTENOIDS

Chlorophylls a and *b* consist of a magnesium porphyrin complex with a long hydrophobic side chain, whereas chlorophyll c is actually a chlorophyllide that lacks the phytol tail. Carotenoids are long polyisoprenoids having conjugated double bonds with unsaturated unsubstituted cyclohexane rings at each end of the molecule.

There are two classes of carotenoids: carotenes, which are hydrocarbons, and xanthophylls, which contain oxygen atoms in their terminal rings. Chlorophylls can be characterized spectrophotometrically as having relatively sharp absorption maxima in both the blue and red spectral regions.

The carotenoids, in contrast, usually have a broad yellow absorption band, perhaps with several local maxima within this broad band. Chlorophylls and carotenoids can be extracted in organic solvents: acetone has been the solvent of choice for oceanographers, although investigators who study macroalgae and freshwater phytoplankton prefer the more polar solvent methanol, which provides a higher extraction efficiency.

Macroalgal samples are blotted dry, cut into small pieces, and extracted by grinding tissues in a mixture of solvent and an abrasive such as sand, whereas microalgae are commonly concentrated by filtration, followed by homogenization in a solvent using a tissue grinder.

Solubilized pigments are separated from residual material by centrifugation or filtration. The homogenization step is sometimes omitted in analyses of microalgae in order to decrease the processing time.

Specifically, a sample can be concentrated onto a filter, placed in a vial containing solvent, and allowed to extract overnight in the cold at 4°C or in a deep freeze at -20°C. Phinney and Yentsch (1985) recommend direct injections of samples into 100% acetone (to obtain a final concentration of 85%) for pigment extraction of microalgae.

Incomplete pigment extraction may be encountered with less laborintensive procedures, particularly when chlorophytes and cyanobacteria are present in samples extracted with 90% acetone. Complete extraction from microalgal samples can be obtained with either hot 100% methanol or a 1:1 mixture of dimethyl sulfoxide (DMSO) and acetone.

Complete extraction of pigments from macroalgae presents more problems, and an initial extraction with DMSO following by extraction with acetone or methanol has become a method of choice for extracting pigments from recalcitrant species (Duncan and Harrison, 1982).

Plant physiologists have found that N_0N-dimethylfo-rmamide (DMF) is an effective solvent for extracting chlorophylls a and b from vascular plants. This solvent may also prove useful for macroalgal samples. Chlorophylls and carotenoids are labile compounds that may decompose when exposed to light, acids, or oxygen. Precautions must be taken to avoid chemical degradation and photooxidation: these include working at low temperature under subdued illumination or darkness and using deoxygenated solvents.

Addition of H_2S to methanol is commonly recommended, and $MgCO_3$ is often added to the sample prior to extraction to neutralize organic acids, which may be released when tissues are disrupted. The principal breakdown products of chlorophylls a and b are pheophytins, chlorophyllides, and pheophorbides.

Acidification of chlorophyll leads to pheophytin product-ion through removal of magnesium from the porphyrin ring. Chlorophyllide is produced by the removal of the phytol chain from chlorophyll a by chlorophyllase. Pheophorbide is produced by the removal of both magnesium and phytol.

Pheophytins and pheophorbides may be present at large concentrations in natural samples as a result of zooplankton grazing, senescence, and/or decomposition.

Chlorophyllide may be produced during sample extract-ion because chlorophyllase remains active in aqueous organic solvents. In addition, pheophytin or pheophorbide may be produced if organic acids are not neutralized during extraction.

Chlorophyllase is active even in 90% acetone, and extraction in 100% acetone has been recommended to inhibit chlorophyllase activity. Even this may not be sufficient, and Suzuki and Fujita (1986) suggest a brief exposure to heat (65°C) to completely inactivate chlorophyllase.

QUANTIFICATION OF CHLOROPHYLLS AND CAROTENOIDS

Pigments are commonly identified by their absorption spectra, and routine methods for determining pigment concentrations in solvent extracts rely on spectrophotometric measurements. Several different expressions are used to quantitatively describe the absorption characteristics of pigments.

Much of the older data is reported as specific extinction coefficients designated E_{1cm}, where 1 cm refers to the pathlength of the spectrophotometer cell used to measure absorbance. More recently, molar and weight-specific absorption coefficients have become the preferred units. The following relationship can be used to convert among these different expressions:

$$A^* = A_m/M = E_{1cm}10 \quad (4.1)$$

where: A^* is the $\log_o$ weight-specific absorption coefficient ($m^2 g^{-1}$), A_m is the molar absorption coefficient ($m^2 mol^{-1}$), E_{1cm} is the specific extinction coefficient ($dm^3 \cdot g^{-1} \cdot cm^{-1} = 0.1\ m^2\ g^{-1}$), and M is the molecular weight ($g \cdot mol^{-1}$) of the pigment.

The weight of pigment in a pure sample (such is would be obtained following separation by thin-layer chromatograDhy) can be calculated from the specific absorption coefficient as follows:

$$W/V = D/(A^*1) \quad (4.2)$$

where W is the weight of pigment (in grams), V is the volume of solution (in cubic meters), D is the absorbance

Table 4.1:Specific absorption coefficients, molecular weights and absorption maxima of chlorophylls, chlorophylla degradation products and selected carotenoids.

Pigment	*Solvent*	*max (nm)*	*A*(max) ($m^2 \cdot g^{-1}$)*	*Molecular Weight ($g \cdot mol^{-1}$)*
Chlorophyll	Diethyl ether	423	12.8	893
Diethyl ether	662	9.85		
Acetone	666	8.90		
90% Acetone	664	8.77		
80% Acetone	664	7.68		
Methanol	664	7.14		
Chlorophyllide	90% Acetone	664	12.7	615
Pheophytin a	90% Acetone	667	5.12	869
Pheophorbide	90% Acetone	667	7.42	591
Chlorophyll	Diethyl ether	453	17.5	907
Diethyl ether	643	6.1		
90% Acetone	647	5.14		
80% Acetone	647	4.70		
Methanol	652	3.86		
Chlorophyll	Acetone/pyridine	447	34.9e	611
Acetone/pyridine	630	3.93		
Acetone	629	3.92		
90% Acetone	630	4.26		
Chlorophyll	Acetone/pyridine	447	32.2	609
Acetone/pyridine	630	3.73		
Acetone	631	3.72		
90% Acetone	631	4.26		
β-carotene	Petroleum ether	453	25.92	537
γ-carotene	Petroleum ether	462	31.00	537
Diadinoxanthin	Acetone	453	23.0	659

(Table 4.1 Contd.)

Pigment	Solvent	max (nm)	A*(max) ($m^2 \cdot g^{-1}$)	Molecular Weight ($g \cdot mol^{-1}$)
Fucoxanthin	Acetone	449	16.0	659
Lutein	Acetone	445	25.0	569
Peridinin	Acetone	466	13.4	630
Violaxanthin	Acetone	442	24.0	601
Zeaxanthin	Acetone	452	23.4	569

measured in a spectrophotometer cell with pathlength 1(in meters), and A^* is the specific-absorption coefficient.

By substituting the specific-absorption coefficient for the red absorption maximum of chlorophyll a into Eq. 4.2, one can calculate the concentration of chlorophyll a in extracts from rhodophytes and cyanobacteria, which lack accessory chlorophylls *b* and *c*.

However, Eq. 4.2 cannot be used where absorption bands of several pigments overlap. Series of equations have been developed to allow estimation of chlorophylls a and *b* or chlorophylls a and c in unialgal samples, as well as for the simultaneous estimation of all three chlorophylls in mixed assemblages.

The trichromatic equations of Jeffrey and Humphrey are based on reliable estimates of specific absorption coefficients and yield satisfactory results when applied to mixed algal assemblages.

Determination of chlorophyll concentrations by spectrophotometry in samples that contain degradation products is problematic. Chlorophyl-lides have nearly identical absorption spectra to undegraded chlorophylls and thus can only be separated by chromatography.

Pheophytins and pheophorbides show reduced absorption when compared to chlorophylls: this is associated with the loss of magnesium from the center of porphyrin ring of chlorophyll. A crude estimation of chlorophyll a and pheop-

Table 4.2: Spectrophotometric equations for estimating chlorophyll concentrations.

Jeffrey and Humphrey's (1975) equations for 90% acetone extracts.

Chlorophylls *a* and *b*

$Chl\textit{a} = 11.93\ D_{664} - 1.93\ D_{647}$

$Chl\textit{b} = -5.50\ D_{664} + 20.36\ D_{647}$

Chlorophylls *a* and *c*

$Chla = 11.47\ D_{664} - 0.4\ D_{630}$

$Chic = -3.73D_{664} + 24.36\ D_{630}$

Chlorophylls *a*, *b* and *c*

$Chla = 11.85\ D_{664} - 1.54\ D_{64} - 0.08\ D_{630}$

$Chlb = -5.43\ D_{664} + 21.03\ D_{64} - 2.66D_{630}$

$Chic = -1.67\ D_{664} - 7.60\ D_{64} + 24.52D_{630}$

Lorenzen's (1967) equations for 90% acetone extracts.

Chlorophyll *a* and pheophytin *a*

$Chla = 26.7\ [D_{665}(o) - D_{665}(a)]$

$Pheoa = 26.7\ [1.7D_{665}(a) - D_{665}(o)]$

where $D_{665(o)}$ is the absorbance of a 90% acetone extract and $D_{665(a)}$ is the absorbance of the 90% acetone extract following acidification to pH 2.7.

Jeffrey and Haxo's (1968) equations for 100% methanol extracts.

Chlorophylls *a* and *c*

$Chla = 13.8\ D_{668} - 1.3\ D_{635}$

$Chic = -14.1\ D_{668} - {}^{67.3}\ D_{635}$

Porra et al. (1989) equations for 100% methanol extracts.

Chlorophylls *a* and *b*

$Chla = 16.29\ D_{665} - {}^{8.54}\ D_{652}$

$Chlb = -13.58\ D_{665} + 30.66\ D_{652}$

horbide a concentrations is possible by measuring the absorption at 665 nm before and after acidification of a 90% acetone extract.

The method does not allow discrimination of chlorophyll *a* from chlorophyllide *a,* nor pheophytin *a* from pheophorbide a. In addition, there is no spectrophotometric technique for simultaneously estimating chlorophylls a, *b,* and c and their degradation products.

Samples for spectrophotometric pigment determination can be readily obtained from macroalgal thalli, which have chlorophyll a concentrations of > 100 $mg \cdot m^{-2}$.

However, relatively large volumes of natural phytoplankton assemb-lages, in which chlorophyll a concentrations can be < 0.1 $\mu g\text{-}dm^{-3,}$ may need to be concentrated to obtain enough material for spectrophotometric analysis.

A major improvement in routine estimation of chlorophyll concentration in open ocean waters was provided by the introduction of a fluorometric technique that allows up to a 100-fold increased sensitivity over spectrophotometric methods.

A comparison of spectrophotometric and fluorometric determinations of chlorophyll a from ocean waters indicated agreement between the two techniques to within ± 20%.

Measurement of fluorescence before and after acidification of a sample enables the determination of chlorophyll *a* and pheophorbide *a*, but, unfortunately, as routinely employed, the fluorescence technique does not allow the determination of chlorophylls *b* and *c*.

Unlike the spectrophotometric methods, which give an absolute measure of concentration based on the specific absorption coefficients of the pigments under investigation, the fluorescence methods give a relative measure of pigment concentration and must be calibrated with solutions of known composition.

Fluorescence techniques were originally calibrated against acetone extracts of log-phase algal cultures in which chlorophyll a concentration was determined by a spectrophotometric procedure. However, the relationship between chlorophyll a and fluorescence depends on the accessory pigments that are present, and thus the calibration can vary with the algae used to obtain the pigment extract.

To overcome this problem, many investigators prefer calibration against purified chlorophyll a, which provides an objective standard, even though this may lead to a bias in the estimation of chlorophyll a concentration.

Holm-Hansen et al. (1965) recognized that errors in estimating chlorophyll a by the fluorometric technique could result from interference by other pigments that also fluoresce red when excited by blue light. Using data of Lorenzen and Jeffrey (1980), Trees et al. (1985) were able to provide an equation for predicting the effects of other pigments on the concentration of chlorophyll *a* determined by fluorometry.

The equation relating the chlorophyll *a* concentration obtained by the fluorometric technique of Holm-Hansen et al. (1965) to the pigments present is:

$$C_m = 0.974\ (\text{chlorophyll } a) - 0.282\ (\text{chlorophyll } b) + 0.380\ (\text{chlorophyll } c) + 0.0793\ (\text{pheophorbide } a) + 1.392\ (\text{chlorophyllide } a) \quad (5.3)$$

where C_m, is the measured chlorophyll a concentration and the parentheses are used to indicate the true concentrations of the indicated pigments. Thus, the presence of significant chlorophyll *b* in a sample will lead to underestimates of the chlorophyll a concentration, whereas the presence of significant amounts of chlorophyll c or the degradation products chlorophyllide *a* or pheophorbide *a* will lead to overestimates of the chlorophyll a concentration.

Chromatographic Separation of Pigments

To completely characterize the pigment composition of a sample, it is necessary to chromatographically separate

Table 4.3: Spectral characterization of various phycobiliproteins.

Absorption Phycobiliprotein	Emission λ_{max}	Fluorescence Molecular λ_{max}	Weight (g-mol^{-1})
C-phycocyanin	620	650	120,000
R-phycocyanin	553, 615	640	130,000
Cryptomonad phycocyanins			
phycocyanin-615	585, 615	—	—
-630	585, 630	—	—
-645	585, 620, 645	—	—
phycoerythrocyanin	568, 590	610	103,000
allophycocyanin B	618, 673	680	98,000
allophycocyanin I	654	680	145,000
allophycocyanin II	650	680	105,000
allophycocyanin 111	650	680	105,000
R-phycoerythrin	498, 542, 565	578	260,000
B-phycoerythrin	498, 545, 563	575	260,000
b-phycoerythrin	545, 563	575	—
C-phycoerythrin	565	578	—
C-phycoerythrin I	555	578	—
C-phycoerythrin II	540, 568	578	—
Cryptomonad phycoerythrins			
Phycoerythrin-544	544, 565	—	—
-555	555	—	—
-568	508	—	—
C-phycoerythrins			
Synechococcus WH7803	500, 545	560	—
Synechococcus WH8018	551	570	—
Trichodesmium	498, 557	—	—
Gloeobacter violacea	501, 564	574, 577	—

Table 4.4: Specific absorption coefficients (a*, with units of $m^2 \cdot g^{-1}$ pigment) of some phycobiliproteins in phosphate buffer.

Biliprotein	λ_{max}	*Molecular Weight*	*a**
C-phycocyanin	618	—	0.724
C-phycocyanin	615	224,000	0.770
C-phycocyanin	620	—	0.650
R-phycocyanin	615	273,000	0.660
allophycocyanin	650	—	0.603
allophycocyanin	650	90,000	0.650
B-phycoerythrin	565	290,000	0.820
B-phycoerythrin	545	—	0.878
C-phycoerythrin	565	226,000	1.250
C-phycoerythrin	550	—	1.250
R-phycoerythrin	565	298,000	0.810
R-phycoerythrin	565	—	0.802
phycoerythrin	545	—	1.260
phycoerythrin	548	—	1.050
phycoerythrin	551	—	0.800
phycoerythrin (M)	492	264,000	1.05
	543	—	0.432

pigments prior to identification and quantification. Quantitative thin-layer chromatography was first used on algal pigments by Jeffrey (1968) and was subsequently improved.

More recently, reverse-phase highperformance liquid chromatography (HPLC) techniques have been developed for routinely separating chlorophylls, chlorophyll degradation products, and carotenoids. Mantoura and Lewellyri s (1983) method required a 20min run to separate pigments using a two-mobile-phase solvent system on a 250 × 5 mm C-18 column (5-μm particle size).

Increasing column diameter and solvent flow rate Trees

et al. (1986) achieved separation of chlorophylls and their degradation products in a 10-min run. Recently, de los Rivas et al. (1989) describe a new three-phase solvent system and a 10 x 8 mm radial compression column, which allows separation of terrestrial vascular plant pigments within a 10-min run.

Widespread application of HPLC and thin-layer chromatography in recent years has led to the identification of previously unknown pigments and to the recognition of the importance of these pigments in various algal groups. A consideration of this research is beyond the scope of this review, and further discussion will be limited to a comparison of HPLC and other methods for measuring chlorophyll *a*.

In general, HPLC and other techniques lead to comparable estimates of chlorophyll concentration, although individual estimates may be greatly at variance. For example, Murray et al. (1986) compared two HPLC techniques, a fluorometric method and a spectrophotometric method for estimating chlorophyll a in 29 plankton samples with chlorophyll a concentrations ranging from 0.02 to 30 $\mu g\text{-}dm^{-3.}$

The chlorophyll a peak accounted for only 57% of the spectrophotometer response and 72% of the fluorescence response. However, including chlorophyll allomers in the comparison led to a one-to-one correspondence of spectrophotometric and HPLC methods.

In sediments with chlorophyll a and pheopigment concentrations of 1-30 $\mu g\text{-}g^{-1}$ dry weight, Riaux-Gobin et al. (1987) found that the fluorescence measurements underestimated chlorophyll a and pheopigments by 30% to 40% relative to the HPLC measurements.

Trees et al. (1985) found that fluorometric determinations of chlorophyll a were in error by from -68% to +53% when compared with values obtained from a HPLC method. They found that errors in the fluorometric determination varied between stations within a given oceanographic region, and between regions.

When data from various oceanographic regions were combined, chlorophyll a determined from HPLC and fluorometric techniques were highly correlated with a correlation coefficient of 0.961. Despite the high correlation obtained when measurements over a large range of chlorophyll a concentrations (< 10-40,000 $ng \cdot dm^{-3}$) were compared, individual estimates of chlorophyll a by the fluorometric technique were as much as three times lower or 1.5 times greater than the true value.

The increased discrimination available from HPLC analysis of phytoplankton pigments has also proven useful in ecological investigations. Aside from providing qualitative information on the major taxa present, a quantitative estimate of the relative contribution of phytoplankton with different accessory pigments to total chlorophyll a can be obtained from the application of a multiple regression analysis to quantitative pigment determinations.

Changes in the concentrations of accessory pigments can also be used to characterize the growth and loss rates of different phytoplankton taxa in grazing experiments.

EXTRACTION AND QUANTIFICATION OF PHYCOBILIPROTEINS

Phycobiliproteins are water-soluble light-harvesting pigment proteins found in the rhodophytes, cryptomonads, and cyanobacteria. The major classes of phycobiliproteins are phycocyanin (PC), phycoerythrin (PE), allophycocyanin (APC), and phycoerythrocyanin (PEC) (Gantt, 1981). Within each of these classes are phycobiliproteins with several related spectral forms.

The phycobiliproteins consist of open-chain tetrapyrrole chromophores (referred to as bilins or phycobilins) covalently bound to proteins. The main chromophore types are (1) phycocyanobilin, found in PC and APC, (2) phycoerythrobilin found in PE, and (3) phycourobilin found in some PEs.

There is no routine method generally used for determining phycobiliprotein concentrations. However, as in the case of lipophilic pigments, most methods employ extraction of pigment molecules, followed by spectrophotometric or fluorometric determination of chromophore concentration.

Extraction of phycobiliproteins can be achieved by mechanical and/or enzymatic cell disruption, which releases phycobiliproteins into aqueous solution. Laboratory cultures of microalgae and cyanobacteria are commonly disrupted by repeated cycles of freeze-thaw treatment and passage through a French press, or by prolonged sonication.

Phytoplankton can be concentrated onto membrane filters and disrupted by mechanical shearing and lysozyme treatment, although recoveries may not be complete in recalcitrant organisms. Particularly troublesome in this regard are the small coccoid cyanobacteria, which are resistant to mechanical disruption.

Wyman (unpublished) sought to overcome this problem when measuring phycoerythrin in marine *Synechococcus spp.* by measuring in vivo fluorescence of samples resuspended in 50% glycerol.

Glycerol effectively uncouples phycoerythrin from photosynthetic energy transduction enhancing fluorescence by up to 15-fold relative to untreated cells. A constant maximum fluorescence yield under these circumstances allows calibration against extracted phycoerythrin.

The technique is simple, rapid and has been used for routine measurements at sea. Variations in the magnitude of the package effect may preclude a simple quantitative relationship between glycerol enha-nced fluorescence and phycoerythrin in large cyanobacteria, but this effect should be insignificant for the *Synechococcus spp.* examined by Wyman. Although different phycobiliproteins can be identified by characteristic absorbance and/or fluorescence emission spectra, the diversity of these pigments complicates quantification. An indication of the range of specific absorption coefficients that have been obtained is given in Table elsewhere in this chapter.

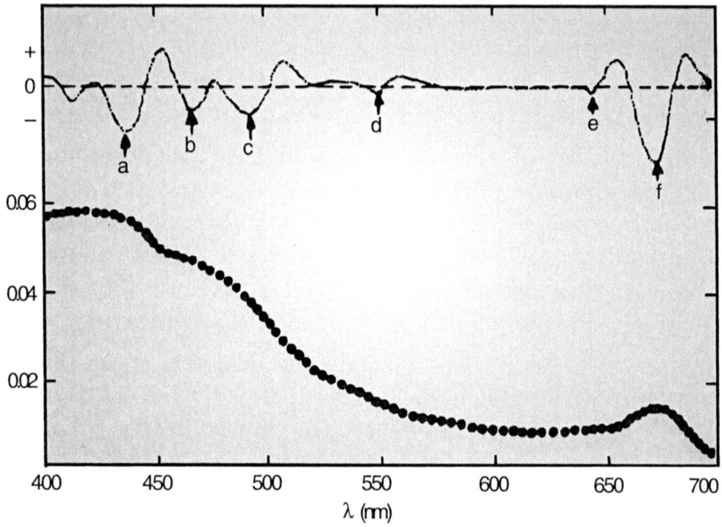

Figure 4.1: Spectral variations in the absorption coefficient of a natural phytoplankton assemblage and their second derivative spectra. The letters a-f denote the derivative positions of the major pigments, chlorophyll a (a) , chlorophyll c (b), phycobiliproteins (c,d), chlorophyll b (e) and the red absorbing form of chlorophyll a (f), which are not clearly identifiable in the original in vivo absorption spectra.

Bennett and Bogorad (1973) and Kursar and Alberte (1983) developed trichromatic equations that account for spectral overlap for estimating phycocyanin, allophycocyanin, and phycoerythrin concentrations from absorption measurements in aqueous extracts.

These equations are specific to the organisms under investigation, and, for maximum accuracy, individual equations need to be derived for each particular application.

In Vivo Fluorescence for Estimating Chlorophyll *a*

Measuring the red fluorescence of chlorophyll a when algae are illuminated with blue light has become a standard method of determining microalgal abundance in natural samples and unialgal cultures.

Although subject to some uncertainty because of variations in fluorescence emission, in situ determination of relative phytoplankton abundance is possible, and absolute abundance can be obtained if these measurements are calibrated against extracted chlorophyll *a*.

At physiological temperatures, in vivo chlorophyll a fluorescence arises predominantly from photosystem 2 and is characterized by a peak in the emission spectrum at about 685 nm. Fluorescence at shorter wavelengths in phycobiliphytes and cryptomonads arises largely from inefficiencies in energy transfer within phycobiliproteins.

Although in vitro fluorescence of pigments in organic or aqueous solvents depends only on the structure of the pigment molecule, in vivo fluorescence also depends on localized interactions with specific proteins and lipids, together with cell structural and metabolic variations.

As a consequence, the ratio of in vivo fluorescence to extracted chlorophyll a can vary by approximately an order of magnitude. The relationship between fluorescence emission and chlorophyll a concentration can be considered as the product of the *in vivo* chlorophyll a-specific absorption coefficient (a*), the photon yield of fluorescence (ϕ_f) and the incident irradiance (E),

$$F_{chl} = \mathrm{a}^*\phi_f \mathrm{E}/2.303 = a^*\phi_f E \tag{4.4}$$

where F_{chl} is the chlorophyll-a-specific fluorescence emission. The absorption coefficient, a*, is influenced by factors that affect light absorption, whereas ϕ_f may be affected by a range of physiological variables.

The chlorophyll a-specific fluorescence emission has been shown to have a size dependence in microalgal cultures and natural phytoplankton assemblages. Specifically, F_{chl} is found to vary approximately by a factor of five between picoplankton (2 μm diam) and net plankton (> 20 μm diam), consistent with expectations based on the relationship between a* and cell size that are predicted by the package effect.

In addition to a dependence on cell size, F_{chl} varies by a factor of two to four due to physiological responses to irradiance and nutrient availability. Chloroplast aggregation in response to high irradiances resulted in decreases of both absorption (λ 440 nm) and fluorescence in the large diatom *Lauderia borealis*.

Changes in ϕ_f may also influence $F_{chl.}$ For example, F_{chl} tends to be higher in stationary-phase cultures than in exponential cultures, and is related to a reduction in the photon yield of photosynthesis under nutrient-starved conditions.

Up to an order of magnitude diel variation in F_{chl} in which F_{chl} is highest at night and lowest during the day, may also reflect changes in $\phi_{f.}$ Significantly, the diel variation in F_{chl} is opposite to that observed for photosynthesis rates, suggesting complimentary variations in the photon yield of fluorescence and photosynthesis.

FLUORESCENCE MICROSCOPY

Epifluorescence microscopy has only recently become a standard tool for examining microalgal samples despite the introduction of fluorescence techniques to phycological research over 30 years ago. In early applications, Wood (1955) employed transmitted light fluorescence microscopy in plankton studies, and Jones (1974) used epifluorescence microscopy to identify living algae on the surfaces of stones.

Epifluorescence microscopy has many advantages over transmitted-light, phase-contrast, or interference-contrast microscopy for examining plankton samples. Small organisms can be identified as algae by their red fluorescence, whereas cyanobacteria, cryptomonads, and rhodophytes can be characterized by distinctive orange or yellow fluorescence, enabling the separate enumeration of photosynthetic from heterotrophic forms.

Use of this technique indicates that between 10 and 90% of oceanic nanoplankton (approximately 2-20 μm diam) are photosynthetic, with autotrophs typically accounting for 50% of total counts. In another application of fluorescence microscopy, Lessard and Swift (1986) found that approximately 40% of oceanic dinoflagellate taxa lack chlorophyll *a,* indicating a large phagotrophic component in a group traditionally regarded as autotrophic.

Quantitative determinations of the chlorophyll or phycobiliprotein content of single cells may be possible when a fluorescence microscope is used as a microspectro fluorometer. However, variations in the photon yield of fluorescence that hamper the in vivo determinations of chlorophyll concentration of cell suspensions will also influence measurements made with single cells.

USE OF DERIVATIVE SPECTRA IN PIGMENT ANALYSIS

Faust and Norris describe an in vivo spectrophotometric technique for determining chlorophylls *a, b,* and c on intact phytoplankton. The technique rests on the observation that taking the second derivative of the absorption spectrum leads to considerably greater detail than is evident in the original data.

The second derivative yields the rate of change of the slope of the absorption spectrum and so accentuates differences in curvature associated with in vivo absorption peaks. In its original application to microalgae, regression analysis was used to find the optimum wavelengths for determining chlorophylls *a, b,* and c from second derivative absorption spectra of samples concentrated on glass-fiber filters.

The method was calibrated with a mixture of microalgae from major taxonomic groups: that is, the cyanobacterium *Anabaena flos-aquae,* the green *Chlorella sp.,* the cryptomonad *Cryptomonas ovata,* and the dinoflagellate *Prorocentrum mariae-lebouriae.*

As employed by Faust and Norris (1982), the technique is strictly correlative, requiring calibration of the in vivo spectra against chlorophyll a, b, and c concentrations determined in solvent extracts of the same samples.

Optimum wavelengths for determining these chlorophylls from second derivative spectra differed from the wavelengths of peak absorption in vivo, presumably because of overlap of absorption bands of chlorophylls and other pigments and absorption flattening, which causes nonlinearities at wavelengths of maximum absorption.

Bidigare et al. (1989) used second and fourth derivative analysis to locate in vivo absorption peaks of pigments in open ocean phytoplankton. Peaks for chlorophylls a, b, and c, as well as for phycoerythrobilin and phycourobilin were apparent in these spectra, despite the lack of features in the original in vivo absorption spectra, which were dominated by the contribution of detrital material.

In contrast to the empirical approach of Faust and Norris (1982; 1985) described above, Bidigare et al. (1989) chose to examine the relations between the most prominent peaks in the derivative spectra (which corresponded to known in vivo absorption maxima) and the concentrations of these pigments.

Chapter 5

PROCESS OF PHOTOSYNTHESIS

The process in which certain carbohydrates are synthesized from carbon dioxide and water by chlorophyllous cells in the presence of light, oxygen being a by-product, is generally called *photosynthesis.* On the continent of Europe and to a lesser extent in Great Britain, the terms *carbon assimilation* and *assimilation* are often used to designate this process.

The common use of the world "*assimilation*" to denote the process in which foods are incorporated into the structures of the plant body makes the employment of this term or carbon assimilation as a synonym for photosynthesis undesirable.

The *summary* equation representing the process of photsynthesis is conventionally, written as follows 673 kg. cal of radiant energy

$$6CO_2 + 6H_2O \xrightarrow[\text{chlorophyllous cells}]{\text{673 kg-cal of radiant energy}} C_6H_{12}O_6 + 6O_2$$

It should be clearly understood that this equation does not purport to indicate the mechanism of the process, but is merely a statement of the net exchanges which occur in the shorthand of chemical symbols.

As usually written, a hexose sugar is designated as the carbohydrate formed in photosynthesis, but this is by no means certain.

The value 673 kg-cal. is, strictly speaking, correct only for glucose; the energy requirement of the reaction is approximately the same, per CH_2O group, however, for the synthesis of any of the hexoses, or for any disaccharide or polysaccharide derived from hexoses.

Photosynthesis (Cr. *Photos* light; *synthesis= putting* together) is an anabolic process of manufacture of organic compounds inside the cell, containing *chlorophyll,* from carbon dioxide and water with the help of sunlight as an energy source.

Basically, photosynthesis is the absorption of light energy and its conversion into chemical potential.

Historical Background

1. *Aristotle and Theophrastus* (*320 B.C.*). Thought that plants derive all their nourishment directly from soil.
2. *Bales* (*1727*). Concluded that plants are nourished, in part, from atmoshere.
3. *Joseph Pristley* (*1772*). Discovered the evolution of oxygen by plants. He also showed that oxygen is consumed by animals.
4. *Janingen-Housz* (*1779-96*). Purification of air is carried out by green plants only and that light is essential to the process. He associated these reactions with the green parts of plants.
5. *Jean Senebier* (*1782*). The rate of purification of air by green plants depends upon the concentration of foul air.
6. *Nicolas de Saussure* (*1804*). Noted that water is involved in photosynthesis, plants pick up carbon dioxide and release oxygen.
7. *Dutrochet* (*1837*). Established connection between photosynthesis and *chlorophyll.*
8. *Leibig* (*1845*). Organic matter synthesized during photosynthesis is derived from dioxide and water.

9. *Von Mayer* (*1845*). Green plants convert solar energy into chemical energy during photosynthesis.
10. *Sachs* (*1882*). Proved that starch is synthesized by plants in light dependent reaction i.e., photosynthesis.
11. *Englemann* (*1882*). Showed that red light is the most efficient stimulator of photosynthesis.
12. *Mayer* (*1883*). First described details of chloroplast structure.
13. *Blackman* (*1905*). Propounded the principle of limiting factors. He also proposed the occurrence of a dark phase in photosynthesis.
14. *Wilstaller and Stoll* (*1913*). Isolated chlorophyll and later determine its structure.
15. *Warburg* (*1919*). Found that the efficiency of photosynthesis is higher with intermittent light.
16. *Warburg and Nagelein* (*1922*). First measured the efficiency of photosynthesis.
17. *Thunberg* (*1923*). Recognized that carbon dioxide is reduced and water oxidized during photosynthesis.
18. *Emerson and Arnold* (*1932*). Performed flashing light experiments at differrent temperature and found out the existence of light and dark phases of photosynthesis.
19. *Wood and Werkman* (*1936*). Distinguished between the light reaction and dark reaction.
20. *Hill* (*1938*). Evolution of oxygen occurs in light reaction performed by isolated illuminated choloroplasts in the presence of suitable electron acceptors and the absence of carbon dioxide.
21. *Ruben, Randall, Kamen and Hyde* (*1941*). Showed that the oxygen liberated during photosynthesis comes from water and not from carbon dioxide.
22. *Calvin and Benson* (*1948*). Showed that phosphoglycerate is an early product of carbon dioxide fixation.

23. *Calvin (1954-55)*. Traced the pathway of carbon dioxide fixation by using $^{11}OO_2$ and gave the q cycle, now known as *Calvin Cycle. Calvin* was awarded Nobel Prize in *1960.*
24. *Hatch and Slick (1965)*. Discovered supplementary mechanism of carbon dioxide fixation called C_4 pathway in certain topical plants.
25. *Huber et al (1985)*. Crystallized and analysed the photocentre of *Rhodabactor* through X-ray differection technique. They were awarded Nobel Prize in 1988.

THE STRUCTURE OF THE LEAF

Since the leaf is the chief site of the photosynthetic process, information on the structure of this organ is fundamental to a 4 full understanding of the leaf activities.

The leaf is commonly studied in cross section—that is by 'cutting through the leaf at right angles to the midvein Figure elsewhere in this chpater.

The tissues of the leaf may be classified as:

(1) *epidermis,*

(2) *mesophyll and*

(3) *vascular bundles.*

Epidermis

The epidermis is composed of a single layer of interlocked cells and contains no chloplasts. It is continuous over both surfaces of the leaf and is therefore distinguished into *upper* and *lower* epidermis.

It is covered by the *cuticle,* a waxy layer, or film, which retards the movement of water and gases into and out of the leaf. The cuticle varies in thickness in different species; when it is thick, it is not appreciably penetrated by oxygen and carbon dioxide, but in leaves with thin cuticles there is some evidence of movement of gases through the epidermal cells.

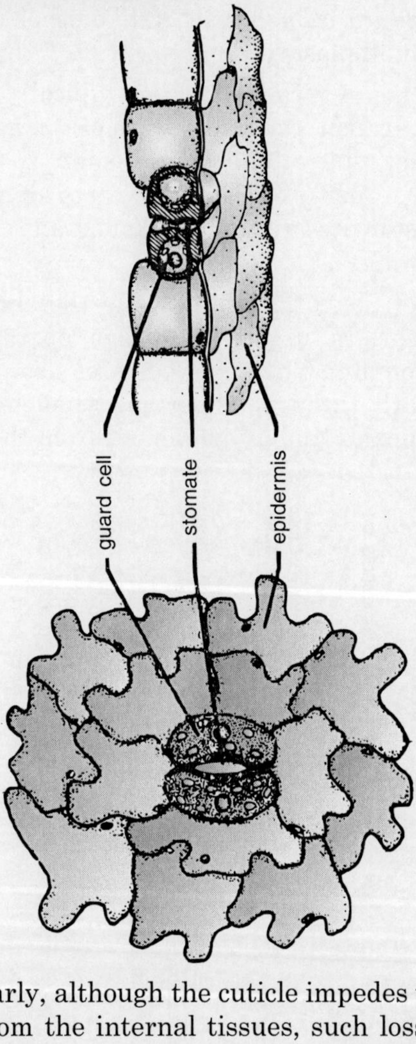

Figure 5.1: The stomates. Left: Surface view. Right: As Benin cross section

Similarly, although the cuticle impedes the loss of water vapour from the internal tissues, such loss, under certain conditions, may nevertheless be considerable.

The epidermis is perforated by numerous lens-shaped openings, called *stomates*, which open into large intercelluar spaces within the leaf. Stomates are also found in the epidermis of young twigs and herbaceous stems. The stomate is really an intercellular space formed by the splitting of the cell wall between two specialised epidermal cells known *as guard cells.* These, unlike other epidermal cells, contain -chloroplasts.

The guard cells, in surface view, are typically -crescent-shaped. In cross section, the inner walls of the guard cells, those which face the stomate, are seen to be much thickened. The upper and lower corners of the walls adjacent to the stomate are also thickened and frequently form projecting ridges.

As a result of these thickenings and the shape of the guard cells, changes in turgor within them operate to open and close the stomate. When the stomates are open, they are the chief path through which gases, such as water vapour, corbon dioxide and oxygen, move from the leaf into the air and *vice versa.*

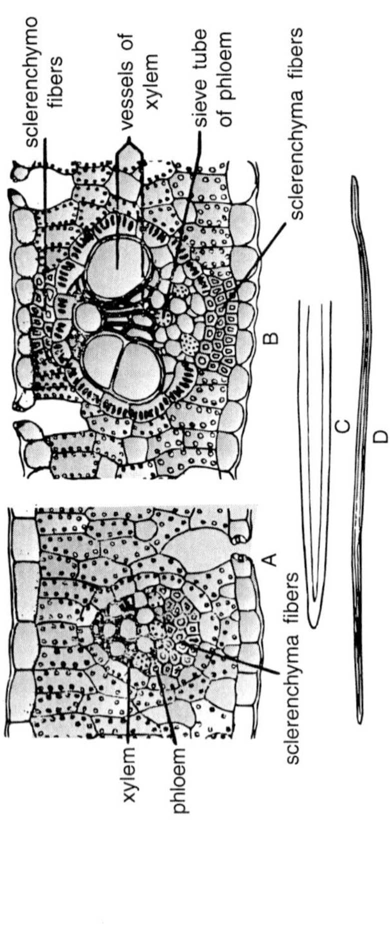

Figure 5.2: Sclerenchyma fibers in the leaf. A. Diagram of a vascular bundle with a cap of sclerenchyma fibers. B Cross section of a small portion of a corn leaf, showing fibers on both the upper and lower sides of the bundle. The mesophyll is undifferentiated into palisade and spongy tissue. C. Portion of sclerenchyma fiber, enlarged. D. Entire sclerenchyma fiber.

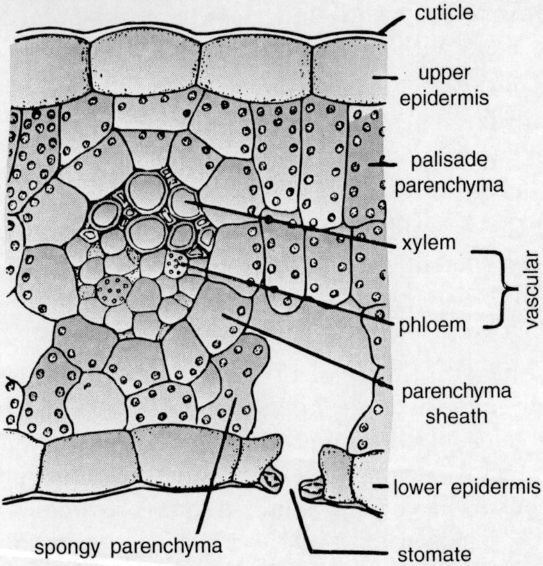

Figure 5.3: Vascular bundle, as seen in cross section of the leaf.

Stomates may be present in both the upper and lower epidermis, but the number in the lower epidermis is usually greater than in the upper. Many, perhaps most, woody plants, have no stomates in the upper epidermis.

Mesophyll

Withia the leaf, photosynthesis is localised in the mesophyll. This tissue, with the exception of the vascular bundles, comprises all the cells between the upper and lower epidermis.

The cells of the mesopnyll are thin-walled and, when mature, retain living protoplasm and a nucleus. Such thin-walled cells make up parenchyma tissue similar to the cells forming the softer parts of roots, stems, flowers, and fruits.

The mesophyll is usually divided into two parts. The cells toward the upper side of the leaf are elongated at right angles to the surface and form one to three layers. These cells make up the *palisade parenchyma*, so called because of the resemblance of these cells to a palisade, or row of stakes forming a wall. Below the palisade cells, and extending to the lower epidermis, is, a zone of a irregularly shaped cells with large intercellular spaces.

These cells form the *spongy parenchyma.* The intercellular spaces of this tissue, together with similar but smaller spaces between the palisade cells, form a system of air passages extending throughout the leaf.

All the mesophyll cells contain chloroplasts, embedded in the cytoplasm surrounding a large central vacuole. The chloroplasts are most numerous in the palisade cells, perhaps two to three times as many as in the spongy tissue.

In the sun flower leaf, for example, the cells of the palisade layer average 77 chloroplasts per cell, those of the spongy mesophyll 27 per cell. Estimating about 400,000 chloroplasts to each square millimeter of an eltn leaf—a very conservative appraisal—it has been calculated that the total exposed area of the chloroplasts in the leaves of a matbre elm tree may amount to as much as 140 square miles.

In some plants, such as corn and other grasses, many aquatic plants, and conifers, the mesophyll is undifferentiated or only slightly differentiated into palisade and spongy tissue.

Parenchyma cells containing chloroplasts are found in other parts of'the plant, such as herbaceous stems, young twigs, and unripe fruits. The terms *chlorenchyma* is applied to such cells, whether they are found in the leaf or in other organs.

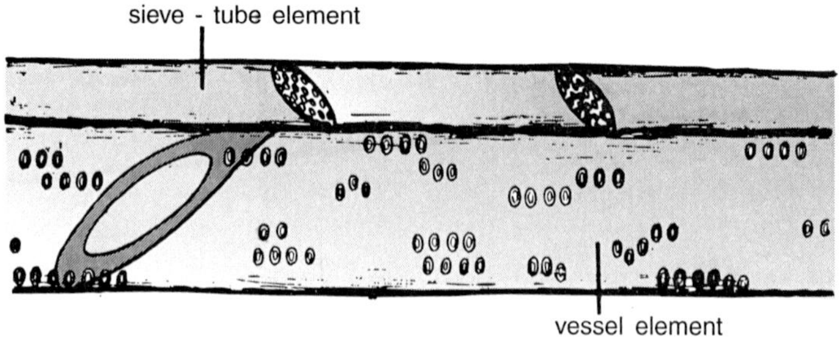

Figur 5.4: Principal cells of xylem and phlcem of oak leaf, as seen in longitudinal view.

Vascular Bundles

Vascular budles are specialised strands of tissue which function both in support and conduction. The larger bundles within the leaf can be seen on the surface as the, main veins. One or several bundles enter the base of the leaf from the *petiole*, which connects the blade of the leaf with thestem of the plant.

The petiole contains one or more vascular bundles, supporting tissue, and parenchyma. In the leaf, the, vascular bundles divide and subdivide to form smaller and smaller strands which extend to all parts of the leaf.

These smaller bundles are not isolated but are connected at frequent intervals to form a netlike system. In most cross sections of the leaf, therefore, vascular bundles may be seen both in end and in side view. The vascular bundles are usually located about halfway between the upper and lower epidermis. They are composed of two fundamental kinds of tissue, the *xylem* and *phloem*. Together these constitute the *vascular tissues* found in. roots, stems, leaves, flowers, and fruits.

The xylem and phloem are composed of elongated cells adapted to the movement of materials through the plants. The thick-walled xylem conducts water and supplies mechanical support. The phloem, is composed chiefly of thinner-walled cells and is the channel through which soluble foods are conducted.

The xylem of flowering plants is composed of several kinds of cells. The most important, from the standpoint of conduction, is the *vessel element*, a somewhat elongated cell with open ends. A continuous series of such cells is termed a *vessel*.

In some vessel elements the secondary wall is incomplete and is laid down in a pattern of rings or spirals inside the primary wall. When mature, the vessel element is nonliving and consists only of the cell wall.

The most important conducting cells of the phloem are the *sieve-tube elements*, so named because of the presence of sievelike openings in the end and frequently the side walls. Sieve-tube elements in the flowering plants are, like vessel elements, arranged end to end, forming *sieve tubes.*

The smaller vascular bundles of the leaf are commonly surrounded by a sheath of thin-walled parenchyma. The cells of this sheath are in direct contact with both palisade and spongy tissue and probably facilitate the movement of materials between the vascular bundles and the mesophyll.

They may also serve as a temporary storage tissue for reserve foods. The vascular bundles end blindly in the tissues of the leaf. As they terminate, they consist only of one or two xylem cells, together with a few parenchyma cells. Sieve tubes are absent.

So numerous are the smaller vascular branches that most cells of the mesophyll are only a few cells removed from conducting tissue. Water and mineral salts from the soil are continuously delivered to the mesophyll cells of the leaf through the xylem; food, manufactured in the mesophyll, moves in the opposite direction.

Where sieve tubes are absent in the bundle ends, the food materials enter the parenchyma cells associated with the xylem and are transported through these cells to the nearest sieve tubes.

In addition to the xylem, the leaf may also contain *sclerenhyma fibres,* thick-walled, greatly elongated cells with tapering ends. Like the vessel elements, the fibers are, at maturity, devoid of protoplasm.

Sclerenchyma fibers do not conduct but furnish mechanical support. They assist the leaf to withstand collapse following loss of water, and they also resist the beating effects of wind and rain. In the leaves of some species, the fibers occur as a cap on the lower side of the vascular bundle, adjacent to the phloem.

In the leaves of other species, fibers extend from both the upper and lower sides of the larger bundles to the epidermis, thus constituting a girderlike structure, effective in support. Selerenchyma fibers are also found in the petiole. stem, and other parts of the plant.

THE LEAF TRACES

The vascular bundles of the blade are branches of the bundles of the petiole. These, in turn, are connected with the vascular tissues of the stem. Such tissues in the stem may be arranged in a hollow cylinder or in separate vascular bundles, as in the leaf.

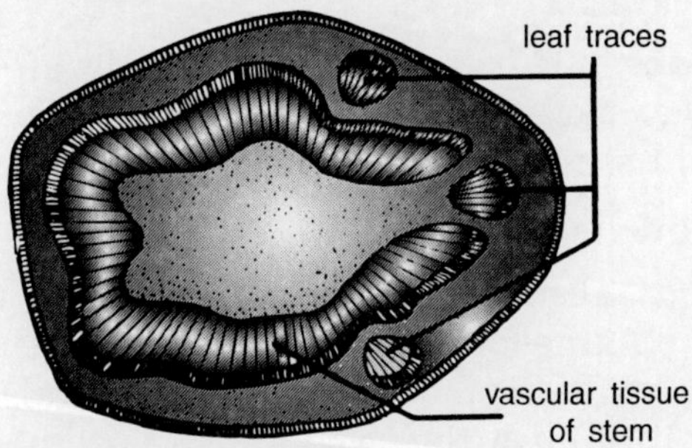

Figure 5.5: Diagram of cross section section of red oak twig through the nodal region, showing the leaf traces.

The bundles which connect the vascular tissues of the stem and petiole are known as *leaf traces*. They vary in number in different species. One and three leaf traces are common, but the grasses and palms have many.

Such bundles usually depart from the vascular system of the stem some distance below the junction of the leaf and, taking an upward course through the outer tissues of the stem, finally enter the petiole.

The leaf traces are the pathway along which water and other materials enter the leaf and foods pass from the leaf into the stem. In woody plants the leaf traces appear as bundle scars within the leaf scars on the twig, following the fall of the leaf.

LEAF ABSCISSION

The falling of leaves is characteristic of woody plants. The fall, or *abscission*, of the leaf is related to the formation of the separation layer, a zone of specialisedd parenchyma cells extending across the base of the petiole. Toward the end of the growing season, the pectins of the cell walls of this layer dissolve through enzymatic action.

The cells then separate and the petiole remains attached chiefly by the vascular bundles. The fall of the leaf is hastened by environmental factors, such as the shrin-kage of the petiole on warm, sunny days, the impact of rain upon the leaf, or the formation of ice crystal within the separation layer.

Before the fall of the leaf, or shortly afterwards, a protective layer of cork, which prevents the drying out of the exposed tissues, forms just below the separation layer.

Raw Materials

1. *Carbon Dioxide.* In terrestrial plants, the carbon dioxide is obtained from the atmosphere through the stomata. A small amount of carbonates are also absorbed from the soil through the roots.

Aquatic plants obtain carbon dioxide supply from the aquatic environment as bicarbonates. These bicarbonates are absorbed by the hydrophytes through their general surface.

2. *Water.* In 1924, *Van Niel* proposed a mechanism accounting for the dual nature of photosynthetic reaction based owhis observation of bacterial photosynthesis.

The bacteria required hydrogen sulphide for their carbon fixation. There was no evolution of oxygen. Sulphur globules accumulated ."as waste product.

$$6CO_2 + 12H_2S \rightarrow C_6H_{12}O_6 + 6H_2O + 12S$$

Van Niel suggested that water was a substance from which H^+ ions and electrons could be derived for the reduction o• carbon dioxide in oxygenic photosynthesis of all organisms.

$$2H_2O \xrightarrow{\text{light}} O_2 + 4(H)$$
$$4(H) + CO_2 \longrightarrow CH_2O + H_2O$$

The nature of the reductant was not known, and it was clear that the second reaction was complex and probably involved several steps.

Ruben and *Kamen* (1941) were able to use isotopically enriched oxygen ($^{18}O_2$) to established that all of the oxygen produced in photosynthesis was derived from water and none from carbon dioxide.

Hill (1937) illuminated the isolated chloroplasts of *Stellariamedia* in the presence of leaf extract or hydrogen acceptors is the absence of carbon dioxide. The chloroplast evolved oxygen.

The reaction involving the production of oxygen by the illuminated chloroplasts in the absence of carbon dioxide fixation is called *Hill reaction.* The hydrogen acceptor of Hill reaction is nicotinamide adenine dinucleotide phosphate (NADP).

$$2NADP^+ + 2H_2O \xrightarrow[\text{light}]{\text{chlorophyll}} 2NADPH + 2H^+ + O_2$$

3. *Light.* Since the primary reactions of photosynthesis involve the absorption of light by pigments. It is necesary to examine some of its basic properties. Light is electromagnetic energy propagated in discrete corpuscles called *photons* or *quanta.* As the energetics of chemical reactions are usually described in terms of kilocalories per molecule of the chemicals (1 mole=6.02 × 10^{28} quanta).

The colour of the light is determined by the wavelength (λ) of light radiation. At any given wavelength, all the quanta have the same energy. The energy (E) of a quantum is,, inversely proportional to its wavelength.

Depending upon the wavelength electromagnetic spectrum consists of eight types of radiations-cosmic rays, gamma rays, X-rays, ultra-voilet rays, light spectrum, infrared rays, electric rays and radio rays. Visible light consists of radiations having a wave length between 390-760 urn. It can be resolved into light of different colours-violet (390-430 nm), *blue* (430-470 nm), *bluegreen* (470-500 nm), *green* (500-580 nm), *yellow* (580600 nm), *orange* (600-650 nm), *orange-red* (650-660 nm) and *red* (660-760 nm). Red light above 700 nm is called *infrared.*

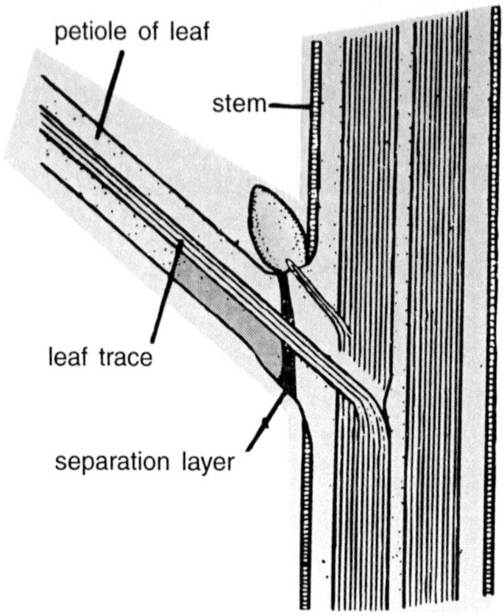

Figure 5.6: Diagram showing position of separation layer.

Infrared rays having wavelength of 760-10,000 nm. Radiations shorter than those of violet are called *ultra violet rays* having a wavelength of 100-390 nut.

Solar radiations or sunlight reaching the earth have wavelength between 300-2600 nm. The proportion of light energy that is available in photosynthesis has long been a matter of controvercy. Much attention was focused in the period 1930-1950 on the quantum requirement of photosynthesis, a measure of the efficiency of the process.

The initial thought was that, since 1 quantum can conduct only one molecular reaction, the number of quanta absorbed per molecule of oxygen produced might indicate the number of reaction steps involved.

In complex experiments *Warburg* found quantum requirements of 4 quanta per molecule of oxygen produced: This means 1 quantum per (H) derived from H_2O for the reduction of carbon dioxide. The enerny required to derive one reducing equivalent from H_2O is close, to 30 K cal/mole, and the energy available in quanta of red light, which *Warburg* used in his experiments is only about 40 kcal/ einstein.

4. *Photosynthetic Pigments.* The photosynthetic pigments are those which occur inside the chloroplasts and can take part in absorption of light energy for the purpose of photosynthesis. There are two catagories of these pigments *chlorophyll* and *carotenoids.*

(*i*) *Chlorophyll.* So far the only light—absorbing pigment we have mentioned is chlorophyll. Initially the green pigment of plants was recognised as the substance responsible for light absorption in photosyn-thesis, absorbing red and blue light but not green. There are five types of chlorophyll occuring in plants. These are chlorophyll a,b,c,d and e. Becteria possess two types of related pigments.

These are bacteriochlorophyll and bacterioviridin. In highter plants only chlorophyll a and b are present. Chlorophyll a occurs in all the photosynthetic plants. It is bluish green in the pure state. Its imperical formula is $C_{55}H_{72}O_5N_4$ Mg. Chlorophyll b is olive green in pure state and its empirical formula is $C_{55}H_{70}O_5N_4Mg$. Both the chlorophylls are soluble in fat solvents such as ether, chloroform, carbon tetrachloride, alcohols etc. Chlorophyll a is more soluble in ether whereas chlorophyll b in methyl alcohol.

In 1912, the structure of chlorophyll was studied by Wilstatter, Stoll and Fischer. The chlorophyll is a tetrapyrrole and bears a close resemblance to the chemical structure of heme and the cytochromes. Chlorophyll differs from these iron enzymes in that it contains an atom of magnesium, which does not appear to participate directly in electron transfer reactions-as does the iron of cytochromes.

The chlorophyll has a tadpole-like structure, with a head called porphyrin and a tail (made up of long chain alcohol called phytol). Use head is made up of four pyrrole rings which are linked by methine bridges (—CH=). The skeleton of each pyrrole ring is made up of 5 atoms-4 carbon and -one -nitrogen.

The nitrogen lies towards the centre. A megnisium atom is held in the centre of porphyrin head by nitrogen atoms of pyrrole rungs (with the help of 2 covalent and,2 coordinate bonds). The external carbon atoms of the pyrrole rings have been given specific numbers, 1-8 carbon atoms 1,3,5 and 8 have methyl groups (—CH_3).

Carbon atom 2 possesses a vinyl ,group (—CH=CH_2) while carbon atom 4 has an ethyl group (=CH_2—CH_3). Carbon atom 6 is attached to methine group by an acetoacetic group. Carbon atom 7 is connected to the phytol tail through a propionic acid residue.

Chlorophyll b differs from chlorophyll a in having formyt group (—CHO) instead of methyl (—CH_s) group at carbon atom 3. Chlorophyll b is present in most green plants, but its place is taken by phycocyanin blue-green algae, fucoxanthin in brown algae and phycoerythrin in red-algae.

These are called accessory phycobilin pigments. The chemical structure of these accessory phycobilin pigments is similar to that of chlorophyll in-that they are tetrapyrrole compounds; however, they differ in being linear instead of cyclic in structure, and they do not have a metal component.

(*ii*) *Carotenolds*. The carotenoids are a group of yellow, brownish is reddish pigments which are associated with the chlorophyll inside the chloroplast. These remain alone inside the chromoplasts. Like chlorophyll b these are also called accessory photosynthetic pigments. They hand over the energy to chlorophyll a absorbed by them. The carotenoids are of two types

(*a*) *Carotenes*: These are closely related to the vitamin A and are bisictily long-dhain lipophiiic molecules with a more active terminal group at each end. The empirical formula is $C_{40}H_{56}O$ i.e., cryptoxanthin and $C_{10}H_{56}O_2$ i.e., zeaxanthin.

The carotenoids are suluble in fat solvents like ether, chloroform, acetone, carbon disulphide.

Fluorescence. The fluroscence is the property of emmission -of radiations absorbed by a substance and the substance which can emit back the absorbed radiations is called *fluroscent substance*. It has been noted that all the photosynthetic pigments are fluroscent substances. However, most of the fluroscence emitted by photosynthetic organs is due to chlorophyll *a* because other pigments hand over their absorbed energy to it through resonance.

The normal state of the atoms or molecules is called *ground state* or *singlet state,* when an electron of a molecule or atom absorbs a quantum of light, it is raised to a higher energy level which is called *excited second singlet state.*

The excited state is unstable and lasts for about 10^{-9} second. The excited electron may return to ground state in two ways (*a*) either losing its remaining energy in the form of heat or (b), by losing extra -energy in the form of radiation energy.

This later process is called fluorescence. The fluroscent substances emit fluroscent light only during the period they are exposed to incident light. The fluroscent light is of higher wave length than the incident light.

Absorption spectrum of Chlorophyll. If a substance is extracted and illuminated with light of various wavelengths, it is possible to determine its absorption spectrum, the amount of light of different wavelengths that the substance absorbs or does not absorb.

Chlorophyll's absorption spectrum has peaks in the blue and red regions, which means that light of these wavelengths in absorbed. The major peak at 675 nm and minor peak at 450 nm. The unabsorbed or reflected light appears green, thus making chlorophyll, the chloroplasts and the leaves that contain it, appear green to our eye.

Action spectrum. The curve showing the relative rates of photosynthesis at different wavelengths of light is called action spectrum. The curve shows that maximum photosynthesis occurs in red part and blue-violet part of light.

Thus the action spectrum of photosynthesis corresponds closely to absorption spectra of chlorophyll a and *b* showing the chlorophyll *a* as well as b are the main photosynthetic pigments, however, photosynthesis also occurs in the mid part of light spectrum where carotenoid are active.

Photosynthetic Units (PSU)-Quantosome

As already stated that light travels in the form of waves of different wavelengths. In certain respects light behaves as if it consists of tiny particles called *photons* or *quanta.* The quanta is indivisible units. Using the technique of intermittent light in their experiments,

Emerson and *Arnold* found that the evolution of one molecule of oxygen by *Chlorella* required the functioning of approximately 2500 molecules of chlorophyll.

It was also estimated that in reduction of one molecule of carbon dioxide and the liberation of one molecule of oxygen eight quanta of light energy are consumed. Putting these observations together it is easy to deduce that a group of 300 pigment molecules is the smallest unit that is capable of utilising one quantum of light energy.

This is called the *photosynthetic unit.* Under electron microscope made by *Park* and *Biggins* showed that minute structures about 100 A in diameter are attached to the cbloroplast lamellae.

These strips of lamellae contained about 230 chlorophyll molecules each and represented photosynthetic units to which they gave the name of *quantosome.*

The quantosome has a *photocentre* or *reaction centre* which is fed by about 200 harvesting pigment molecules. The photocentre consists of a special chlorophyll *a* molecule.

It absorbs light energy at longer wave lengths. The harvesting molecules are of two types, the *antenna molecules* and *core molecules.*

The antenna molecules get excited by absorbing light of various wavelengths but shorter than that of trap centre. The antenna molecules come to ground state by hand over their energy to the core molecules.

The energy picked up by core molecules is supplied to the reaction centre. On absorption of this energy, the reaction centre gets excited and extrudes an electron after which it comes to ground state to repeat the cycle.

Photosystems or Pigment Systems

Photosynthetic units occur in the form of two distinct groups called *photosystems* I and II or *pigment systems* I and II.

In pigments system I, there are different types of molecules of chlorophyll a which absorb photons of light. On the basis of type of wavelength of light absorbed by these chlorophyll a molecules they are known as *chi-660, ch1—670, chi-680 and chl690.*

At the end of this energy gathering pigment system is present a special type of chlorophyll *a* molecule called *P-700* which absorbs 700 nm of wavelength of light which functions as reaction centre. In *P-700* photochemical reaction takes place.

Pigment system I has a reducing agent Fe5 centre A, Fe5 centre B (ferrodoxine), plastoquinone, cytochrome complex and plastocyanin. Normally it derives an electron from pigment system II to $NADP^+$ for cyclic pbotaphosphorylation independently. The pigment system I is located on both the non-appressed part of grana thylakoids and stromal thylakoids.

In pigment system II, the photocentre is a special chloro phyll *a* molecule called P-680. Besides it contains *chi-650, chl-660, chl-670, ch1—678.* It is surrounded by chlorophyll *b* and carotenoid molecules. Pigment system II also contains Mg^{++}, Cl^-, Quencher molecule Q, plastoquinone, cytochrome complex and plastocyanin.

It picks up electrons released during photolysis of water. In this system photons of lower wavelength of light are absorbed. It is inactive in infrared light. This system is located in the appressed part of grana thylakoids only.

Mechanism of Photosynthesis

Photosynthesis is an oxidation-reduction process, in which water is oxidised to release oxygen and carbon dioxide is reduced to form carbohydrates. Photosynthesis occurs in two phases, plutochemical reactions (also called light or HIM reader) and biochemical reactions (also called dark or Blackman's reaction).

The Light or Photochemical reaction in Photosynthesis Evidences for Light Reaction

Following evidences indicate that the over all reaction in photosynthesis takes place in two steps: one is light mediated and the other is light independent.

1. *Temperature coefficient studies.* The rate of photosynthesis of two groups of plants were compared. Both were supplied with an adequate concentration of carbon dioxide, but one group was kept under light of high intensity and other group in light of low intensty. When the rates of photosynthesis were measured at different temperatures.

It was found that *high light* group had a Q_{19}=2 but the *low light* group Q_1 = 1. Strictly, chemical reactions characteristically have a Q10 from 2 to 3. This fact indicates that at least one of the reaction involved in photosynthesis is of a purely chemical, type.

Since it was first pointed out by *Blackman,* this reaction, is called as dark reaction. The other reaction of Q_{10} indicates that one of the reactions proceeds only at the expanse of absorbed light. It is called dark reaction. The Q_{19} of light reaction is 1.

2. *Flashing light experiments.* Photosynthesis involves photochemical and biochemical reactions is also shown by the results of investigations in which plants are exposed to intermittent light. *Warburg* obtained higher rates of photosynthesis in *Chlorella* when it was exposed to rapid and alternate periods of light and darkness instead of continuous illumination.

Emerson and *Arnold* found that at *25 °C,* the maximum photosynthesis took place when light and dark periods were respectively 10^{-5} second and 0.055 second. At 1.1°C maximum photosynthesis could be obtained with the same light period but the dark period had to be increased to 0.4 second. It means that temperature influences reactions of the dark period and reactions of the light phase are photochemical.

Operation of Photosystem II. The main function of PS 11 is the pbotolysis of water to release oxygen. In this act, when pigments of PS II absorb light, electrons are released from this system, in this manner chlorophyll molecules get oxidised. Oxidised pigments then take electrons from OH^- ions and are again reduced.

The OH (hydroxyl radical) is left from OH^- and 4(OH) radicals give rise to two molecules of water and one molecule of oxygen. In the above process H^+ atoms are released which are used for the reduction of $NADP^+$. Manganese ions play an important role in this process.

$$4H_2O \longrightarrow 4H^+ + 4OH^-$$
$$40H^- \longrightarrow 4(OH)+4e$$
$$4(OH) \longrightarrow 2H_2O + O_2$$
$$2H_2O \longrightarrow O_2 + 4e^- + 4H+$$

"Electrons released in PS II reduced quencher molecule Q which has a potential (E′o) of about 0-01. V. From reduced Q the electrons are accepted by B (an unknown substance) which is reduced. From reduced B the electrons are accepted by plastoquinone (PQ). Electrons from reduced PQ are passed to the cytochrome *f* which is now reduced.

Again the electrons from reduced cytochrome *f* are accepted by plastocyanin, (a copper enzyme that has an E'o close to 0.4 V), which is thus reduced. Finanlly, the electrons from reduced plastocyanin are accepted by P-700 f photosystem I. P-700 is now reduced. In this way plastocyanin works as a middle man between PS 11 and PS 1. Electrons from water are passed on to $NADP^+$, to reduce it into NADPH + H^+.

Operation of photosystem I. Photons of light hit P-700, By absorbing quantum energy of photons $4e^-$ of P-700, attain an excited state. Due to high energy of these electrons, they are released from chlorophyll which, is thus oxidised.

Electrons are now accepted by iron-protein complex, Fe5-A. It has a negative potential (E′o= -0.5 - 0.6 V). Fe5-A thus reduced. The next electron acceptor is Fe5-B (Ferrodoxin) which is reduced. From reduced ferrodoxin, the electrons are accepted by flavin-adenine dinucleotide (FAD^+) which is reduced to FADH $+H^+$. Finally, the electrons and hydrogen ion is accepted by $NADP^+$ and it is reduced to NADPH + H^+.

In this manner, the excited electrons are released from P"100 are accepted by $NADP^+$ which is reduced to NADPH + H^+. Hydrogen attached to reduced NADPH + H+ is used for reduction of carbon dioxide in the dark or biochemical reaction. Thus NADPH + H^+ is called the *reducing power* of the cell.

Photo-phosphorylation

According to *Arnon et. al.,* the light reaction is concerned with the production of adenosine triphosphate (ATP) and NADPH + H^+, which is the reduced form of nicotinamide adenine dinucleotide phosphate.

ATP, is a high energy compound and is formed by the addition of an inorganic phosphate group to adenine diphosphate (ADP) by a process called photophosphorylation.

Photophosphorylation takes place in two ways

1. *Cyclic photophoipkorylation.* It takes place most efficiently when the Hill reaction is prevented, f.e., the medium is devoid of the hydrogen acceptor NADP. Here the electrons released from P-700 move through Fe5-A to cytochrome b_6, to plastoquinone to cytochrome -f to plastocyanin and again return to P-700. While passing between ferrodoxin andplastoquinone, the electrons lose sufficient energy to form -ATP from ADP and inorganic phosphate (P_i).

$$ADP + P_i \xrightarrow[\text{chlorophyll}]{\text{light}} ATP$$

well-known poisons of photosynthesis 3-(3, 4 dichlorophenyl) dimethyl urea (DCMU) do not inhibit the cyclic photophosphorylation.

2. ***Non-cyclic photophosphorylation.*** It is the normal process of photophosphorylation and is unindirectional. It

is carried out in collaboration of both photosystems I and II. Photoexcited chlorophyll molecules in photosystem II donate electrons to acceptors.

The extruded electron has an energy equivalent to 23 kcal/mole. The electrons pass through Q, B, PQ cyto-: chrome-f, plastocyania and enter of P-700. While passing over plastoquinone to cytochrome f, the electron loses sufficient energy for the synthesis of ATP.

The overall photochemical reaction results in the production of ATP and reduced NADP and the oxygen is released to the atmosphere. The products of photochemical reaction are utilised in the reduction of carbon dioxide to the carbohydrate level.

II. Dark reaction or Biosynthetic phase or Blackman's Reaction

The dark reaction does not require light, although this takes place in light also, that is why this is called dark reaction. This process takes place in the stroma of chloroplasts There are two main pathways for the dark reaction.

I. Calvin-Benson cycle

II. Hatch-Slack pathway.

Calvin-Benson **Cycle**

During the last four decades considerable progress has been made in the understanding of the dark reaction in phytosynthesis with the help of tracer techniques and paper chromatography. The path of carbon was studied with the help of radioactive tracer technique using $C^{14}O_2$ in a unicellular alga, *Chlorella* Radioactive carbon C^1s has a half life of 5200 years. Therefore, the path of CO_2 fixation can be easily traced with its help.

Here the radioactive carbon is provided in a solution of bicarbonate to photosynthesizing cells. At regular intervals of time, the cells are killed and analysed quantitatively by chromatography for various compounds containing C^{14}. In cells killed immediately after one second expose to the light C^{14} is found mainly in phosphoglyceric acid (PGA). In cells killed after five seconds expose to the light, C^{14} appears in traces of PGA, alanine, aspartic acid and malic acid. In cells killed after 15 seconds of illumination, in addition to the above substances, faint traces of sucrose containing C^{14}.

It may also be detected in some pentose, glucose phosphate and fructose phosphate. After one minute of illumination, in the killed cells abundant C^{14} occurs in glucose phosphate and fructose phosphate. In lipids and proteins also, the C^{14} appears after 5 minutes of illumination.

Thus radioactive C^{14} obtained from $C^{14}O_2$ is rapidly spread in all the compounds found in plant cell.

After many panstaking calculations, *Calvin* worked out the pathway of carbon dioxide fixation. The acceptor molecule was found to be ribulose-1, 5 biphosphate. The followings are the steps taking place in dark reaction of photosynthesis.

1. *Phosphorylation I.* Carbon dioxide reduction starts with 5-carbon sugar i.e., ribulose monophospbate. Six molecules of ATP (produced during light reaction) to form 6 molecules of *ribxlose 1, 5 biphosphate* and 6 molecules of ADP.

$$\text{6 Ribulose-5-phosphate+6ATP} \xrightarrow{\text{Phosphopentokinase}} \text{6 ribulose-1,5 biphosphate+ 6ADP}$$

2. *Carboxylattvr.* Ribulose 1, 5 biphosphate (RuBP) acts as ~CO, and 6 molecules of water giving rise 12 molecules of 3phosphoglyceric acid.

$$\text{6 Ribulose - 5 - phosphate} + 6CO_2 + 6H_2O \xrightarrow[\text{Carboxylase}]{\text{Ribulose 1, 5 biphosphate}} \text{3-phosphoglyceric acid (12 molecule)}$$

3. *Phosphorylation II.* 12 molecules of 3-phosphoglyceric acid react with 12 molecules of ATP giving rise to 12 molecules of 1, 3-diphosphoglyceric acid and 12 molecules of ADP.

$$\underset{\text{(12 molecules)}}{\text{3-phosphoglyceric acid}} + 12\text{ ATP} \xrightarrow[\text{Kinase}]{\text{Phosphoglyceric}} \underset{\text{(12 molecule)}}{\text{1,3-diphosphoglyceric acid}} + 12\text{ADP}$$

4. *Reduction.* 12 molecules of NADPH + H^+ produced in light reaction are now used to reduces 12 molecules of 1, 3diphosphoglyceric acid leading to the formation of 12 molecules each of 3-phosphoglyceraldehyde or glyceraldehyde3-phosphate, NADP+ and phosphoric acid.

$$\underset{\text{(12 molecules)}}{\text{1,3 diphosphoglyceric acid}} + 12\text{ NADPH}+H^+ \xrightarrow[\text{dehydrogenase}]{\text{Triose phosphate}}$$

$$\underset{\text{(12 molecules)}}{\text{3-phosphoglyceraldehyde}} + 12\text{ NADP}^+ 12H_3PO_4$$

In this way by the reduction of carbon dioxide 12 moleculesof 3-phosphoglyceraldehyde are formed. Out of these 12 molecules only two molecules go to synthesize sugar and rest 10 molecules are recycled to produce 6 molecules of ribulose 5-phosphate.

5. One molecule of 3-phosphoglyceraldehyde isomerise into dihydr-oxyacetone phosphate.

$$\text{3-phosphoglyceraldehyde} \xrightleftharpoons[\text{isomerase}]{\text{Triose phosphate}} \text{3-dihydroxy-acetone phosphate}$$

6. One molecules of 3-phosphoglyceraldehyde unite with 3-dihydrox-yacetone phosphate in the presence of aldolase to form fructose- 1, 6-diphosphate.

3-phosphoglyceraldehyde+3-dihydroxyacetone phosphate

$\xrightarrow{\text{Aldolase}}$ Fructose-1,6-diphosphate

7. Three molecules of phosphoric acid are released from one molecule of fructose-1, 6-diphosphate to form one moleculefructose-6-phosphate in the presence of phosphatase.

Fructose-1,6-diphosphate+HO2

$\xrightarrow{\text{phosphatase}}$ Fructose-6-phosphate $+3H_2PO_4$

8. Fructose -6-phosphate is converted to fructose- l-phosphate which forms glucose-I-phosphate.

Fructose-6-phosphate → fructose-1-phosphate

fructose-1-phosphate → Glucose-1-phosphate.

9. Fructose-I-phosphate and glucose-1-phosphate condense to form sucrose.

Fructose-6-phosphate + Glucose-1-phosphate

$\xrightarrow{\text{phosphatase}}$ sucrose.

10. *Regeneration of riboluse-5 phosphate.* Remaining 10 molecules of 3-phosphoglyceraldehyde regenerate 6 molecules of riboluse-6-phosphate after a series of complex reactions as follows.

(a) 3-phosphoglyceraldehyde reacts with fructose-6phosphate to yield a pentose (5-carbon) xylu lose-5- phosphate and a triose (4-carbon) erythrose-4-phosphate in the presence of transketolase.

Fructose-6-phosphate+3-phosphoglyceraldehyde

$\xrightarrow{\text{Transketolase}}$ Xylulose -5-phosphate+Erythrose-4-phosphate.

Xylulose-5-phospbate readily isomerizes to ribulose-5 phosphate.

(b) Erythorose-4phosphate combines with dihydroxya-

Figure 5.7: Release of oxygen during photosynthesis. Bubbles of gas are given off from the green plant in the sunlight.

cetone phosphate in the presence of aldolase to form sedoheptulose 1, 7-diphosphate, a 7-carbon sugar.

Erythrose-4-phosphate+Dihydroxyacetone phosphate

$\xrightarrow{\text{Aldolase}}$ Sedoheptulose -1, 7-diphosphate

(c) Sedoheptulose-1. 7-diphosphate looses one phosphate group in the presence of phosphotase to form sedoheptulose -7-phosphate.

Sedoheptulose -1,7-diphosphate $\xrightarrow{\text{phosphatase}}$

Sedoheptulose-7-phosphate

Distinction between green plant photosynthesis and bacterial photosynthesis.

	Green plant photosynthesis		Bacterial photosynthesis
1.	*Photosystems :* Consists of two photosystems (PSI and PSII) connected in series.	1.	Consists of two photo systems connected parallely.
2.	*Electron donor in PSII* : Water is the only electron donor for photoreduction.	2.	H_2S, malate and succinate are the usual electron donors in photoreduction.
3.	*Gas evolution :* Oxygen is evolved.	3.	Oxygen is not evolved.
4.	*Reductant :* The reductant of CO_2 is NADPH.	4.	The reductant of CO_2 is NAD-PH.
5.	Electron transport chain: (*a*) Cytochrome *b*, c present (*b*) Plastocyanin is all the time present. (c) P_{700} and P_{690} are the reaction centres of PSI and PSII respectively.	5.	(*a*) Cytochrome *b* is lacking. (*b*) Plastocyanin is absent. (c) One of the reaction centres is P_{890} the other, if any, is not known.
6.	Wavelength of light at which it occurs: 400-700 nm.	6.	Above 700 nm.
7.	*Emerson enhancement effect:* Detacted.	7.	Not detected.
8.	*Special features:* Can be converted into bacteria type photosynthesis, if the plants are allowed to photosynthesize in an atmos-phere of hydrogen.	8.	Can not be converted into green plant's type photosynthesis.

Distinction between cytochrome and phytochrome

	Cytochrome		*Phytochrome*
1.	It is one of the electron carr-iers of mitochondrial membrane system, associated with phosphorylation.	1.	It is a morphogenetic pigment found in all growing cells.

2.	It is an iron containing cyclic tetrapyrrolic compound. It has different forms -Cyt b, Cyt c, Cyt a, Cyt a_3 etc.	2.	It is a linear tetrapyrrole compound associated with protein. It has two absorb-ing *forms-phytochrome* red form (P,) and *phytochrome* far red form (Pf,). Both for-ms are interconvertible. P_r Red light / Far red light of darkness P_f,
3.	It carries $2e^-$ at a time as noticed in both photophosphorylations (PSII) and oxidative phospborylation. It is also associated with salt respiration, nitrate reduction etc.	3.	It performs a number of physiological function such as, (a) morphogenesis and differentiation (b) flowering (c) germination of seeds etc.

Distinction between absorption spectrum and action spectrum

Absorption spectrum	*Action spectrum*
All photosynthetic organisms contain one or more organic pigments capable of absorbing visible radiation which will initiate the photochemical reactions of photosynthesis. The absorption of some wavelengths of light by such pigments is termed as absorption spectrum, which varies from pigment to pigment. For photochemical reactions involving single pigment the action spectrum has the same general shape as the absorption spectrum of that pigment, otherwise both are quite distinct.	The efficiency of photosynthesis by monochromatic light as a function of the wavelength of light is known as action spectrum of photosynthesis.

By shining lights of specific wavelength through a solution of a substance, and measuring the fraction absorbed, one obtains the absorption spectrum of that substa-nce. Each type of molecule has a characteristic absorption spectrum, and measuring the absorption spect-rum can be useful in identifying some unknown substance isolated from a plant or animal cell.

Distinction between photosynthesis and respiration

	Photosynthesis		*Respiration*
1.	*Celluar site*: Chloroplast.	1.	Mitochondria
2.	*Substrates*: CO_2 and water are converted to hexose sugar glucose ($C_6H_{12}O_6$) and other carbohydrates in the presence of light.	2.	Glucose ($C_6H_{12}O_6$) is broken down into CO_2 and H_2O and energy is released. It takes place mostly in the presence of oxygen.
3.	*Products*: Glucose and other polysaccharides like starch, cellulose etc.	3.	$CO_2.H_2O$ and energy in aero-bic respiration; alcohol and lactic acid etc. in an aerobic or fermentative reactions.
4.	*Nature of reaction*: Reduct-ive process.	4.	Oxidative process.
5.	*Change of energy*: Kinetic energy (solar radiation) is converted to potential ener-gy.	5.	Potential energy is released in the form of kinetic energy (i.e., beat or ATP).

(d) Sedoheptulose-7-phosphate reacts with 3-phosphoglyceraldhyde in the presence of transketolase to form xylulose5-phosphate and ribose-5-phosphate.

Sedoheptulose-7-phosphate+3-phosphoglyceraldehyde

$\xrightarrow{\text{transketolase}}$ Xylulose-5-phosphate-f-ribose-5-phosph-ate.

(e) Xylulose-5-phosphate is converted into ribulose-5 phosphate (5-carbon sugar) in the presence of phosphoketopentose epimerase.

$$\text{Xylulose-5-phosphate} \xrightarrow[\text{epimerase}]{\text{Phosphoketopendose}} \text{Ribulose-5-phosphate}$$

(f) Ribose-5-phosphate is also converted in ribulose-5 phosphate in the presence of phosphopentose isomerase.

$$\text{Ribose-5-phospbate} \xrightarrow[\text{isomerase}]{\text{phosphopentose}} \text{Ribulose-5-phosphate}$$

(g) Ribulose-5-phosphate is finally converted into ribulose1,5-diphospbate in the presence of phosphopentose kinase and ATP.

Phosphopentose Ribulose-5-phosphate+ATP

$$\xrightarrow[\text{Kinase}]{\text{Phosphopentose}} \text{Ribulose-l, 5-diphosphate+ADP.}$$

In this manner the Calvin's cycle is completed. The net reaction of C_3 dark fixation of CO_2 is

$$6RuBP+6CO_2+18\ ATP+12NADP_2H \rightarrow 6RuBP+12NADP^+ +C_6H_{19}O_s+ 18ADP+ 18P$$

II. *The Hatch-slack Cycle or C_4 Pathway. It* was worked out by *Hatch* and *Slack* (*1965, 1967*). *Kortschak et. al.* first of all found that lebelled carbon dioxide ($C^{14}O_2$) assimilated by sugarcane leaves first appeared in 4-carbon compound *i.e.* oxaloacetic acid.

Hatch and *Slack* found it a regular mode of carbon dioxide fixation in a number of tropical plants such as maize, Sorghum, *Salsola, Atriplex, Amaranthus* etc. These plants are called C^4 plants because of the first stable photosynthetic product being a 4-carbon compound.

These plants live in hot, arid and as the mesophyll is undifferentiated and its cells occur in concentric layers around vascular bundles. In C[4] plants, initial fixation of CO2 occurs in mesophyll cells. In this cycle, the primary acceptor of CO_2 is phosphoenol pyruvic acid. (PEP).

1-XII Enzymes : I, Carboxydismutase, II, 2-phosphoglycerate kinase, I-II. NADP+glyceraldehyde-3-phosphate dehydrogenase, IV. Triose phosphate isomerase, V. Vldolase IV. Fructose- 1,6-diphosphate, VII. Transketolase, VIII. Ribulose 5-phosphate-3-epimerase, IX. Aldolase, X. Sedoheptulose-1,7disphosphate, XI. Transketolase, XII. Ribosephosphate isomerase, XIII. Phosphoribulokinase.

1. The first step involves the carboxylation in phosphoenol pyruvic acid in the chloroplasts of mesophyll cells to form oxaloacetic acid and phosphoric acid in the presence of phosphoenol pyruvic acid carboxylase.

$$\text{Phosphoenol pyruvic PEP}+CO_2+H_2O \xrightarrow[\text{acid carbodxylase}]{\text{Phosphoenol pyruvic}} \text{Oxaloacetic acid}+H_2PO_4$$

2. Oxaloacetic acid is reduced to malic acid or aminated to form aspartic acid in the presence of transaminase and malate dehydrogenase respectively.

$$\text{Oxaloacetic acid} + NADPH_2 \xrightarrow{\text{Malat dehydrogenese}} \text{Aspartic acid} + NADP^+ + H_2O$$

3. From chloroplasts of mesophyll cells, the malic acid or aspartic acid is translocated to the chloroplasts of bundle sheath cells where it is decarboxylated as in malic acid or deaminated as in aspartic acid to form pyruvic acid and carbon dioxide.

$$\text{Malic acid}+NADP \xrightarrow{\text{decarboxylase}} \text{Pyruvic acid} + CO_2 + NADPH_2$$

4. Now second carboxylation occurs in the chloroplasts of bundle sheath cells through Calvin cycle. RuBP of Calvin cycle is called *final* or *secondary* acceptor of CO_2 in C[4] plants.

The pyruvic acid produced above is sent back to mesophyll cells. Here it is phosphorylated to regenerate phosphoenol pyruvic acid. Energy is required for this. It is provided by ATP.

$$\text{Pyravic acid} + P_i + \text{ATP} \xrightarrow[\text{Kinase}]{\text{Pyruvate } P_i}$$

Phosphoenol pyruvic acid +AMP + PP_i (Pyrophosphate)

Ribulose-diphosphate accepts CO, produced in step 3 in the presence of carboxydimutase system and ultimately yields 3-phosphoglyceric acid as mentioned above in Calvin cycle. Some of the 3-phosphoglyceric acid is utilised in the formation -of glucose-6-phosphate and sucrose while rest regenerates ribulose-l,5-biphosphate in the system.

In the Calvin cycle 3 ATP molecule are required for the C^4 plants, 5 ATP molecules are required for the fixation of CO_2. For the formation of a glucose molecules C_4 plants require 30 ATP while q plants utilize only 18 ATP.

6-phosphoenol pyruvic acid+6RuBP+30 ATP+ 12 NADPH
→ 6 phosphoenol pyruvic acid +6RuBP +

$$C_6H_{12}O_6 + 30ADP + 12NADP^+ + 30H_3PO_4$$

Significance of Hatch-Slack Pathway

(*i*) This pathway is a modification of Calvin cycle and is advantageous to plants growing in dense, stands of tropical vegetation where the carbon dioxide concentration may be very much reduced.

(*ii*) Concentric arrangement of mesophyll cell produce a smaller area in relation to volume for better utalization of available water and reduce the intensity of solar radiations.

(*iii*) Normal oxygen concentration is not inhibitory for thegrowth in contrast to C_3 plants.

Glycolic Acid or C_3 Pathway

Calvin et. al. reported that glycolic acid in labelled early during photosynthesis with $C^{14}O_2$. When the carbon dioxide concentration of the air is lowered below 1 % glycolic acid is formed in large amount. Glycolic acid may be formed from ribulose-5-phosphate and, therefore, may be a secondary product of the photosynthetic carbon-reduction cycle, but, on the other hand, it may be direct product of photosynthesis.

At high concentrations of carbon dioxide in' the atmosphere,, the synthesis of glycolic acid is inhibited and the phospboglyceric acid is the favoured product. The mechanism of glycolic acid pathway is unknown.

According to *Gibbs*, biosynthesis of glycolic acid during photosynthesis coupling of photosynthetic carbonreduction cycle to the light reactions maybe associated either with PS-I or PS-II.

Measurement of Photosynthesis

Several methods have been used to measure the rate of photosynthesis. In one important and relatively accurate method, a single leaf, still attached to the plant, is enclosed in a small chamber and placed in the light.

A continuous stream of air is then passed through the chamber, and the amount of carbon dioxide in the outgoing air is measured. This is compared with the amount of carbon dioxide in an identical stream of normal air.

A reduction in the amount of carbon dioxide leaving the chamber as compared to the amount entering do.s not, however, indicate the real, or true, rate of photosynthesis but is termed the *apparent* photosynthesis. It is not the true rate of photosynthesis because the living tissues of the leaf are, at the same time, oxidizing food in the process of respiration.

In this energy-yielding process, oxygen is utilised and carbon dioxide released. Since this carbon dioxide, as well as that derived directly from the atmosphere, is used in photosynthesis, the amount of carbon dioxide released in respiration must also be determined and added to the apparent rate to determine the true rate.

The true rate is therefore higher than the apparent rate. Another method of studying the rate of photosynthesis involves placing an aquatic plant in a jar of water in the sunlight. Bubbles of gas soon arise from the cut end of the stem.

If the plant is covered with a glass funnel and an inverted test tube filled with water placed over it, the gas will be collected as it displaces the water in the test tube. When a glowing wood splint is thrust into the test tube, it bursts into flame, indicating a high concentration of oxygen.

The rate at which the bubbles arise roughly indicates the rate of photosynthesis. This, however, is subject to error, for thegas is not necessarily pure oxygen but may also contain nitrogen derived from the intercellular spaces of the leaf and stem. Moreover, some of the oxygen released in photosynthesis diffues into the surrounding water and thus will not appear in bubble form.

The rate at which organic matter in a plant increases during a given period of time may also be used as an index of the rate of photosynthesis. Several methods are used. In one of these, disks with an area of about 1 square centimeter are removed from one side of a leaf in the morning.

The *dry weight* of these disks is then obtained by placing them in an oven at 100°C. and heating them until the weight no longer decreases. This takes about 24 hours. At the end of the day an equal number of disks is removed from the other half of the leaf and their dry weight determined.

The difference in average dry weight between the disks removed in the morning and those removed in the late afternoon is taken to represent the carbohydrate manufactured in an area the size of the sample during the day. This figure, however, is also subject to error, because:

(1) some of the sugar was respired during the day-that is, a gain in weight is a measure only of apparent photosynthesis;

(2) some sugar and other foods were moved to other parts of the plant; and

(3) the area of the leaf may shrink during the day as a result of loss of water.

The "*twin-leaf*" method, a variation of the above, uses :plants in which the leaves are opposite, arranged in pairs. A number of pairs are selected. The area of one leaf of each pair is determined. One member of each pair is removed early in the morning and its dry weight determined. This is compared with the dry weight of opposite leaves removed in the late afternoon. Any gain in dry weight is clearly evident.

In spite of the fact that some of the sugar of the plant is lost in respiration, more than 90 per cent of the dry weight of the plant results, directly or indirectly, from the photosynthetic activity of the leaves. In terms of leaf area, the gain in dry weight may vary from 0.5 to 2 grams per square meter per hour. The magnitude of the photosynthetic process may better be visualised by the calculation that an acre of corn plants, producing 100 bushels, will manufacture on the average 200 pounds of sugar a day. Only about one third of this is deposited in the grain and thus becomes directly available as food for man.

Even so, the products of photosynthesis are prodigious and it is obvious that investigations on the rate of this process are of practical importance.

The Products of Photosynthesis

The products of photosynthesis are generally considered to be the carbohydrates and oxygen. Most of the latter diffuses out of the cells in which it is set free and plays no further part in the metabolism of the plant. Some of the oxygen, however, may be chemically intercepted and utilised in respiration within the cells. The products of importance in plant nutrition are the energy-rich carbohydrates which are built up in the chloroplasts.

Only four carbohydrates commonly appear in leaf cells during or immediately after photosynthesis. These are the hexoses, D-glucose and D-fructose, the disaccharide sucrose, and the polysaccharide starch.

Numerous attempts have been made to determine how many of these carbohydrates are direct products of photosynthesis and also which is the "4first product in this process, but to date there is no entirely satisfactory answer to this question.

It appears quite probable, in fact, that the products of photosynthesis may differ somewhat from one photosynthetic tissue to another. The work of some investigators seems to indicate that the principal leaf carbohydrates are formed sequentially in the order of their complexity. Weevers, *for* example, showed that if geranium plants, the leaves of which bad been depleted of sugars by keeping them in the dark, were allowed to photosynthesize for a very short period, only hexoses accumulated. A longer exposure was required for the appearance of sucrose, and a still longer one for the appearance of starch.

On the other hand, a number of investigators have claimed that sucrose ($C_{12}H_{22}O_{11}$) is the first sugar to be formed in photosynthesis. The fact that the sucrose content of the leaves of a number of species increases during periods of active photosynthesis and decreases rapidly upon the cessation of photosynthesis, while the hexose content of those same leaves remains much more nearly constant throughout the day, has been, taken as evidence for this postulation.

Further evidence that sucrose is probably the first free carbohydrate to be formed .in photosynthesis, at least in some species, is given later under the discussion of the carbon pathway in photosynthesis.

Still different results were obtained by Smith. He found that sucrose and starch are formed simultaneously during photosynthesis in sunflower leaves, presumably from a common precursor, and also obtained evidence that most of the hexoses present in the leaf cells arise from the digestion of sucrose, rather than as direct products of photosynthesis.

Both starch and sucrose serve principally as temporary storage carbohydrates in mesophyll cells. Sucrose is readily translocated from the leaves as such. Starch, however, being insoluble, is immobile until digested to simpler, soluble carbohydrates which can move out of the mesophyll cells.

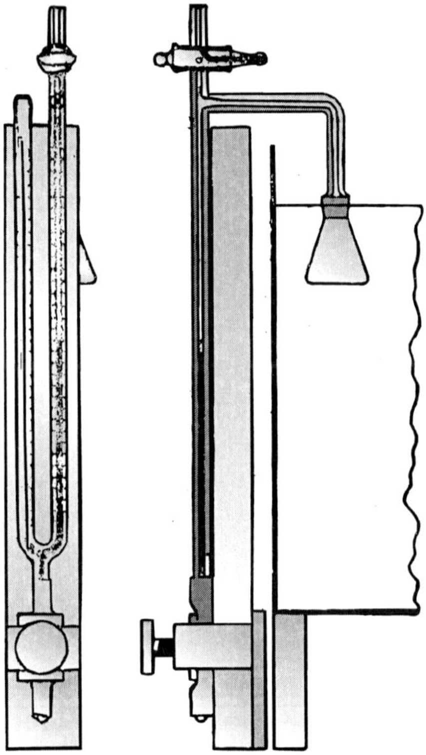

Figure 5.8: Warburg manometer. Left, front view. Right, side view, showing attached flask which is immersed in, and oscillates in, a constant temperature bath. In the simplest application of this method to the measurement of photosynthesis, algae or other small units of photosynthetic tissue are suspended in a bicarbonate buffer (which serves as the CO_2 source) in the flask, and the rate of O_2 evolution, measured mano-metrically, taken as the index of the rate of apparent p4otosynthesis. The same type of apparatus is also widely used for the measurement of the rates of repiration as indicated by the rate of O_2 consumption.

There is some evidence that other types of stable organic compounds may arise more or less directly in the photosynthetic process, at least under some conditions or in some species. Burstrom's results with young, excised wheat leaves indicate that a direct reduction of nitrates resulting in the formation of amino acids or related compounds may occur as an integral part of photosynthesis.

Indications of a similar close relationship between nitrogen metabolism and photos) nthesis has also been found in *Chlorella.* Evidence of an intermeshing of the processes of photosynthesis and amino acid synthesis also comes from studies of the carbon pathway in photosynthesis as revealed by the use of radioactive isotopes.

Results indicating that amino acid synthesis occurs in young leaves of at least some species as an apparently integral part of photosynthesis contrasts with the results, who found an exact equivanlece between the quantity of carbon dioxide photosynthesized and the quantity of carbohydrates made in sunflower leaves. It seems highly probable that the course of photosynthesis is not exactly the same in all photosynthetic tissues. The process may follow a different course in young, growing leaves, for example, than it does in older and more mature leaves, even in the same species.

Starch Synthesis

One of the most familiar facts about photosynthesis is that starch accumulates in the chloroplasts of many species shortly, if not immediately, after the onset of the process at any appreciable rate. Although the possibility of the direct formation of starch in photosynthesis in, some species cannot be excluded, in general starch synthesis and photosynthesis are independent processes. Since starch is insoluble, in water the presence of starch grains a cell must signify that the grains have been built up in that cell.

Starch grains often occur abundantly in the cells of non-green tissues or in the tissues of roots or other plant organs which are never exposed to light. Obviously photosynthesis cannot take place in such cells and the starch present must have been synthesized from sugars translocated to them from the green organs of the plant.

Since starch synthesis in the non-green cells of plants is obviously a distinct process from photosynthesis, it seems probable that this is also true of the starch synthesis which occurs in green cells. The fact that starch synthesis will take place in the chloroplasts of green leaves floated on a sugar solution in the dark also supports this view.

Photosynthesis occurs only in the presence of light and in the higher plants, only in the chloroplasts. Starch synthesis may occur in the chloroplasts, most probably as the product of a secondary, but also may take place in many non-green cells and in either the light or dark. In non-green cells starch is synthesized in the leucoplasts.

The critical concentration of simple sugars required for starch formation in the leaves of many species is very low and has been reported to be less than 0.5g. per 100 g. of fresh leaves in-some species.

In the mesophyll cells of most species, therefore, starch formetion in the leaves quickly follow photosynthesis, much of the sugar made in the latter process being converted into starch.

Under conditions favourable to photosynthesis the starch content of the leaves of most species usually increases during much of the daylight period.

During the night hours the starch content of leaves usually decreases because of digestion of girt or all of the starch back to glucose and translocation out of the cells in the form of this sugar or ,other soluble carbohydrates produced therefrom.

That starch synthesis is an entirely independent process from photosynthesis is also indicated by the fact that this process does not occur in the mesophyll cells of a number of species of plants, yet photosynthesis takes place in these cells in the same manner as in all other green plants.

Failure of the leaves to synthesize starch is a characteristic feature of the metabolism of many species of the Liliaceae, Amaryllidaceae, Gentianaceae, Compositae, and Umbelliferae.

Similarly the non-green portions of at least some kinds of variegated leaves do not normally synthesize starch. However, if the sugar concentration within the chlorophyll-free cells is artificially increased by floating such leaves on glucose solutions, starch synthesis can be induced.

For the leaves of the variegated geranium a glucose solution of about 0.5 M concentration has been found to be optimum for the induction of starch synthesis in the non-green portions.

The Measurement of Photosynthesis

Measurements of photosynthesis are complicated by the fact that certain other processes involving the same materials are proceding in the cells at the same time. The process of respiration is continually in progress in all cells, resulting in an oxidation of part of the carbohydrates synthesized in photosynthesis.

This introduces an error which is inherent in all methods of measuring photosynthesis. Determinations of the quantity of photosynthete formed in a given time are always less than the true value by the amount of carbohydrate which has been consumed in respiration. In many measurements of photosynthesis the simultaneous occurrence of respiration is disregarded, and the results obtained are designated as the *apparent* or *net* photosynthetic rate, in other words, as the rate of photosynthesis minus the rate of respiration.

Since in rapidly pbotosynthesizing tissues the rate of photosynthesis is often ten to twenty times as great as the rate of respiration, the apparent photosynthetic rate is often not greatly less than the true rate. For many purposes measurements of the rate of apparent photosynthesis have as great or greater significance as determinations of the "true"' rate.

Values for the actual rate of photosynthesis are obtained by correcting apparent rates for the quantity of carbohydrates consumed in respiration during the period of the measurement. The values used for such corrections are obtained by measuring the respiration rate of the same plant or organ when treated so that photosynthesis cannot occur-as, for example, by subjection to complete darkness.

Quantitative measurements of photosynthesis in terrestrial plants are usually based on determinations of the rate of oxygen evolution or rate of carbon dioxide consumption. The plants or parts of plants are enclosed in transparent chambers, or leaf cups are attached to the leaves. Outside air is passed through the chambers or leaf cups at a relatively rapid rate. The air is collected upon emergence from the chamber and analysed for oxygen, or carbon dioxide, or both. Another procedure is to analyze small samples of the air for these gases at frequent intervals. By a comparison of the results of these analyses with similar analyses of the outside atmosphere, the rate of carbon dioxide consumption or oxygen evolution can be computed, either of which will serve as an index of the rate of apparent photosynthesis.

The rate of carbon dioxide consumption, under field conditions favourable for photosynthesis, is usually between 10 and 20 mg. CO_2 per $dm.^2$ of leaf area per hr.

Many of the most fundamental investigations of photosynthetic rates have been made by very sensitive manometric techniques which are intrinsically limited in their application to determinations of photosynthesis in small units of plant tissue.

Manometric methods of measuring photosynthesis have been used most widely with suspensions of algae such as *Chlorella*. In these techniques the rate of oxygen evolution, or carbon . dioxide consumption, or both, are measured by pressure changes in a closed system in which the photosynthesizing. tissue is enclosed.

The simplest method of making rough quantitative measurements of the rate of photosynthesis in terrestrial plants is to determine the increase in the dry weight of leaves during a given interval of time. One method of procedure is as follows a representative sample of disks, usually 100 or more, is cut from the leaves by means of a cork borer at the beginnh g of the period for which the determination is to be made.

These disks are transferred to an oven and dried to constant weight. At the end of a chosed period of time, the plant having been meanwhile exposed to the desired environmental conditions, a second sample consisting of the same number of disks as the first is cut from the leaves.

Various precaution must be taken to insure the two samples being as nearly comparable as possible. The dry weight of the second sample of disks is also determined. Any gain in dry weight is considered to represent carbohydrates which have accumulated in the leaves as a result of photosynthesis. This methods is subject to several serious errors and yields only approximate results.

The gain in dry weight of leaves under conditions favourable for photosynthesis is usually between 0.5 and 2.0 g. per square meter per hour. The "twin leaf" method described by Denny is a variation of this method.

The Use of Isotopes as Tracers in Physiological Investigations. The atoms of most chemical elements exist in more than one variety. Each kind of a given element has a different atomic weight, but all of them carry the same nuclear charge. For example, there are three different kinds of magnesium atoms with atomic weights of 24, 25, and 26, respectively. Suchdifferent varieties of atoms of a given element are called *isotopes.* Differences in the chemical behaviour of two isotopes of the same element are so slight as to be barely detectable, and ordinarily they cannot be separated by chemical methcds.

The chemical properties of all isotopes of a given element are virtually identical, because all have the same electron configuration; one isotope differs from another only in the constitution of the atomic nucleus which is composed of protons and neutrons.

In addition to the stable isotopes described above there aremany radioactive isotopes of various elements. Radioactive isotopes of certain heavy elements: such as uranium and radi im oecur in nature.

The atoms of many elements not normally radioactive may be made so by bombardments with various types of elementary particles such as neutrcus, protons, deuterons, and alpha particles. Such bombaidu Ms us usually accomplisbed with the aid of a cyclotrost or an uranium pile reactor.

Atoms of all radioactive elements gradually disintegrate, emitting charged particles and radiations in the process. Forthe artificially radioactive elements which are of greatest significance in biological sciences, the charged particles emitted are electrons and positrons.

As a result of the loss of particles and radiations by radioactive isotopes one element is transmuted into another. Radioactive Na^{24}, for example, with the loss of an electron, is converted into the stable naturally occuring Mg^{24} isotope.

The *half-life* of a radioactive isotope is the length of time required for half of any given weight of the isotope to be converted into the kind of atom into which it is degraded.

The half-lives of radioactive isotopes range from less than a second to many hundreds of years.

The situation with regard to isotopes is well illustrated by the biologically important element carbon. Naturally occurring carbon consists almost entirely of the stable C^{12} isotope.

The C^{12} isotope is also stable and occurs in traces in nature. The atomic weight of naturally occurring carbon is a little more than 12, because of the presence of a slight admixture of the C^{12} isotope.

In addition, three radioactive isotopes can be made: C^{10}, with a half-life of 9 sec., C^{11}, with a half-life of 21 min.; and

C^{14}, with a half-life of about 5000 years.

A radioactive isotope betrays its presence wherever it may be by the continual emission of charged particles which can be detected with an electroscope or Geiger counter. Similarly, the presence of any of the rarer stable isotopes in a system can be detected, because of their unusual mass, by means of the instrument known as the mass spectograph.

Hence, if molecules of any compound are tagged, by incorporating into them atoms that are radioactive or atoms of the rarer kinds of stable isotopes, it is possible to trace such molecules through a system.

After the absorption or ingestion of such molecules by an organism it is possible to follow their subsequent distribution through the organism and often to determine the reactions in which they participate.

This is not possible by ordinary methods of chemical analysis because by such methods it is impossible to distinguish between introduced molecules and others of the same species which were already present in the organism.

Chapter 6

EFFECTS OF LIGHT

Instantaneous rates of photosynthesis may be controlled by external factors, including irradiance, temperature, and the concentrations of CO_2 and O_2, by the molecular composition of the photosynthetic apparatus, including the concentrations or activities of pigments, catalysts of electron transport, and enzymes of CO_2 fixation, or by other factors, such as the concentration of metabolites, or the demands for photosynthetic products.

Photosynthesis-factor response curves, such as the photosynthesis-irradiance, photosynthesis-CO_2, and photosynthesis-temperature relations describe the response of photosynthesis rates to external factors. In addition, the interpretation of these curves often provides important information on regulatory control of photosynthesis by the composition of the photosynthetic apparatus and other internal factors.

Interpretation of resource-response relations rests on the basic principle formulated by Blackman (1905) that an abrupt break in the response curve indicates a switch in control of photosynthesis between two different external factors.

Often, these external factors have their dominant influence on different components of the photosynthetic apparatus. For example, the efficiency of utilization of irradiance often limits the initial slope of the photosynthesis-irradiance (PI) curve, but temperature or CO_2 availability often determines the light-saturated rate.

In other words, the initial slope is often determined by light harvesting and the maximum rate by carboxylation. Usually, the simple resource-response relation envisaged by Blackman or a form based on Michaelis-Menten kinetics is not observed, in part because the concentrations of CO_2 and O_2 or irradiance at the site of photosynthesis within a microalgal cell or macroalgal thallus differs from that in the external environment.

In an attempt to deal with this problem, plant physiologists have developed models based on a mechanistic description of transport and fixation of CO_2 and irradiance distribution within leaves.

Although gradients in irradiance and resistances to CO_2 diffusion may be particularly important in macroalgae, models similar to those employed with terrestrial vascular plants have not been applied to the algae.

The response of photosynthesis to irradiance can be considered over the short and long term. Instantaneous observations of CO_2 or O_2 exchange made over the short term are often considered to be uncoupled from growth, whereas the cumulative rate of photosynthesis should be consistent with the measured growth rate.

In practice, however, it is often difficult to separate photosynthesis from growth. Many techniques require finite time intervals for carrying out photosynthesis measurements during which growth can occur.

Although it is often taken for granted that algal growth rate can be predicted from measurements of photosynthesis rate, it was not until 1979 that Bannister demonstrated that measurements of growth and photosynthesis in the green algae *Chlorella pyrenoidosa* were internally consistent.

The difficulty in relating growth to photosynthesis arises largely from phenotypic, genotypic, and ontogenetic

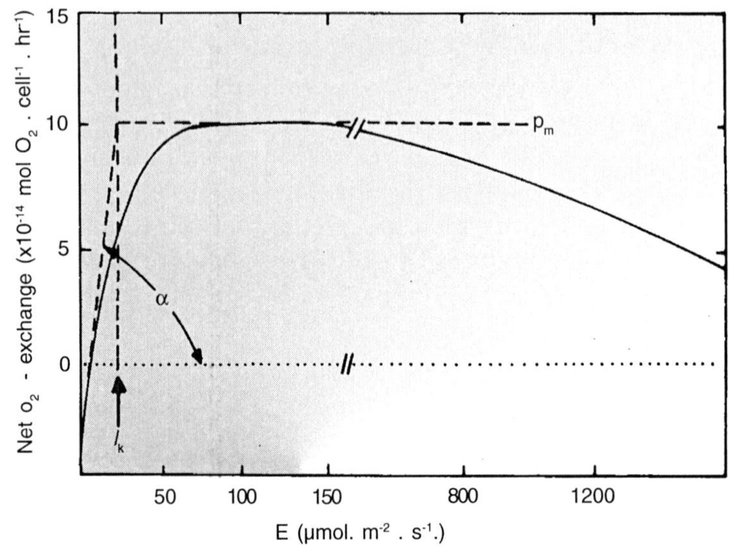

Figure 6.1: Influence of irradiance on the photosynthetic rate of Chlamydomonas rheinhardtii previously grown at 15 μmol-$m^{-2}s^{-1}$. P_m is the maximum rate of light saturated photosynthesis, α is the initial slope, and I_k ($I_k=P_m/\alpha$) is the irradiance at the onset of light saturation.

changes in the size and composition of the photosynthetic apparatus with consequent changes in biomass-specific photosynthesis rates. Interpretation of the response of algal growth to irradiance has been given a mechanistic foundation in terms of the energetic efficiency and size of the photosynthetic apparatus.

The PI curve plays a central role in measuring, modeling, and predicting algal photosynthesis, and in assessing both intra- and interspecific variations in photos-ynthetic physiology.

It contains important information on the functioning of various components of the photosynthetic apparatus and their response to environmental variables.

This chapter considers the equations that are used to describe the PI curve, the range of variability of the parameters of the PI curve, and problems encountered in measuring the PI curve.

Table 6.1: Different formulations of the photosynthesis-light response curve for gross photosynthesis in the absence of photoinhibition.

$P = \alpha E$	$E \leq P_m/\alpha$	(6.1)
$P = P_m$	$E > P_m/\alpha$	
$P = \dfrac{P_m \alpha E}{P_m + \alpha E}$		(6.2)
$P = \dfrac{P_m \alpha E}{[P^2_m + (\alpha E)^2]^{0.5}}$		(6.3)
$P = \alpha E \exp\, (\alpha E/P_m e)$		(6.4)
$P = \alpha E \exp\, (-\alpha E/P_m e)$	$E \leq P_m e/\alpha$	
$P = P_m$	$E > P_m e/\alpha$	(6.5)
$P = P_m\, [1 - \exp\, (\alpha E/P_m)]$		(6.6)
$P = \alpha E - [\alpha E - (\alpha E)^2]/4P_m$	$E \leq 2P_m/\alpha$	(6.7)
$P = P_m$	$E > 2P_m/\alpha$	
$P = P_m \tanh\, (\alpha E/P_m)$		(6.8)

MATHEMATICAL DESCRIPTIONS OF THE PHOTOSYNTHESIS-IRRADIANCE CURVE

The relationship between net gas exchange and irradiance can be broken up into three regions; these are a light-limited region in which photosynthesis increases with increasing irradiance, a light-saturated region in which photosynthesis is independent of irradiance and a photoinhibited region in which photosynthesis decreases with further increases in irradiance.

In addition some workers have identified an intermediate region, where there is either a gradual or abrupt transition from lightlimited to light-saturated photosynthesis. The photosynthesis-light response (PI) curve is constructed by plotting the biomass-specific rate of net photosynthesis against irradiance.

Biomass may be expressed in terms of a number of possible variables including chlorophyll a, total pigment content, organic carbon, organic nitrogen, or dry weight.

Mathematical descriptions or models of the PI curve are empirical in that they attempt to describe the influences of all of the factors that may affect photosynthesis rates in terms of the minimum number of parameters required to adequately describe the PI curve.

Most models of the PI curve characterize the light-limited and light-saturated regions with three parameters: these are the initial slope (α), the dark respiration rate (R), taken as the extrapolation of the initial slope to darkness, and the light-saturated photosynthesis rate (P_m). Inclusion of the photoinhibited region requires additional coefficients in the mathematical formulation and complicates the interpretation of the meaning of the parameters.

This section begins with a consideration of light-limited and light-saturated photosynthesis and then proceeds to an examination of the complete PI curve, including photoinhibition. The quantitative description of the light-dependence of photosynthesis dates from Blackmari s (1905) studies of limiting factors in plant production.

Blackman considered the rate of plant production to be linearly dependent on the availability of a single limiting factor at low resource supply and independent of the availability of this factor above some threshold value.

It was soon recognized that the transition between limiting and saturating resource availability may not be as abrupt as postulated by Blackman kinetics, and a number of different formulations of the PI curve were proposed by plant physiologists, oceanographers, and limnologists.

Although algal physiologists often take the shape of the PI curve as fixed, it may in fact be variable, and vascular plant physiologists often explicitly employ a shape factor. Abrupt transitions in the PI curve are thought to result from extremely efficient regulatory controls over the activity of the primary carboxylating enzyme RUBISCO, although these may be obscured due to gradients in the internal light environment. Variations in the relative importance of these biochemical and nonbio-chemical factors could have important consequences for mathematical descriptions of photosynthetic responses to irradiance as the greatest imprecision in current models is often found in the transition region.

In analogy with the Michaelis-Menton description of enzyme kinetics, the rectangular hyperbola has been used to simulate the photosynthesis-light response in ecological models. Unfortunately, this equation consistently yields a poor fit to experimental data, especially in the transition region from light limitation to light saturation, because the rectangular hyperbola does not allow a rapid enough transition from light-limited to light-saturated photosynthesis.

A modified rectangular hyperbola provides a much better fit to the experimental data by using higher order terms in the denominator, but this equation has no greater mechanistic justification than any of a number of other possible formulations.

The most popular models currently employed to describe experimental PI curves are the hyperbolic tangent function and an exponential model. The hyperbolic tangent function was originally introduced as a purely empirical function, but has found theoretical justification in an analysis by Chalker.

The exponential function is mathematically identical to the cumulative one-hit Poisson distribution used to describe the relationship between flash yield and flash intensity. Jassby and Platt (1976) reformulated eight models of gross photosynthesis, so that they were expressed in terms of the same two parameters.

These parameters are α, defined here as the light-limited initial slope of the PI curve at low incident irradiances and P., the lightsaturated maximum photosynthesis rate. To account for negative values of net photosynthesis in darkness, the authors needed a third parameter, R, the dark respiration rate. The various formulations of the PI curve differ in the abruptness of the transition from light-limited to lightsaturated photosynthesis.

When P_m, α, and R are assumed to have fixed values, the Blackman formulation greatly overestimates photosynthesis and the rectangular hyperbola greatly underestimates photosynthesis at intermediate light levels, relative to the other six models.

The accuracy with which the different models describe the PI curve has been considered for free-living and symbiotic microalgae and macroalgae. Working with ^{14}C-uptake data for natural assemblages of marine phytoplankton, Jassby and Platt concluded that the hyperbolic tangent function provided the best fit to the data.

However, a reanalysis of their data with improved curve-fitting techniques indicated that most models could not be distinguished on a criterion of goodness of fit, although Blackman kinetics and the Michaelis-Menton equation were clearly inferior descriptions of the PI curve.

Chalker (1981) concluded that the hyperbolic tangent function and the exponential function provided more accurate estimates of α and P_m in the reefbuilding corals than did Blackman kinetics or the rectangular hyperbola, consistent with Lederman and Tett's (1981) analysis for phytoplankton.

Coutinho and Zingmark (1987) reported that the hyperbolic tangent provided the best fit to PI curves of marine macroalgae based on both the criteria of goodness of fit and minimizing residuals. Surprisingly, a recent investigation of the PI curve in marine macroalgae found poor fit and low precision in estimates of a and P. using the hyperbolic tangent function.

Researchers involved in terrestrial plant photosynthesis have circumvented the problem of choosing the most appropriate model by introducing the concept of convexity, in which the shape of the PI curve is determined by a parameter, which, like P_m or α, needs to be independently assessed. In the first application of the concept of convexity to algae, Leverenz et al. (1990) demonstrated that the shape of the PI curve depended on the degree of photoinhibition in *Chlamydomonas reinhardtii.*

The transition from light-limitation to light-saturation became less abrupt with increased photoinhibition.

ALTERNATIVE FORMS OF THE PHOTOSYNTHESIS

Most investigators express photosynthesis rates on a unit chlorophyll *a* basis because chlorophyll *a* is a readily measured index of the size of the photosynthetic apparatus.

However, some investigators prefer to express photosynthesis rates in terms of the optical cross section and turnover time of a photosynthetic unit (PSU) rather than in terms of the chlorophyll *a* specific maximum rate P_m^{chl} and the initial slope α^{chl}.

The analysis of steady-state photosynthesis in terms of PSUs is derived from the treatment of O_2 flash yield versus flash irradiance curves.

$$\gamma/\gamma_m = 1 - \exp\left(-\sigma^{PSU}E\right) \tag{6.9}$$

where γ is the yield of O_2 per flash, γ. is the maximum yield of O_2 in a saturating flash, σ^{PSU} is the 'optical' cross-section of a PSU and *E* is the flash irradiance (μmol photons $\cdot m^{-2} \cdot flash^{-1}$). In this section, we show that the two approaches are equivalent when an exponential model is employed.

Following Mauzerall and Greenbaum (1989), the optical cross-section (σ^{PSU}) can be considered to equal the product of the maximum photon yield for O_2 evolution, the *in vivo* absorption coefficient of a chlorophyll *a* molecule and the size of the PSU:

$$\sigma^{PSU} = \phi_m a^* / N^{PSU} \tag{6.10}$$

where ϕ_m is the maximum photon yield (mol O_2.mol^{-1}.photons), a* is the *in vivo* absorption coefficient normalized to chlorophyll a and N^{PSU} is the amount of chlorophyll a in a PSU. Thus, σ^{PSU} is analogous to the initial slope of the PI curve when photosynthesis is normalized to PSUs rather than to chlorophyll *a*; specifically,

$$\sigma^{PSU} = \phi_m a^*_{PSU} = \Phi_m a^* N^{PSU} \tag{6.11}$$

where a_{PSU} is the specific absorption coefficient normalized to a photosynthetic unit.

Based on Mauzerall's treatment of the flash yield versus flash irradiance curve, Dubinsky et al. (1986) proposed the following form for a continuous light PI curve:

$$P / P_m = 1 - \exp\left(-\sigma^{PSU} \tau E\right) \tag{6.12}$$

where σ^{PSU} is the optical cross section of a PSU, τ is the turnover time of a PSU in continuous light, and E is the irradiance (μmol$\cdot$m^{-2} s^{-1}). Noting that by definition P_m^{PSU} = $1/\tau$ and $\sigma^{PSU} = \sigma^{PSU}$ allows Eq. 6.18 to be rewritten as

$$P^{PSU} = P_m^{PSU} \left(1 - \exp\left(\alpha^{PSU} E / P_m^{PSU}\right)\right) \tag{6.13}$$

This is mathematically analogous to Eq. 6.14. By noting the identities

$$\begin{aligned} P^{chl} &\equiv P^{PSU} N^{PSU} \\ \alpha^{chl} &\equiv \alpha^{PSU} N^{PSU} \\ P_m^{chl} &\equiv P_m^{PSU} N^{PSU} \end{aligned} \tag{6.14}$$

Equation 6.6 is readily obtained from Eq. 6.13.

One advantage gained by expressing both the initial slope and lightsaturated rate of photosynthesis in terms of the number of photosynthetic units is the explicit recognition that α and P_m are not necessarily functionally independent.

The often-observed covariation of α and P_m can be most readily explained in terms of changes in the number of active photosynthetic units, all other factors remaining unchanged.

When α and P_m vary independently, it becomes necessary to invoke changes in τ, a^*_{PSU}, or ϕ_m.

Table 6.2. Stoichiometry of electron transport chain components and RUBISCO in microalgae.

Species	Irradiance $\mu mol.m^{-2}.s^{-1}$	RCII:	cytb/f:	RCI	RUBI-SCO
Chlarnydomonas	47	1.3	1.4	1.0	—
reinhardtii	200	2.2	—	1.0	—
400	2.6	2.8	—	1.0	—
Chlorella	low	1.4	—	1.0	—
pyrenoidosa	high	1.3	—	1.0	—
Dunaliella tertiolecta	45	0.9	—	1.0	—
		600	0.8	—	1.0
—					
Dunaliella tertiolecta	80-1,900	0.8	1.4	1.0	0.9-3.5
Mantoniella	5	3.7	1.2	1.0	—
squarnata	100	2.4	1.8	1.0	—
Isochrysis galbana	30-600	2.0	—	1.0	
Isochrysis galbana	(N-limitation)	1.2	4.0	1.0	5.3-14.4
Skeletonema	30	2.3	—	1.0	—
costaturn	200	1.4	—	1.0	—
		600	1.1	—	1.0
—					
Ny17	27	0.89	—	1.0	—
		274	0.76	—	1.0
—					
UP45	27	0.44	—	1.0	—
		274	0.52	—	1.0
—					
Skel	27	0.85	—	1.0	—
		274	0.63	—	1.0
—					
Thalassiosira weisflogii	30-600	2.0	—	1.0	—
Prorocentrum micans	70-600	1.4	—	1.0	—

MECHANISTIC INTERPRETATION OF THE PHOTOSYNTHESIS

As described above, the parameters of the PI curve are strictly empirical coefficients. To gain a greater understanding of the environmental or physiologic factors that regulate photosynthesis, it is desirable to relate these parameters to more fundamental processes.

For the remainder of this discussion, we assume that the PI curve can be described by the exponential function:

$$P^{\text{chl}} = P_m^{\text{chl}}\left[1-\exp\left(-\alpha^{\text{chl}}E/P_m^{\text{chl}}\right)\right] \tag{6.15}$$

Both the initial slope (α^{chl}) and the light-saturated rate (P_m^{chl}) have been described in terms of underlying biochemical and biophysical events.

At low irradiance, the photosynthesis rate is proportional to the amount of light intercepted by the photosynthetic apparatus, and the proportionality constant is the initial slope α^{chl}.

The initial slope can thus be equated to the product of a chlorophyll *a*-specific absorption coefficient and the maximum realized photon yield of photosynthesis

$$\alpha^{\text{chl}} = a^{*}\phi_m \tag{6.16}$$

Absorption coefficients are often defined per unit chlorophyll a but can also be normalized to units of per cell or per unit mass.

Much of the variation in α^{chl} in actively growing microalgae appears to be due to variations in light absorption (a*), rather than to variations of the photon yield (ϕ_m).

However, the initial slope has been observed to decrease under adverse growth conditions due to a decline of ϕ_m, and interspecific variations of ϕ_m have been reported.

During phenotypic responses to irradiance or nutrient limitation, compensating changes in ϕ_m and a^* may lead to the situation where there is less variation in α^{chl} than in either ϕ_m or a^*. Typically, the photon yield is calculated from measurements of the initial slope and the absorption coefficient by rearranging Eq. 6.16.

Only in the experiments of Welschmeyer and Lorenzen (1981) and Cleveland and Perry (1987) has ϕ_m been obtained directly from simultaneous measurements of absorption and photosynthesis using an integrating sphere (i.e., from the initial slope of a plot of photosynthesis versus absorbed light).

Whether measured directly or indirectly, all estimates of ϕ_m are subject to potential errors in the measurements of light absorption outlined in elsewhere in this book. In addition, variations in gas exchange rates due to induction phenomena, changes in mitochondrial respiration between

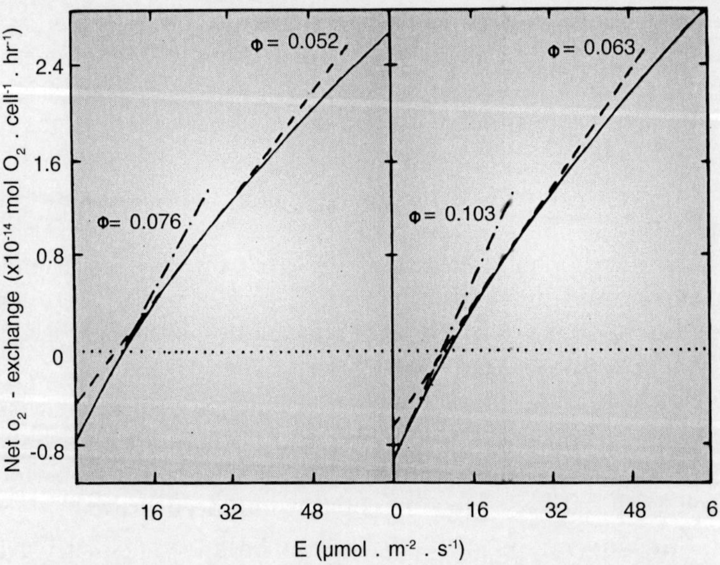

***Figure** 6.2: The response of photosynthesis to limiting irradiance in the cyanobacteriium Anacystis nidulans previously grown at 200 μmol-m.s*$^{-1}$ *to indicate the influence of the Kok effect on the photon yield (*ϕ_m*) of photosynthesis in the absence (a) or presence (b) of nitrate. Figures next to the dashed lines in (a) and (b) represent the calculated slopes of the linear least-squares regression analysis of the photon yield above (—) and* **(.-.)** *below the light compensation point.*

light and darkness, and changes in gas exchange with irradiance due to photorespiration produce ambiguities that confound an accurate estimate of ϕ_m.

With material acclimated to low irradiances or nutrient-deficient conditions, light-limited rates of photosynthesis may only be marginally greater than the light compensation point, making it difficult to estimate the initial slope accurately.

These uncertainties are manifested by a continuing controversy over the absolute upper limit of ϕ_m. According to the Z-scheme for photosynthesis, a minimum of eight photons are required per molecule of O_2 evolved, giving a maximum upper limit for ϕ_m of 0.125 mol O_2.mol^{-1}.photon.

The value of 0.125 is an upper limit, which is unlikely to be realized in practice because of expected inefficiencies in photosynthetic electron transport. Although many investigators report values for $\phi_m < 0.125$, a number of investigations are inconsistent with the Z scheme in that values of $\phi_m > 0.125$ have been observed.

In view of recently expressed reservations about the operation of the two photosystems and the demonstration of the direct photoreduction of $NADP^+$ by PS2, additional experimental determinations of ϕ_m under well-controlled conditions that are free of the experimental artifacts discussed above are clearly warranted.

Largely as a consequence of problems associated with transitory gas exchange phenomena, some workers have suggested that the maximum value for ϕ_m can only be estimated with actively growing cells in balanced growth.

Measurements of ϕ_m based on balanced growth are technically more difficult than estimates based on gas exchange, because of the need to maintain stable conditions of biomass and irradiance over several division cycles (i.e., days to weeks). It is, therefore, not surprising that only a few studies have attempted to estimate ϕ_m from measurements of light absorption and growth.

Unfortunately, even these measurements do not provide unequivocal estimates of ϕ_m because of difficulties associated with the determination of metabolic costs associated with cell synthetic activity.

A finite amount of time is required for transfer of an electron from H_2O to CO_2, and that time interval (T) is referred to as the turnover time of a PSU. Light saturation of photosynthesis occurs when T exceeds the time interval between successive excitations.

Photosynthetic unit size was originally defined in terms of the number of PS2 reaction centers, determined from oxygen flash yield experiments, and, until recently, it was assumed that the ratio of PS2:cyt b_6/f:PS1 was fixed at unity, based on the Z scheme for photosynthetic electron flow.

It is now known that the photosynthetic electron transport chain is less rigidly defined than is required by a literal interpretation of the Z scheme, and various stoichiometries of reaction centers and electron transport chain catalysts have been observed.

When dealing with intact cells, the photosynthetic unit can be empirically defined as all of the catalysts or compounds associated with a PS2 reaction center that are required for whole-chain electron flow from H_2O to CO_2, resulting in the evolution of one O_2 molecule. Thus, $P_m{}^{chl}$ can be expressed as:

$$p_m^{\text{chl}} = 1/\tau N^{\text{PSU}} \tag{6.17}$$

One disadvantage of describing whole-chain electron flow in terms of photosynthetic unit number and turnover time of an entire PSU is that this approach avoids the question of what process actually sets the limit on PSU turnover during steady photosynthesis in continuous light.

Light-saturated photosynthesis, as determined by net gas exchange techniques, may be set by reactions downstream and to some extent independent of photosynthetic electron transport.

Extending the concept of the photosynthetic unit to include the catalysts of these downstream reactions would greatly dilute the original intent in defining the PSU in terms of a component of photosynthetic light harvesting and electron transport.

Use of ^{18}O techniques to obtain true rates of gross oxygen evolution should lead to an increased understanding of the factors that regulate light-saturated photosynthesis. Significant rates of light-dependent oxygen consumption at light saturation may indicate an excess of electron transport capacity over carboxylation capacity.

PHOTOSYNTHESIS AT IRRADIANCES NEAR THE LIGHT COMPENSATION POINT

The light compensation point is that irradiance at which net gas exchange is zero because gross photosynthesis and respiration rates are in balance. The compensation irradiance can be related to the initial slope and respiration rate as follows:

$$E_0 = R^{chl} / \alpha^{chl} \qquad (7.18)$$

where E_o is the compensation irradiance (μmol photons.$m^{-2}.s^{-1}$); R^{chl} is the respiration rate (μmol O_2-mg chl$a^{-1}.s^{-1}$) and, α^{chl} is the initial slope of the PI curve based on chlorophyll content (mol O_2.mol^{-1} photons.m^{-2}.mg^{-1}chla). The compensation irradiance is not fixed but varies primarily due to R^{chl} and to a lesser extent α^{chl}, both of which will depend on the environmental conditions (irradiance, nutrient availability, temperature), under which the algae were growing.

A careful examination of photosynthesis rates at irradiances near the compensation point often reveals a break in the initial slope, in which the slope abruptly increases at low irradiances. The change in slope is referred to as the Kok-effect in recognition of the contributions of the investigator who first studied this phenomenon.

The Kok effect can be overlooked if the PI curve is poorly resolved near the compensation irradiance and is ignored in all mathematical treatments of the PI curve, such as those summarized in Table elsewhere in this chapter. However, the Kok effect may provide considerable insight into the relationship between photosynthetic and respiratory metabolism.

Kok (1948) found that the ratio of the slopes below and above the break in *Chlorella* varied with physiological condition by up to a factor of two; in the extreme case, an extrapolation of the upper line to zero irradiance gave an estimate of respiration that was only half that of the observed dark respiration rate. Kok (1948) initially interpreted the change in slope as a reflection of changes in the photon yield of photosynthesis (ϕ_m).

However, it is now thought that the higher slope below the compensation point reflects a partial light inhibition of the respiration rate at low irradiances. The Kok effect is not always observed, suggesting that light-inhibition of respiration may be transitory or only occur under certain physiological conditions.

It has also been suggested that the efficiency of metabolite transport across the chloroplast envelope and the rate of cytosolic ATP consumption may determine the magnitude of the Kok effect. Osborne and Geider (1987a) hypothesized that the Kok effect would be particularly vvidcnt following addition of nitrate to nitrogen-starved cells, as has recently been confirmed for the cyanobacterium *Anacystis nidulans*.

MODELS THAT INCLUDE PHOTOINHIBITION

Reductions of biomass-specific photosynthesis rates in samples incubated at or near the surface are often observed under in situ or simulated in situ conditions. Equations that account for this high irradiance inhibition of photosynthesis have been developed by several investigators working in both fresh and salt waters. Platt et al. (1980) extended the exponential formulation to account for

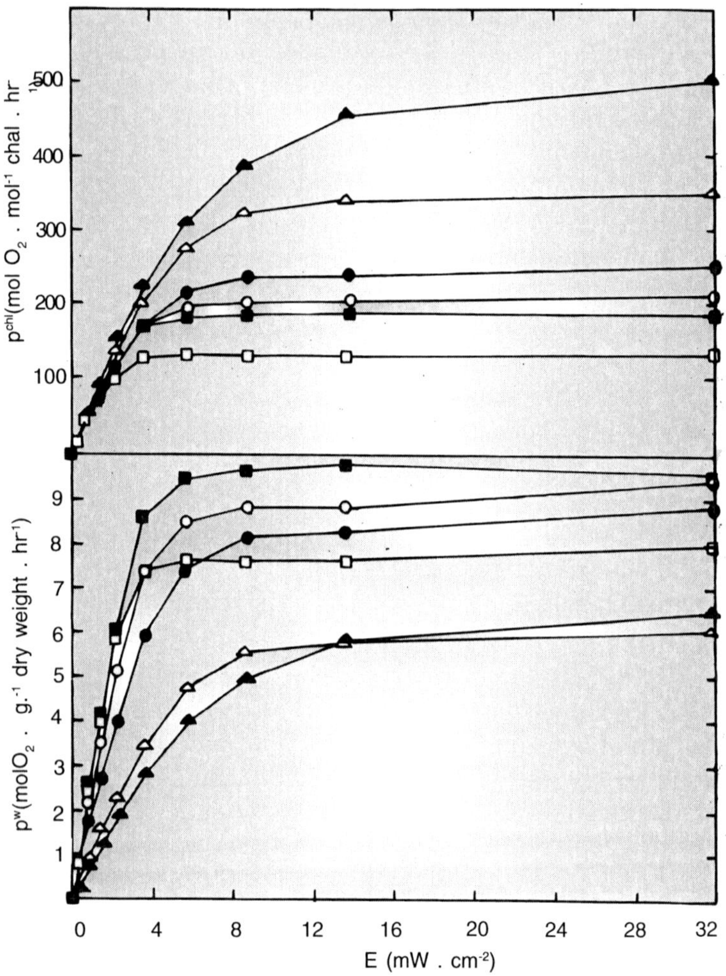

Figure 6.3: Response of the photosynthesis-irradiance (PI) curve to light-limited growth in Chlorella pyrenoidosa.

photoinhibition as follows:

$$P = P_s\left[1 - \exp(-aE)\right]\exp(-bE) \qquad (6.19)$$

where $a = \alpha/P_S$ and $b = \beta/P_5$. In this formulation P_s is not necessarily equivalent to the P_m of Eq. 6.6. When photoinhibition is not observed $P_m = P_s$. However, when photoinhibition is observed $P_s > P_m$. Furthermore, the value of α determined from just the nonphotoinhibited portion of the PI curve will equal the sum $\alpha + \beta$ determined from a complete PI curve that includes photoinhibition.

The three-parameter model of gross photosynthesis works well in many environments, but fails to adequately describe the extended plateau observed in some samples. Coutinho and Zingmark (1987) report that Eq. 6.19 provides a good fit to those PI curves of marine macrophytes that exhibit photoinhibition.

Fasham and Platt (1983) derived a four-parameter model of gross photosynthesis, including photoinhibition, which allowed more flexibility than previous models.

Although derived from a description of the light reactions of photosynthesis that are typified by time constants of less than a second, the model was applied to data obtained from 4 to 6hr incubations. This mismatch in time scales between the mechanistic processes incorporated into the model and the observations to which the model was applied may limit the usefulness of this model in other situations.

Megard et al. (1984) employed a three-parameter model that extended the rectangular hyperbola to include photoinhibition through addition of an E^2 term in the denominator,

$$P = P_s / \left(K_1 + E + E^2 / K^2\right) \tag{6.20}$$

This equation is identical to Haldane's (1930) formulation for enzyme reactions that are inhibited by high substrate concentrations. A mechanistic derivation involving light-dependent activation and inactivation of PS2 was provided by Megard et al. (1984), and a somewhat different formulation of the same model was proposed by Peeters and Eilers (1978).

Reduced gas exchange rates at high irradiance are due largely to two processes: photoinhibition and photorespiration. Photoinhibition is a time-dependent process that

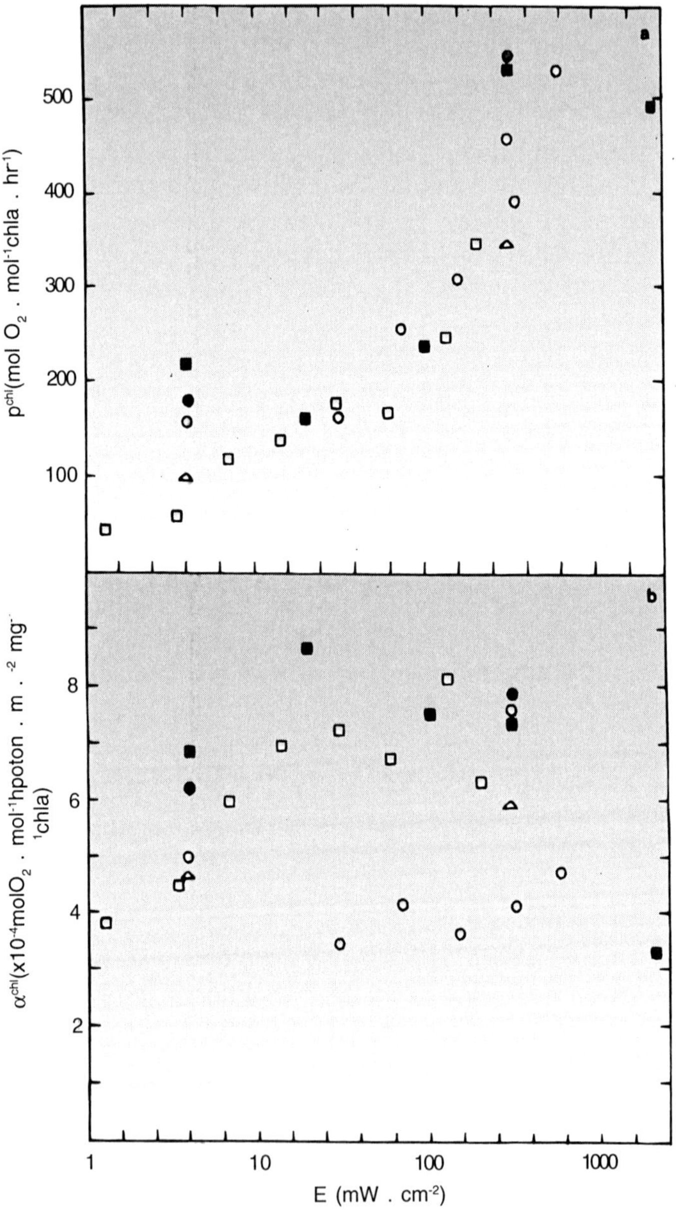

Figure 6.4: Responses of (a) chlorophyll-specific, light-saturated photosynthesis (P_m^{chl}) and (b) the initial slope (α^{chl}) of the PI curve to preconditioning irradiance.

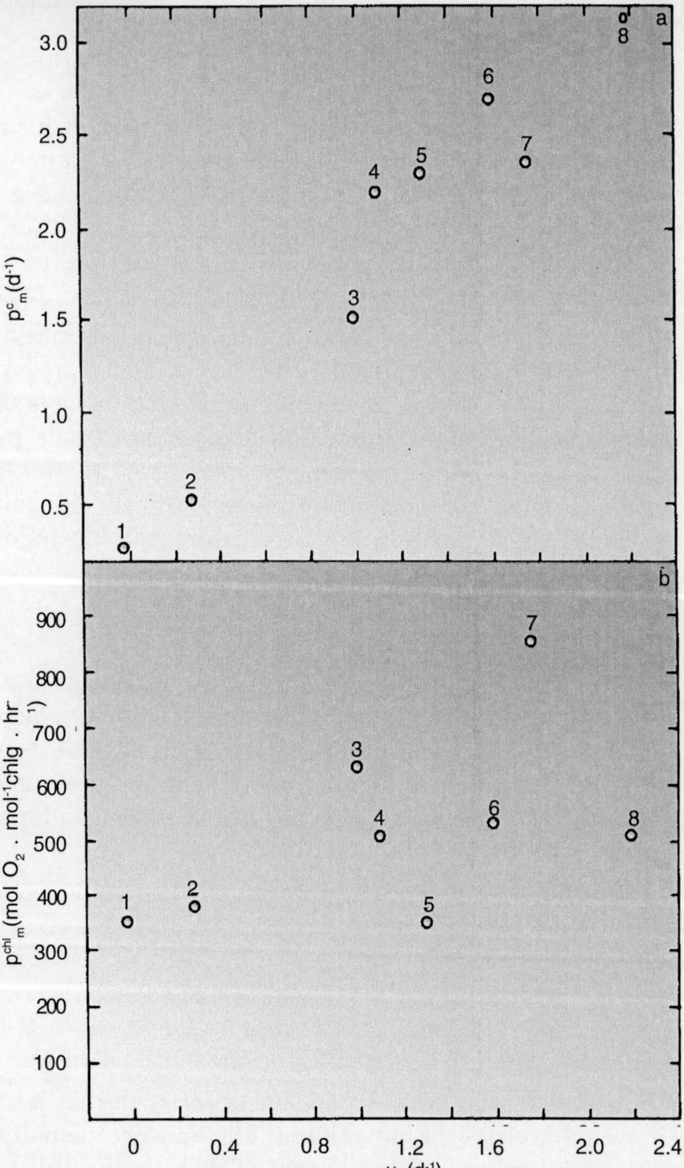

Figure 6.5: Response of carbon-specific, light-saturated photosynth-esis to growth rate (μ_m) in light-and nutrient-saturated cultures. P is linearly related to the resource-unlimited growth rate suggesting that the potential for growth may limit the maximum biomassspe-cific rate of photosynthesis.

appears to involve a reversible or irreversible inactivation of PS2.

Photorespiration is caused by the oxygenase reaction of ribulose bisphosphate carboxylase-oxygenase, which is increased under high light and/or reduced CO_2 supply or increased O_2 concentration. An additional oxygen-consuming reaction in illuminated plants, the Mehler reaction, may play a role in the protection of the photosynthetic apparatus from photoinhibition.

High light inhibition of photosynthesis occurs on a time scale that is commensurate with the time required to determine the PI curve. It is thus likely that models that characterize high light inhibition of photosynthesis by a single, time-invariant parameter may not adequately describe the light-dependence of photosynthesis on shorter time scales. This question has been addressed by Gallegos and Platt (1985).

INTERSPECIFIC AND INTRASPECIFIC VARIATIONS IN P_m AND α

Photosynthesis rates are normalized to some measure of biomass to allow comparisons between organisms with widely different sizes and thus to account for the general observation that the rate of photosynthesis scales with plant biomass.

The choice of a biomass unit for normalizing photosynthesis rates is often based on convenience, but this choice is important in making interspecific and intraspecific comparisons. In microalgae, photosynthesis rates are often expressed as cell-specific or chlorophyll-specific rates or more rarely as carbon-specific or mass-specific rates.

In macroalgae, photosynthesis is often normalized to unit area, dry weight or chlorophyll, and occasionally to unit wet weight or carbon content. The PI curve will have the same shape whatever the unit of biomass to which photosynthesis rates are normalized.

However, changes in the absolute values of biomass-specific photosynthesis rates in response to environmental factors will depend on the unit of biomass to which photosynthesis rates have been normalized.

One goal of algal photosynthesis research is to determine the magnitude of phenotypic and genotypic variations in the parameters of the photosynthesis-light response curve.

Phenotypic variation can be examined by comparing the attributes of genetically identical organisms grown under a range of environmental conditions, whereas genotypic variation is investigated by comparing photosynthesis and biomass of a range of genetically unique organisms grown under identical and well-defined conditions.

Phenotypic responses to irradiance have been best characterized, whereas responses to light quality, nutrient availability, and temperature are not well understood. The effects of both phenotypic and genotypic variability of the photosynthetic apparatus of algae have rarely been examined in the same investigation, although the work of Gallagher et al. (1984) is a notable exception.

The remainder of this section attempts to summarize our current understanding of the influence of phenotypic and genotypic variations on photosynthetic physiology.

Photoadaptation of photosynthesis

An examination of the response of the photosynthetic apparatus to irradiance, nutrient availability, or temperature requires that all other factors be controlled. Photosynthetic parameters can vary widely in batch cultures of marine microalgae, demonstrating the importance of ensuring that cells are in balanced growth before attempting to examine photoadaptation.

However, it may take 5-20 generations before phytoplankton become fully acclimated to the prevailing environmental conditions. It is arguable that balanced growth is never achieved in batch cultures, because the organisms are continuously modifying their environment, which will in turn modify growth processes.

Turbidostats can be used to maintain cells in light-limited balanced growth and chemostats can be used to maintain cells in nutrient-limited balanced growth. However, it is possible to maintain cells in nearly balanced growth in both nutrientsufficient and nutrient-limited cultures by frequent subculturing.

Algae commonly respond to reduced irradiance by increasing the quantity of photosynthetic pigments. This can be viewed as an adaptive response in which the components of the light harvesting apparatus increase in abundance when light is a limiting resource.

In nutrientsufficient microalgae, a plot of the carbon-to-chlorophyll a ratio against irradiance is often linear, although the relationship is sensitive to temperature, with

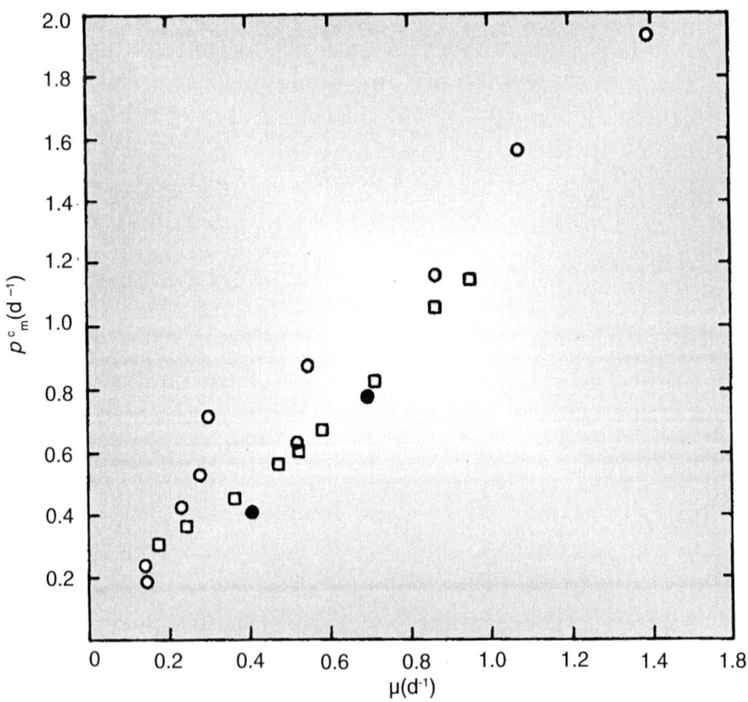

Figure 6.6: Variation in carbon-specific, light-saturated photosynthesis (P_m^c with units of d^{-1}) as a function of growth rate (μ, in units of d^{-1}) for nutrient-limited phytoplankton.

higher carbon-to-chlorophyll a ratios at lower temperatures.

In addition to changes in the size of the photosynthetic apparatus, as indicated by lower carbon-to-chlorophyll a ratios, the response to irradiance may involve changes in the composition of the photosynthetic apparatus. The most common response to low irradiance is an increase in the antennae size of the photosynthetic unit, which is reflected in an increase in the ratio of total chlorophyll a to reaction center P_{700}.

The classic pattern for the acclimation of the PI curve to irradiance is Myer's (1970) data for *Chlorella pyrenoidosa*. To understand this response, it is necessary to consider both chlorophyll a-specific and dryweight-specific photosynthesis rates. Myers (1970) found that the chlorophyll *a*-specific initial slope of the PI curve was largely independent of the irradiance at which the cells were grown but the chlorophyll *a*-specific light-saturated rate (P_m^{chl}) decreased at low irradiance.

In contrast, the dry-weight-specific light-saturated photosynthesis rate (P_m^w) was less dependent on irradiance, but the initial slope (α^w) decreased at low irradiance.

Myer's (1970) observations suggest that light-limited photosynthesis is controlled by the efficiency of light absorption, which covaries with pigment concentration. What controls light-saturated photosynthesis is less clear, but it appears to be the concentration of some component(s) which covary(ies) with algal mass. Foy and Gibson (1982b) found that cell-protein-specific P_m was independent of irradiance in *Oscillatoria agardhii,* whereas dry-weight-specific P_m decreased at high irradiance, presumably because of the accumulation of noncatalytic carbohydrate storage reserves.

It is not surprising that cell protein provides a good predictor of light-saturated photosynthesis given the large contribution of RUBISCO and thylakoid proteins to total cell protein. Other patterns in the response of chlorophyll *a*-specific and weightspecific photosynthesis rates have also been described.

Richardson et al. (1983), for example, list five different types of response of the PI curve—to preconditioning irradiance. It is possible, however, that the range of responses reported by Richardson et al. (1983) is not an inherent property of different algal groups but represents different components of a continuum of photoadaptation along a gradient from light-limitation to photoinhibition.

Chlorophyll-specific, light-saturated photosynthesis rates generally increase in microalgae acclimated to high irradiance. Two- to fivefold changes of P_m^{chl} in response to differences in irradiance have been documented in a wide range of microalgae, including chlorophytes, diatoms, dinoflagellates, cyanobacteria, and a rhodophyte.

An almost linear increase of P_m^{chl} with the logarithm of irradiance is observed in several diatoms grown under nutrient-sufficient conditions in continuous light. In contrast to P_m^{chl}, α^{chl} generally varies little with preconditioning growth irradiance. For example, Foy and Gibson found small changes in α^{chl} in response to an increase in growth irradiance from 30 to 150 $\mu mol.m^{-2}.s^{-1}$ in 20 strains of freshwater cyanobacteria.

The value of α^{chl} increased up to 20% in 5 strains, decreased up to 25% in 15 strains, with a mean overall decrease of 6% when data from all 20 strains are considered.

The phenotypic variability of α^{chl} in response to preconditioning irradiance is generally limited to less than a twofold range, and often differences of less than 25% are observed.

Carbon-specific, light-saturated photosynthesis rates (P_m^{c}) can be considered as the product of P_m^{chl} and ch*la*:C. Because P_m^{chl} and ch*la*:C have the opposite dependencies on irradiance, it is not immediately evident how P_m^{c} will vary with growth irradiance.

Some species show a small dependence of P_m^{c} on irradiance. In *Chlorella pyrenoidosa,* Im varied approximately 1.5-fold, despite a 20-fold change in irradiance and a

7-fold change in μ, whereas P_m^c did not change in *Glenodinium sp.*, despite a 10-fold change in irradiance and a 3-fold change in μ.

However, other species show a pronounced decline in P_m^c at low μ, and/or a decrease as μ approaches μ_m. An interspecific comparison suggests that P_m^c is correlated with the maximum resource-unlimited growth rate.

Diel Patterns of Photosynthesis

Pronounced diel oscillations in phytoplankton photosynthesis complicate the interpretation of the response of the photosynthetic apparatus to variations in irradiance. Diel periodicities are evident in both light-saturated and light-limited photosynthesis rates, with P_m and α undergoing proportional changes in magnitude in both laboratory cultures of marine microalgae, and in phytoplankton populations collected from the field.

This covariation of P_m and α is one of the major patterns that emerges in photosynthesis experiments and may indicate the activation/inactivation of photosynthetic units by endogenous or environmental factors in situ. Diel patterns of P_m and α commonly show maxima during the light period and minima in darkness, although the timing of maximum α and P_m varies between midmorning and midafternoon.

In contrast to the observations for microalgae, in which both P_m and α exhibit diel periodicities, Mishkind et al. (1979) found that only P_m. exhibited a diel variation in *Ulva lactuca,* whereas α did not. The diel variation in P_m was attributed to an endogenous rhythm in the rate of reoxidation of plastoquinone by PSI.

In a comprehensive examination of 24 marine phytoplankton species grown at 15°C and 1,200 $\mu W.m^{-2}$ (approximately 60 $\mu mol.m^{-2}.s^{-1}$) on a 12:12 light-dark cycle, Harding et al. (1981) documented die] variations in 17 species.

A 150-fold difference was observed for P_m in the diatom *Ditylum brightwellii,* and a 50-60-fold difference was observed in *Lauderia borealis.* Of the species that exhibited

Table 6.3: Genotypic (clonal) variations in division rate of various phytoplankters.

Species	Temp C°	Divisions/Day Range	c.v., %	n
Prorocentrum micans	22	0.84-0.92	—	19
Gulf of Maine clone				
	26	0.65-1.1	—	19
Georges Bank clones	22	0.81-0.92	—	9
	26	0.96-1.11	—	9
Emiliania huxleyi				
(Sargasso Sea clones from different locations)				
Population D	16	1.24-1.71	7.9	51
Population N	16	0.94-1.58	13.4	9
Population P	16	1.22-1.71	8.7	11
Population R	16	1.20-1.66	12.2	9
Population D	26	2.05-2.56	6.5	51
Population N	26	2.16-2.28	5.1	9
Population P	26	1.93-2.65	8.6	11
Population R	26	2.27-2.58	3.1	9
Gephyrocapsa oceanica (Sargasso Sea)	16	0.89-1.22	9.0	9
Cyclococcolithina leptopora (Challenger Bank)	20	0.88-1.00	4.1	31
	24	0.67-0.88	6.9	31
Prorocentrum micans (Gulf of Maine)	22	0.84-0.92	3.2	21
	26	0.65-1.11	12.4	21
Dissodinium lunula (Sargasso Sea)	24	0.29-0.37	6.6	41
Gonyaulax tamarensis (Falmouth, Massachusetts)	16	0.19-0.66	10.4	57
Skeletonema costatum (Narragansett Bay, Rhode Island)	20	0.07-3.1	71	12
Thalassiosira rotula (Narragansett Bay, Rhode Island)		2.3-2.4	2.1	6

Table 6.4: Phenotypic and genotypic variability of the photosynthetic apparatus in Skeletonema costatum.

	Clone NY 17		*Clone UP45*		*Clone Skel*	
	27	274	27	274	27	274
10^{-15} mol chla:cell	0.38	0.30	0.74	0.57	0.67	0.40
mol chlc:mol chla	0.31	0.23	0.23	0.20	0.28	0.29
mol fuco:chla	0.52	0.40	0.48	0.29	0.20	0.09
mol chla:mol P_{700}	651	551	1380	951	558	516
mol chla:mol PSU(O_2)	579	416	610	494	478	327
α^{chl} [mol O_2.mol^{-1} chl .min^{-1} (µmol.m^{-2}.s^{-1})$^{-1}$]	3.1	4.0	3.1	2.2	3.8	3.9
P_m^{chl}(mol O_2.mol^{-1} ch*la*.min^{-1})	5.8	7.7	6.2	4.7	9.4	9.9

no diel periodicity, most were small and fast growing and these included three common laboratory "weeds" (i.e., the diatoms *Phaeodactylum tricornutum* and *Skeletonema costatum* and the chlorophyte *Dunaliella tertiolecta*).

In a subsequent investigation using *D. brightwellii,* Harding et al. (1981) showed that diel periodicity in the PI curve was most pronounced in early exponential phase cultures where cell-specific maximum photosynthesis rates (P_m^{cell}) varied from < 10 to 170 pg C.cell^{-1}.h^{-1}, and was least evident in late stationary phase cultures, in which P_m^{cell} varied from 4.5 to 7.5 pg C.cell^{-1}.h^{-1}.

Nutrient Dependence of photosynthesis

The components of the photosynthetic apparatus, namely the pigmentprotein complexes, the carriers of the photosynthetic electron transport chain, and enzymes of the photosynthetic carbon reduction cycle, account for a large fraction of total cell nitrogen in micro- and macroalgae. For example, Falkowski et al. (1989) calculated that 20 to 30% of total cell nitrogen could be attributed to the carboxylating enzyme RUBISCO in nutrient-sufficient *Isochrysis galbana.*

The nitrogen costs of the light-harvesting complexes were determined by Raven (1984) to range from 28 mol nitrogen.mol^{-1} chromophore associated with allophycocyanin in the phycobiliphytes. It is therefore not surprising that algae respond to a reduction in nitrogen availability by reducing the size of the photosynthetic apparatus. This reduction in pigmentation may be adaptive, if it allows a redistribution of nitrogen from light harvesting proteins to other catalysts or if it affords greater protection from photoinhibition when growth processes limit the rate of consumption of the products of photosynthesis.

However, a reduction in the chlorophyll *a:* carbon ratio (chlorosis) appears to be a general response to nutrient limitation, and is not specific to nitrogen limitation and macroalgae. The range of ch*la*:C encountered is likely to depend on both irradiance and temperature, with low temperature and high irradiance contributing to decreases of ch*la*:C, which are most pronounced at low nutrient-limited growth rates.

In addition to a role as light-harvesting accessory pigme-nts, phycobiliproteins have been suggested to be a major intracellular nitrogen reserve in cyanobacteria and red algae. Although efficiently coupled to photosynthesis in low light environments, phycobiliproteins may become uncoup-led from photosynthesis under high irradiances.

Phycobiliproteins decrease to a greater extent than chlorophyll a under nitrogen-limited conditions with much of the nitrogen in the phycobiliproteins presumably being mobilized to allow continued growth in a nitrogen-limited environment.

In contrast to the phycobiliphytes in which the accessory pigment-to-chlorophyll a ratio decreases under nutrient-limited conditions, both chlorophyll c:chlorophyll *a* and carotenoid:chlorophyll *a* increased with increasing N-limitation in *Isochrysis galbana.*

Chlorophyll *a*-specific, light-saturated photosynthesis rates typically decline slightly under moderate nutrient-

Table 6.5: Interspecific variablility of growth rate within higher taxonomic groups of marine and freshwater phytoplankton.

	Light: Dark Period	*T, °C*	*E*	*Max/Min*	*c.v., %*	*n*
Cyanobacteria	C	20	60	5.1	38	22
Diatoms	C	18	320	3.5	49	6
Diatoms	C	21	8	1.6	19	5
	C	21	16	1.5	16	5
	C	21	32	1.2	8	5
	C	21	80	1.4	13	5
	C	21	160	1.4	15	5
	C	21	256	4.9	43	5
Diatoms	C	24	35	—	84	10
	C	24	80	—	79	9
	C	24	350	—	96	10
	C	24	800	—	135	10
	14:10	24	35	1.9	18	10
	14:10	24	80	1.9	19	9
	14:10	24	350	2.5	27	10
	14:10	24	800 .	2.9	33	10
Dinoflagellates	C	21	8	4.2	54	5
	C	21	16	2.4	42	5
	C	21	32	3.8	46	5
	C	21	80	3.9	45	5
	C	21	160	—	79	5
	C	21	256	—	120	5
Dinoflagellates	C	24	35	87	6	
	C	24	80	—	64	
	C	24	350	—	84	7
	C	24	800	—	125	7
	14:10	24	35	—	79	
	14:10	24	80	6.8	53	6

	Light: Dark Period	*T, °C*	*E*	*Max/Min*	*c.v., %*	*n*
	14:10	24	350	—	65	7
	14:10	24	800	115	6	
Coccolithophorids	C	24	35	—	67	4
	C	24	80	—	68	4
	C	24	350	—	70	4
	C	24	800	—	70	4
	14:10	24	35	2.3	32	4
	14:10	24	80	2.0	28	4
	14:10	24	350	2.8	38	4
	14:10	24	800	3.3	51	4
Green algae	C	16	10	1.2	11	4
	C	16	25	2.0	26	4
	C	16	40	2.8	42	4
	C	16	60	2.4	39	4
Green Algae	C	26	10	1.7	22	4
	C	26	25	2.5	43	4
	C	26	40	2.6	53	4
	C	26	60	4.8	54	4

limitation, dropping off markedly only as μ approaches zero. A linear dependence of carbon-specific, light-saturated photosynthesis rates on nutrient-limited growth rate has been observed in several microalgae and a macroalga.

Correlated with the reduction in P_m^c is a decrease in the proportion of cell nitrogen, which is associated with RUBISCO. This response to nutrient limitation involves large reductions in chlorophyll per cell and slight reductions in the chlorophyll-specific lightsaturated photosynthesis rate. In general, chlorophyll *a*-specific rates of light-limited photosynthesis are less affected by nutrient limitation than are light-saturated rates.

The initial slope was independent of growth rate in phosphorus-limited chemostat cultures of *Scenedesmus quadricauda* and phosphorus starved batch cultures of *Anabae-*

na wisconsinense and *Chlorella pyrenoidosa*. However, α^{chl} increased slightly with increasing nitrate-limitation in *Phaeodactylum tricornutum*, and *Isochrysis galbana*.

A large increase in the chlorophyll a-specific absorption coefficient was partially offset by decreases in the maximum photon yield of photosynthesis in these microalgae. Osborne and Geider (1986) observed that α_{chl} increased from 0.0045 to 0.0065 $m^2.mg^{-1}$ chl *a*, but ϕ_m decreased from 0.129 to 0.10 mol O_2 mol^{-1} photons.

Herzig and Falkowski (1989) observed an increase in ϕ_m from 0.0094 to 0.016 $m^2.mg^{-1}$ ch*la*, and a decrease in ϕ_m from 0.08 to 0.06 mol $O_2.mol^{-1}$ photons. In contrast to these observations for nitrate-limited cultures, photon yields were approximately 3—4 times lower in vitamin B_{12} limited *Monochrysis lutheri* than in nutrient-sufficient cultures.

More dramatic declines of ϕ_m and α_{chl} have been observed in stationary phase batch cultures, indicating a large reduction in photosynthetic efficiency under nitrogen-starved conditions.

Temperature Dependence of Photosynthesis

Most investigations of the temperature dependence of photosynthesis have examined the response of photosynthesis rates or enzyme activities immediately following a shift in temperature from the growth tempe ture to a higher or lower experimental temperature.

A theoretical fran work for interpreting these transient responses is provided by the A henius plot in which the natural logarithm of the rate constant of inter is plotted against the inverse of the absolute temperature. The line portion of an Arrhenius plot fits the equation

$$\log_e k \qquad E_d / RT \qquad C \tag{6.21}$$

where k is the rate constant (s^{-1}), E_a is the activation energy (kJ°/mol^{-1}), R is the universal gas constant (8.3 $mol^{-1}.k^{-1}$), T is the absolute temperature (°K) and C is an arbitrary constant. Plots of In k versus 1/T are linear over a range of temperatures near the growth temperature but may show

Table 6.6: Interspecific variability in photosynthesis and chlorophyll a: biomass ratios within higher taxonomic groupings of marine and freshwater phytoplankton.

Taxonomic group	*T,°C*	*E, μmol. $m^{-2}.s^{-1}$*	*Max/ Min*	*c.v., %*	*n*
Cyanobacteria					
P_m^{chl}	20	30	4.7	27	20
P_m^{chl}	20	150	2.3	27	20
α^{chl}	20	30	1.7	18	20
α^{chl}	20	150	1.9	20	20
Diatoms					
P_{chl}	18	320	5.8	52	6
C:chla	18	320	1.7	22	6
C:N	18	320	1.4	13	6
Diatoms					
P_m^{c}	5-8	50	52.0	142	16
α^{chl}	5-8	50	13.0	65	16
C:chla	5-8	50	4.5	54	16
Diatoms					
chla:protein	21	8	2.0	27	5
chla:protein	21	16	1.6	18	5
chla:protein	21	32	1.4	12	5
chla:protein	21	80	1.3	18	5
chla:protein	21	160	2.2	31	5
chla:protein	21	256	3.6	43	4
Dinoflagellates[4]					
chla:protein	21	8	1.5	25	5
chla:protein	21	16	2.4	45	5
chla:protein	21	32	2.4	28	5
chla:protein	21	80	2.1	29	4
chla:protein	21	160	—	70	5
chla:protein	21	256	—	104	5

Table 6.7: Size dependence of growth in microalgae.

	T,°C	*μ*, d^{-1}	r^2	*n*
All taxa included	20	$3.51C^{-0.32}$	0.70	26
All taxa included	15	$2.95C^{-0.28}$	0.59	32
Diatoms	18	$2.60C^{-0.14}$	0.91	56
Diatoms	21	$2.28C^{-0.06}$		5
Diatoms	20	$3.02C^{-0.13}$	0.66	10
Dinoflagellates	21	$1.61C^{-0.16}$		5
Dinoflagellates	21	$1.38C^{-0.15}$	0.75	6
Chlorophytes	16	$1.09C^{-0.19}$	0.72	4

a change in slope within this range.

Outside of this temperature range, *k* declines precipitously. Arrhenius constants for light-saturated photosynthesis and for various partial reactions have been summarized by Raven and Geider (1989).

Light-saturated photosynthesis and the carboxylase activity of RUBISCO are characterized by an E_Q of 54-72 $kJ.mol^{-1}$, which corresponds to a Q_{10} of 2.1-2.7.

This is slightly greater than the Q_{10} for maximum (i.e., resource unlimited) growth (μ,,,) of microalgae obtained from interspecific comparisons, but lower than the Q_{10}, which characterizes the phenotypic response of μ_m to temperature.

When considering a seasonal cycle, temperature is the environmental factor that consistently accounts for the largest component of the variance in P_m^{chl} in marine phytoplankton assemblages with 50% of the variation in P_m^{chl} accounted for by variations in temperature.

Recent investigations demonstrate that α_{chl} shows a similar temperature dependence to phi, immediately following a shift in temperature. This contrasts with the commonly held expectation that light-harvesting and light-limited photosynthesis should be independent of tempera-ture. The temperature dependence of α^{chl} is not limited to short periods following a change in temperature but can be seen in samples from the natural environment, as well.

For example, Cote and Platt (1983) report that temperature can account for 56% of the variance in α^{chl} within the temperature range 5-16°C in Bedford Basin, Canada. This is similar to the proportion of variance in P_m^{chl}, which can be attributed to temperature.

Reductions in α^{chl} at low temperature indicate that the maximum photon yield of photosynthesis (ϕ_m) may be temperature dependent, although it is not possible to confirm this suggestion without independent measurements of the chlorophyll a-specific light absorption coefficient (a^*).

It is now well established that ϕ_m in terrestrial C_3 species is temperature sensitive because of the differential sensitivity of the carboxylase and oxygenase activities of the RUBISCO enzyme to variations in temperature.

Observations that the light-limited growth rate is often reduced at low temperatures to a greater extent than would be expected on the basis of a reduction in pigmentation supports the suggestion that P. is reduced at low temperature.

However, this is not consistent with an effect on RUBISCO kinetics as the oxygenase activity would be predicted to decrease at low temperatures resulting in an increase in ϕ_m.

Other evidence indicating an effect of temperature on ϕ_m is the temperature dependence of growth yields (dry weight of biomass produced per mole of photons absorbed) of *Chlorella vulgaris* and *Chlorogonium sp.,* although in the case of these organisms the temperature effect was attributed to changes in bulk biochemical composition and respiratory metabolism.

There is a clear need for examining the temperature dependence of the photosynthetic energy conversion efficiency and algal growth, because many natural environments are characterized by temperatures considerably lower than the 15-25°C commonly employed in the laboratory.

Acclimation of an organism to a new temperature may modify the properties of catalysts and membranes, or change the relative amounts of different components and so influence photosynthesis rates in ways not predicted by short-term responses to temperature.

The most striking acclimation to different temperatures involves reductions in chla: C and chla $cell^{-1}$ at low temperatures, and increases in the activity of photosynthetic enzymes such as RUBISCO. Davison (1987) demonstrated that light-saturated photosynthesis rates at an assay temperature of 15°C were linearly related to in vitro RUBISCO activities determined at a temperature of 20°C in *Laminaria saccharina* acclimated to temperatures between 0 and 20°C.

He found identical activation energies (i.e., the slope of Arrhenius plot) and temperature dependencies of half saturation constants for TCO_Z uptake in plants previously acclimated to 5°C and 20°C.

GENETIC VARIABILITY

Phenotypic variations in photosynthetic physiology and growth rate in response to environmental conditions were considered in the preceding sections. These phenotypic responses have often formed the basis for modeling growth of algal populations or assemblages.

Good agreement, for instance, was found between the growth rate of natural populations of *Skeletonema costatum* in cage cultures and predictions based on the response of axenic cultures of a single strain of *S. costatum* to irradiance, temperature, and silicate concentration in the laboratory.

However, few rigorous comparisons of predictions based on laboratory experiments and measurements of growth or photosynthesis in nature have been undertaken, and the validity of extrapolating from observations on a relatively few species maintained in the laboratory to mixed assemblages growing under natural conditions has not been firmly established.

One factor that might limit this autoecological approach is genetic variability, both between different clones of morphologically indistingu-ishable organisms and between different taxonomic species. Here we examine the magnitu-de of intraspecific (clonal) and interspecific genetic variab-ility of algal responses to different environmental conditi-ons.

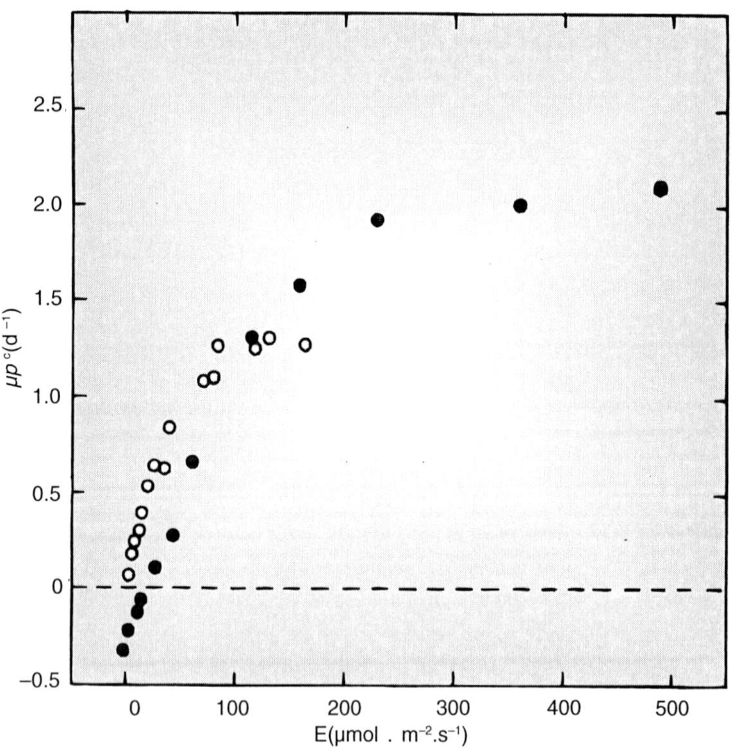

Figure 6.7: Comparison of the photosynthesis-irradiance and growth-irradiance curves of the marine diatom Phaeodactylum tricornutum.

Unfortunately, despite the importance of assessing clonal and interspecific variations in algal physiology, there have been few investigations of the effects of genetic variation on algal photosynthesis. It has been necessary to supplement data on instantaneous photosynthetic respon-ses with information on algal growth in order to address this problem more comprehensively.

Clonal Variability

Clonal variability in the growth rate of various marine phytoplankters has been most extensively examined in a series of investigations undertaken by Brand. Brand (1981) found statistically significant differences in the growth rates of different clones isolated from the same water mass, and significant differences in population growth rates from different water masses. Different populations were characterized by coefficients of variation in reproduction rate, which ranged from 3 to 12% under controlled experimental conditions.

Consistent with these observations, Krawiec (1982) found little clonal variability in maximum reproduction rates and temperature tolerance of six clones of *Thalassiosira rotula* isolated from Narragansett Bay.

A single isolate from Baja, California had a significantly higher maximum division rate and a different temperature tolerance than the Narragansett Bay isolates. However, in both the Baja clone and a Narragansett Bay clone the assimilation number (P^{chl}) showed a similar dependence on temperature and irradiance.

Gallagher (1982) found much higher variability in reproduction rates of *Skeletonema costatum* isolated from Narragansett Bay, with the clones under investigation having a coefficient of variation of reproduction rate of approximately 70%.

However, Gallagher's (1982) cultures were not maintai-ned in balanced growth, and the assessment of the significance of the observed clonal variability is difficult to evaluate. Although variations of up to 10% in growth rate within a population are large by the yardstick of a geneticist, they are relatively small when compared with phenotypic variability.

Phenotypic and genotypic components of variability in the photosynthetic apparatus of *Skeletonema costatum* were investigated by Gallagher et al. (1984). Three clones that varied in maximum specific growth rate and electrophoretic mobility patterns were cultured under conditions of nutrient-sufficient balanced growth at both high and low irradiance.

Significant genotypic and/or phenotypic differences were observed in a number of variables, some of which are summarized in Table elsewhere in this chapter. However, phenotypic variability of P_m^{chl} and α^{chl} showed no consistent pattern.

Both P_m^{chl} and α^{chl} were independent of irradiance in one clone, but were positively related to irradiance in a second clone and inversely related to irradiance in a third. However, covariation of α^{chl} and P_m^{chl} in these clones of *S. costatum* may indicate that changes in the photosy-nthetic apparatus are constrained by similar underlying physiological processes.

A similar covariation of α_{cell} and P_m^{cell} was found in two *Synechococcus* clones cultured under a range of conditions. Ecotypic and developmental differences in the photosynthetic characteristics of *Laminaria saccharina* were investigated by Gerard (1988) with plants taken from shallow- and deep-water sites in Maine and a turbid site in New York State.

Juvenile *L. saccharina* were collected from the field sites and grown 6 weeks at four different light levels (0.065, 0.12, 0.26, and 0.54 of the incident irradiance), with nitrate and phosphate added at 2-d intervals. Gerard (1988) found that area-based measurements of P_m and α were proportional to chlorophyll *a* content, but that plants varied in chlorophyll content, such that the turbid-water ecotype outperformed both the shallow-water and the deep-water forms at all irradiances.

Plants from the deep-water site had lower specific growth rates under both light-saturated and light-limited conditions than plants from the shallow-water site, and plants from the turbid site had the highest growth rates at all irradiances.

Significantly, P_m^{chl}, α^{chl}, and the photon yield of photosynthesis were similar in all three ecotypes. Thus, ecotypic variation in *Laminaria saccharina* was due primarily to differences in pigment content rather than to fundamental differences in the chlorophyllspecific rate of photosynthesis.

Interspecific Variability

Examining interspecific variability in photosynthetic gas exchange rates is complicated by the phenotypic and clonal variability outlined above. However, when organisms are cultured under identical experim-ental conditions, it is possible to examine the variability in specific growth rates, photosynthesis rates, or biochemical composition, which can be attributed to genetic variation.

When such comparisons are made, much of the intersp-ecific variability can be accounted for by higher taxonomic affiliation and organism size in the microalgae and by taxonomic affiliation, size, and form in the macroalgae.

However, there must be a careful consideration of the appropriate physiologic attributes used in any comparison. For example, Dunstan (1973) found that five species of chlorophyll ccontaining microalgae could be characterized by identical values of I_k which implies little interspecific variability, but that chlorophyll a-specific light-saturated photosynthesis and dark respiration rates varied by about a factor of two, implying rather more variability.

This section begins by considering the magnitude of interspecific variability, before proceeding to a discussion of the extent to which interspecific variability is predictable.

Maximum, resource-unlimited growth rates (μ_m) of microalgae, growing under optimal conditions, vary by over an order of magnitude.

For example, at 20°C, μ_m can be expected to range from approxi-mately 0.1 d^{-1} in some large slow-growing dinoflagellates to approximately 3 d^{-1} in some small fast-growing diatoms and green algae. This 30-fold range may approximate an upper limit on the amount of interspecific variability in μ_m that will be observed under controlled conditions. In fact, the range in μ_m is less than fivefold in many interspecific comparisons, even when organisms have been deliberately chosen to include both fastand slow-growing species.

To make meaningful assessments of interspecific variability in growth and photosynthesis, it is necessary to restrict the scope of the comparison to well-defined higher taxonomic groups.

Table elsewhere in this chapter, for example, examines the variability in growth rates within the cyanobacteria, diatoms, dinoflagellates, and green algae. For comparison, Table elsewhere in this chapter examines the variability of some indicators of the size (C:chla, chla:protein) or operating performance (P^{chl}, P_m^{chl}, α^{chl}) of the photosynthetic apparatus.

This information is limited to those studies in which four or more species or clones were cultured under relatively well-defined environmental conditions. Within each of the taxa under consideration, μ_m varied by up to a factor of five and coefficients of variation for μ_m varied by up to 140%. This interspecific variation is considerably greater than that observed for clonal variability in which coefficients of variation of approximately 10% are typically observed.

Photosynthetic characteristics are considerably less variable than μ_m with coefficients of variation of 25 to 50% for P_m^{chl} and α^{chl}, and 10 to 40% for the C:chla and protein: chla ratios. Apparently exceptional in this regard are Taguchi s (1976) observations in which C:chla, P_m^c and α^{chl} vary widely.

Higher taxonomic affiliations can account for a large fraction of the interspecific variability noted above. It is commonly observed that dinoflagellates grow slower than diatoms when cultured under identical environmental conditions, whereas chlorophytes and coccolithophorids appear, on average, to grow at rates comparable to those achieved by the diatoms.

Organism size also appears to account for a significant fraction of interspecific variability. Generally the rates of metabolic processes in both unicellular and multicellular organisms have size dependencies that can be described by an allometric relation of the form

$$rate = aW^{b} \tag{6.22}$$

where *rate* is the rate of some metabolic process, W is a measure of organism size, and a and b are constants. When specific metabolic rates with units of inverse time are plotted against mass, the exponent of Eq. 6.16 usually varies from –0.25 to –0.33.

In other words, specific metabolic rates decrease with increasing organism size. Within the microalgae, the allometric dependence only becomes evident when organisms from a wide range of cell size are considered.

Groups of organisms that meet these criteria and for which sufficient data is available to examine the size dependence of metabolic rates, include the diatoms, dinoflagellates, chlorophytes, and cyanobacteria.

Growth rate is one of the few variables for which a size dependence has been examined in microalgae. When data from all classes of microalgae are included in allometric equations, growth rate scales approximately with mass as $W^{-0.03}$, apparently consistent with observations for other groups of organisms.

However, when data are grouped by higher taxonomic affiliation, the size dependence is markedly reduced as indicated in Table elsewhere in this chapter. Schlesinger et al. (1981) provide evidence for a reduced size dependence of growth under suboptimal environmental conditions previously postulated by Banse (1976). Significantly, organism size can account for approximately 75% of the variance in growth rate.

Bulk biochemical composition shows little size dependence within particular classes of microalgae, although it may vary significantly between higher taxonomic groups.

In particular, dinoflagellates are characterized by lower chlorophyll a:biomass ratio than diatoms, but it is unclear how relative pigment concentrations vary among the other algal classes or in the cyanobacteria. There is some evidence for a reduction in the ratio of chlorovhvll a to biomass as cell size increases, but this reduction in pigmentation does not appear to be sufficient to offset a reduction in chlorophyll *a*-specific photosynthesis rates (P^{chl}) due to a reduced growth rate.

The size-dependence of growth rate discussed above should not be allowed to overshadow the potential use of other functional attributes as predictors of algal growth and photosynthesis, especially in the light of the weak size dependence often observed for specific growth rate. It is well established that a significant proportion of phenotypic variation in growth can be accounted for by differences in the chlorophyll *a*-to-carbon ratio and irradiance.

However, the use of variables such as the chlorophyll a-to-carbon ratio to describe interspecific variations in μ are less well established. An important exception is the observation by Chan (1978) that most of the variation in nutrient-sufficient specific growth rates of diatoms and dinoflagellates could be accounted for by differences in irradiance and the chlorophyll *a*-to-protein ratio.

These results indicate that algal growth rates can be predicted by considering the combined effects of one environmental variable and one physiological variable. Specifically, growth rate was found to be linearly related to the chlorophyll *a*-to-protein ratio at each of the six irradiances examined by Chan (1978).

Underlying this relationship between μ, and the chlorophyll a-to-protein ratio is an implicit limitation on the interspecific variability in the parameters P_m^{chl} and α^{chl} of the photosynthesis-light response curve.

PROBLEMS IN MEASURING PARAMETERS OF THE PHOTOSYNTHESIS

Although often considered to be an attribute solely of the organism being examined under a given set of environmental conditions, the PI curve is not fixed exclusively by these factors, but also depends in a complex manner on the duration of the experiment.

Two extremes in duration can be imagined. At one extreme, the response of growth rate to irradiance is obtained after exposure to continuous, usually constant irradiance, for a period of days to weeks.

At the other extreme, the response of the watersplitting reaction of PS2 to irradiance can be obtained through flash yield experiments in which individual flashes of < 1-μs duration are used to probe the operation of PS2.

It is to be expected that growth rate and PS2 photochemistry will have different dependencies on irradiance due to differing rate limitations and regulatory activities, although direct comparisons of the light-response curves for PS2 activity and growth have not been undertaken.

The Appropriateness of Current Protocols: A Question of Time Scale

Most determinations of the PI curve employ experimental durations of minutes to hours, a range of time scales that is clearly intermediate to the two extremes mentioned above. Transients in the O_2 evolution rate that accompany the onset of illumination, or a large change in irradiance, are well characterized and are typically complete within a period of seconds.

The steady rate of O_2 evolution over a period of minutes that follows these transients is often used in determinations of the PI curve. Myers (1970) was the first to discuss the difference between the photosynthesis—light response curves obtained from these nearly instantaneous observations and the longer term dependence of growth rate on irradiance.

When expressed in the appropriate units, response curves for growth and photosynthesis are expected to cross at the irradiance to which the algae are acclimated. Comparisons of PI and growth irradiance response curves are difficult to make because of differences in the geometries of culture vessels, light sources, and methods employed to measure growth and photosynthesis. A recent comparison for *Phaeodactylum tricornutum* is illustrated in Figure elsewhere in this chapter, where it can be observed that the instantaneous photosynthesis rate exceeds the growth rate at irradiances above that to which the organism was acclimated, but that the growth rate exceeds the photosynthesis rate at lower irradiances.

Even when PI curves are obtained in short-duration experiments, it is found that the rate of photosynthesis at a given irradiance may depend on the previous irradiance. Harris (1973) and Harris and Piccinin (1977) called attention to the problem that instantaneous rates of photosynthesis observed in rising light may exceed rates observed in falling light, and termed the divergence in measured rates of photosynthesis "*hysteresis*."

Harris (1973) noted that hysteresis was more pronounced in samples exposed to saturating and photoinhibiting irradiances than in samples exposed to subsaturating irradiances, and that the magnitude of hysteresis appeared to depend on the duration of exposure to high irradiances.

Hysteresis in net gas exchange measurements has been attributed to several phenomena, including photoinhibition, photorespiration, and variable dark respiration. It is possible that all of these processes contribute to hysteresis to a variable extent depending on the organism under investigation and the experimental conditions.

Clearly, the shape of the PI curve and the magnitude of the parameters that describe this curve may be affected by hysteresis, should it occur to any significant extent. To standardize procedures employed to measure the PI curve, many investigators begin by determining the oxygen consumption rate in darkness followed by measurements of net O_2 evolution at increasing irradiances. This approach should minimize the possibility that photoinhibition will affect the determination of the light-limited photosynthesis rates.

Myers and Graham (1971) recommend that samples be directly transferred from the growth chamber to the cuvette for measurement of gas exchange rate within 10 min of removal from the previous growth condition. This avoids any influence of previous treatments on measured photosynthesis rates, but the precision of the analysis may suffer since measurements of oxygen exchange are made on separate samples taken at separate times.

Determination of the PI curve using “C-bicarbonate assimilation employs parallel incubation of a set of subsamples at a range of irradiances. Thus, each subsample is exposed to a different irradiance for the same time interval, which may range from minutes to hours.

Sample size can vary from 1 cm^{-3} incubated directly in a scintillation vial, to a more typical volume of 50 to 200 cm^{-3}. The preceding discussion indicates that the photosynthetic response of algae may not always be unambiguously described by PI curves.

The utility of the PI curve decreases for algae exposed to very high irradiances for an extended period of time. In particular, photosynthesis rates decline during long exposure to photoinhibiting irradiances, with both the initial rate and the rate of decline dependent on irradiance.

The rate of decline and any subsequent recovery depends not only on the experimental irradiance, but also on the physiological condition of the algae under investigation. As a consequence, the parameters of the PI curve are seen to depend on the duration of the experiment as well as on the characteristics of the sample.

Chapter 7

LIGHT UTILIZATION & OPTICAL PROPERTIES OF ALGAE

In many aquatic systems, the capture of light energy is regarded as the primary factor controlling plant productivity. Measurements of the optical characteristics of algae are essential for estimating the efficiency of photosy-nthetic light utilization, interpreting the in vivo significance of quantitative and qualitative changes in light harvesting pigments, and for determining the role of algae in modifying the transmission and reflection of light by natural waters.

Despite this importance, optical measurements are made infrequently, largely because of difficulties associated with partitioning attenuation into components of absorption and scattering.

In particular, measuring light absorption is complicated when scattering (reflection, refraction, and diffraction) is the dominant process that contributes to light attenuation.

However, techniques are available for determining the optical properties of unicellular and multicellular algae, and it is likely that further progress in areas such as remote sensing and aquatic producti-vity will proceed from a more complete understanding of the absorption and scattering properties of algal cells and tissues.

The angular dependence of the scattered light for homogeneous spheres can be predicted from Mie theory or the simpler anomalous diffraction theory.

Scattering by unicellular algae tends to conform to these predictions, although there is some evidence for a disproport-ionally high percentage of wide-angle scattering in some algal cells. This wide-angle scattering could be due to internal inhomogeneities, such as organelles and other cell structures.

The interaction of a cell with a beam of light is commonly quantified in terms of the cross-sectional area of the incident beam that is modified by the presence of the cell. For scattered photons, this area is called the scattering cross section of the cell (SQ_b), where s is the cross-sectional area of the cell and Q_b is the efficiency factor for scattering.

Dividing the scattering cross section by the geometric cross section gives the efficiency factor for scattering (Q_b). Similar expressions can be used for the absorption cross section (sQ_a) and the efficiency factor for absorption (Q_a). Since the total amount of light attenuated is the sum of scattered and absorbed light, an efficiency factor for attenuation (Q_c) can also be determined:

$$Q_c = Q_a + Q_b \tag{7.1}$$

Interestingly, Q_c, Q_a, or Q_b can theoretically exceed unity, and a cell can influence the light field over an area that is greater than its geometrical cross-sectional area.

This is most likely associated with diffraction and interference phenomena around the periphery of the cell. In practice, however, only measured values for Q_a and Q_b exceed 1, whereas values for Q_a are significantly < 1 indicating that "edge" effects increase scattering more than absorption. Considerably less information exists on the absorption and scattering characteristics of multicellular algae and theoretical descriptions of the optical properties of multicellular tissues have rarely been attempted.

Phenomenologic theories have a limited application and do not provide quantitative descriptions of the influence of tissue dimensions or structures on absorption and scattering. Thick thallii (> 1 mm) of many macrophytes have

Table 7.1: Experimentally determined measurements of a number of optical parameters.

Parameter	*(Minimum)* ($m^2.mg^{-1}$)	*(Maximum)*	*Parameter*	*(Minimum)* (μm^2)	*(Maximum)*	*Parameter*	*(Minimum)* *(dimensionless)*	*(Maximum)*
a*	0.004	0.043	SQ_a	0.024	9.2	Q_a	0.020	0.65
b^*	0.044	0.60	SO_b	39	61	Q_b	0.278	2.5
C*	0.09	0.63	sQ_c	41	72	Q_c	0.308	3.05
b^*_b	0.075×10^{-3}	0.075×10^{-2}	$s_Q bb$	41×10^{-3}	151×10^{-2}	Q_{bb}	1.4×10^{-2}	6.5×10^{-2}

Values are given as the range of reported values. Data taken from Bricaud, Bricaud and Morel, Davies-Colley, Haardt and Maske, Table elsewhere in this chapter of Maske and Haardt, Morel, Morel and Bricaud, and Osborne and Geider. Where reported, cell diameters and intracellular chlorophyll a concentrations varied from 1.5 to 26.5 pm and from 0.3 to 6.16 $kg\text{-}m^{-1}$, respectively. All absorption parameters are for X = 675 nm, whereas the scattering parameters are for values at X = 540-590 nm. For a definition of symbols see Table elsewhere in this chapter.

spectral absorption and reflectance properties that are similar to the leaves of terrestrial vascular plants.

Absorption, reflection and transmission show only small variations with wavelength across the visible spectrum, and differences in pigment content or complement have little effect on light absorption. The flatness of the absorption spectrum between 400 nm and 700 run, which is largely independent of pigment content, is normally ascribed to increases in the pathlength of light within the tissue because of multiple internal reflections.

On this basis, structural features appear to have a greater influence on light absorption than do variations in pigment content. There are, however, few detailed studies on the optical characteristics of macroalgae and many measurements ignore the reflectance component.

The optical properties of macrophytes measured in a fixed position, perpendicular to the incident light, may also be modified in situ because of water movements or variations in the underwater light field. Some algae found appressed to reflective substrates may also show an enhanced absorption in comparison to freely suspended material.

With thin multicellular tissues (< 1 mm thick), absorption often shows a greater dependence on pigment content, although not all macrophytes with tissues comprising only two to three cell layers show this dependence. Absorptance of thick tissues typically equals 90% of incident light and is independent of pigment content.

It is difficult to understand the reasons for the increased synthesis of accessory pigments in multicellular algae in response to reductions in light level or changes in spectral quality, if the function of these pigments is solely a means of increasing the total amount of light absorbed.

There is considerable interest in internal light environments within the photosynthetic tissues of terrestrial plants and their functional significance.

One of the important consequences of the highly

scattering characteristics of plant tissues is that the magnitude of the light gradient is much greater than would be predicted from measurements made with a nonscattering system.

The Kubelka-Munk theory predicts and experiments verify that backscattering results in a higher irradiance just below the tissue surface closest to the light source than the incident irradiance.

Differences in gradients of light within leaves have been correlated with qualitative differences in the response of photosynthesis to light and correlated with changes in tissue biochemistry.

Whether gradients of similar magnitude exist in macrophytic algae awaits experimental investigation. Studies using small fiber-optic probes could be used in measurements on multicellular algae, as could phenomenologic descriptions based on reflection and transmission measurements.

Recent measurements within cyanobacterial mats indicate that the light gradients may be of a similar magnitude to those reported for terrestrial plant species.

CHARACTERIZATION OF THE LIGHT ENVIRONMENT

The major terms used to characterize the underwater light environment are shown in Table elsewhere in this chapter. Since the electromagnetic spectrum is continuous, it is necessary to define the wavelength range used when measuring the light field. Often a broad so-called "*photosynthetically active*" wave-band (λ = 400-700 nm) is used.

Although it is clear that algae can photosynthesize at wavelengths of < 400 nm and > 700 nm, the 400-700 nm waveband is employed because of instrument limitations that preclude extending the upper and lower wavelengths. For many applications it is desirable to resolve spectral variations in the light field, in which case the wavelength

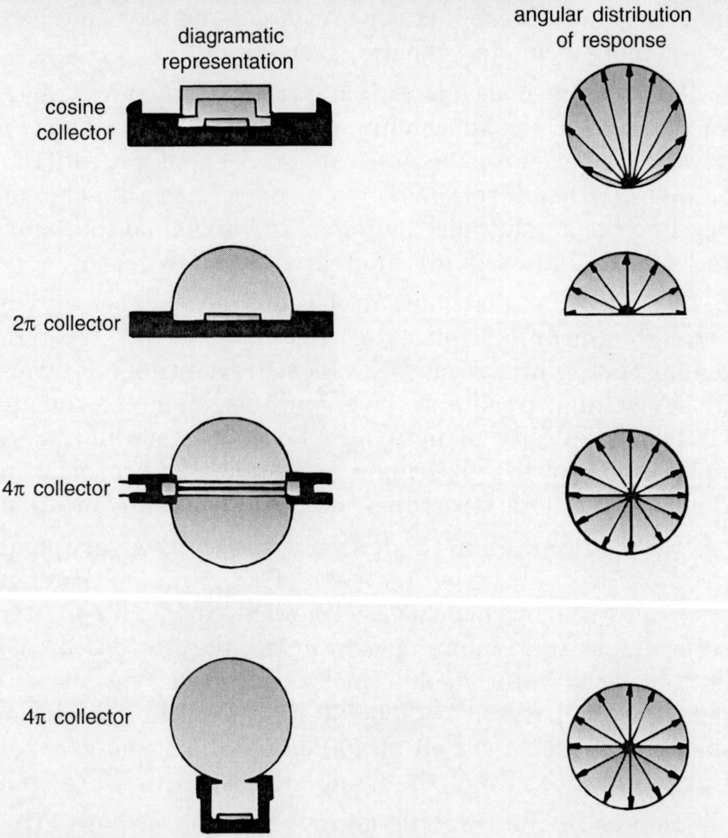

Figure 7.1: Illustration of the types of light detectors used to measure incident irradiance together with the angular distribution of the detector response. Cosine collectors are used to measure horizontal irradiance and exhibit a reduced response to light originating from wide angles; 2π collectors are used to measure hemispheric irradiance over an 180° cone and 4π collectors are used to determine spheric or scalar irradiance over a full 360°. Both 2π and 4π collectors should exhibit an equal response to light of the same flux (photons per second), irrespective of its angular distribution.

under consideration must be designated explicitly. It should also be noted that photon or energy units are often used synonymously, although the conversion between the two is not constant and will depend on the spectral quality of the incident light. The terms *irradiance* and *photon flux density* indicate the incident flux per unit area on either emergent or submerged photosynthetic structures.

They are also used to estimate the flux on an imaginary surface within the suspending medium. In contrast, *scalar irradiance* measures the integrated flux about a point (180° or 360°). Other terms in Table elsewhere in this chapter describe the angular distribution of radiation and the extent to which radiation is attenuated with water depth.

The angular distribution of radiation can be used to estimate the effectiveness of the incident flux for rigid planar photosynthetic surfaces. Measurements of downward (down-welling) irradiance give depth-dependent estimates of the availability of light for photosynthesis and are a consequence of the absorption and scattering properties of the photosynthetic structures and the surrounding medium.

Upward (upwelling) radiation is generally a very small proportion of the downward flux and is due to backscattering by suspended cells, other particulate matter, reflectance from submerged multicellular tissues or the bottom, and water itself. The basic sensor now used to measure light flux (Å= 400-700 nm) is a filtered silicone photodiode with a cut off at 400 and 700 nm and gives an integrated measure of the irradiance over this waveband.

Details of the construction of these sensors are given in Woodward and Sheehy and in the manufacturers literature. Basically, there are three types of sensor/collector, the flat-plate cosine-corrected collector (surface area = πr^2), the 2π collector (surface area = $2\pi r^2$), and the 4rr collector (surface area = $4\pi r^2$).

These differences in collector area are important because the amount of light collected in a *diffuse* light field will be directly proportional to the collector's surface area. Although both the cosine-corrected and the 2π collector measure light over a 180° field of view, they differ because the cosine-corrected collector has a reduced response to light at low solar elevations.

Ideally, this response should obey the Lambert cosine

law, where the light level is equal to the product of the flux on a surface normal to the incident beam and the cosine of the angle of incidence. Most collectors have responses that agree well with theory, except at very low angles of incide-nce. In contrast, the 2π and 4π collectors respond equally to all photons irrespective of their angle of incidence.

There is no unique relationship between recordings from a cosine-corrected and a 4π collector under natural conditions. In a perfectly diffuse radiation field, the response of the sensors should be directly proportional to the surface area of their collectors $(4\pi r^2/\pi r^2)$; however, under experimental situations, the ratio may vary from 1 to 4.

Differences in irradiance measured by sensors having the same type of collector have been largely ascribed to calibration errors, which are beyond the scope of this discussion. There are advantages and disadvantages of each collector, and there is no universally ideal sensor for use in phycological research.

The type of sensor which should be used depends on the spatial arrangement of the light intercepting surface and the angular distribution of the incident light field. Cosine-corrected sensors were developed mainly for work on terrestrial plant species, where the sensor response largely simulates that of a flat, horizontally oriented surface receiving light from above.

Flat, cosine-corrected sensors are most appropriate for studies on some emergent macrophytes and those species in which the photosynthetic structures are found floating on or near the air-water interface or appressed to the substrate.

However, many macroalgae do not have rigid, horizont-ally oriented light intercepting surfaces either in air or water and do not experience unidirectional radiation.

Whether to use a 2π or 4π collector under these situatio-ns depends on whether the light is unidirectional, that is, received on only one surface, in which case a 2π collector is appropriate, or the light is omnidirectional, that is, received on all surfaces, in which case a 4π collector would be appropriate.

For a randomly oriented population of microalgal cells suspended in a diffuse light field, photons are thought to be equally effective for photosynthesis, irrespective of their angular distribution, and a 4π spherical collector would give the most appropriate measure of the incident light level.

However, many of the optical parameters used to characterize the underwater light environment experienced by microalgae are based on light fluxes incident on one side of a horizontal surface, for which 2π collectors, which measure radiation equally over a hemisphere, are used.

Unlike field measurements, in which the sensor is suspended above or in the water, it is necessary to distinguish between the amount of light incident on the surface of a culture and the light level *within* the culture in laboratory studies.

Although the former measurement is often made, the latter measurement is required if laboratory results are to be compared with field investigations. If the light source used in the laboratory is collimated and the incident angle is perpendicular to the flat face of a culture vessel, or the surface of a macrophyte thallus, then the same light level should be found by 2π scalar and cosine-corrected sensors, provided that all other light is excluded.

In practice, the light receiving surfaces of the collectors and the culture vessel must be at the same distance from the light source and a flat cosine-corrected sensor may be more appropriate. If, on the other hand, the light source is completely diffuse, the incident irradiance must be integrated over the whole surface of the culture vessel.

In this case, the incident irradiance can be determined by averaging measurements made with a 2π sensor at several locations over the exterior of the vessel. A small correction will be necessarv for the light attenuated and reflected by the vessel walls. Measurements of irradiance incident *on* the vessel enables the total amount of light absorbed to be calculated, provided that absorptance measurements of the vessel are possible.

This enables comparison of cultures differing in cell numbers and chlorophyll content directly, without the complications associated with differences in the optical geometries of the measuring and culturing vessel. In theory, a diffuse light source could also be used for the measurements.

A sensor immersed within the culture vessel will measure a light level which will be a composite of the absorption and scattering properties of the cells, the optical properties of the culture vessel, and the radiation distribution of the source.

Although a spherical (4π) collector would appear to give the best measurement of mean scalar irradiance within the culture, its practical usefulness depends on the relative size of the vessel in relation to the size of the sensor. Light levels can vary severalfold with position inside a vessel, due to directionality and nonhomogeneity of the external light field and the focusing effects of the container wall, so that the appropriate light level within the culture may be difficult to determine.

The sensors described above measure the amount of light available for photosynthesis in the photosynthetically active waveband, but they give no information on its spectral quality. On the basis of the absorption properties of pigments extracted into organic solvents the probability of a photon being absorbed should depend markedly on wavelength.

In unicellular species and some multicellular plants, absorption is wavelength dependent; however, a thick thallus may have absorption characteristics that are largely wavelength independent, presumably as a result of multiple scattering. Spectral measurements of the incident irradiance are required to assess the significance of differences in light quality.

Measurements of spectral variations in light quality can be made with a spectroradiometer. Typically, this comprises an energy sensor with a monochrometer interposed between the source and the detector.

Commercially available instruments use either irradiance or scalar irradiance collectors and grating or interference monochrometers.

New developments now enable instantaneous spectral measurements to be made using diode array detectors.

Optical Properties of Cells and Tissues

The absorption and scattering characteristics of algal cells and tissues determines how much incident radiant energy is available for photosynthetic processes. Algal abundance may influence the radiant energy available for photosynthesis, because the characteristics of the underwater light field are in part determined by the absorption and scattering properties of the algae themselves.

Light absorption and scattering is also used in a number of experimental techniques for determining the size and composition of algal cells, in remote sensing applications, and for discriminating between phytoplankton species.

Discussions of the optical properties of plants are often complicated because of the wide variety of terms used by workers from different specializations for describing the same optical parameters and because of the misuse of terms such as absorbance and absorptance.

The terminology used to characterize the optical properties of algae is summarized in Table elsewhere in this chapter, which conforms to contemporary usage. Conventional spectrophotometers generally display results as both absorbance and transmittance.

These terms are imprecisely defined, because the optical configu-rations of spectrophotometers, including the distances between sample compartment and detector and the acceptance angle of the detector, vary widely between manufacturers and models. Transmittance (T) is the decimal fraction of the incident flux transmitted through

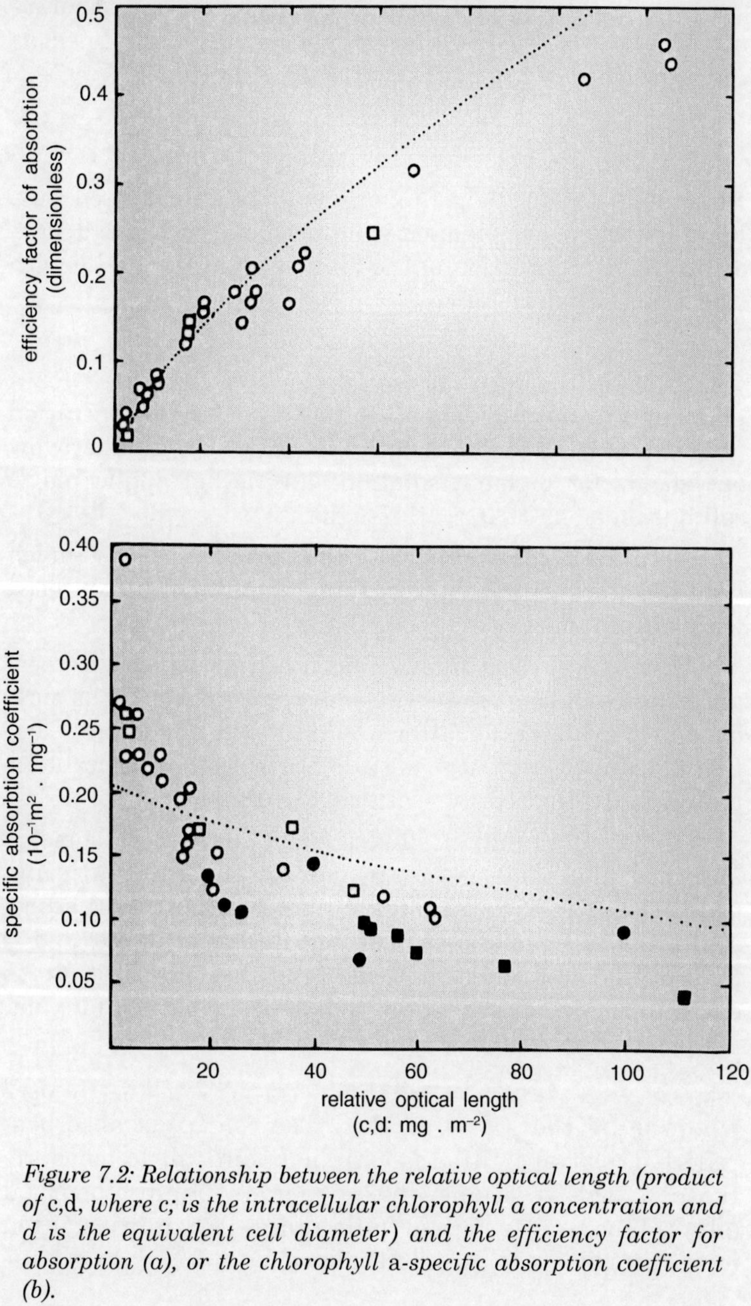

Figure 7.2: Relationship between the relative optical length (product of c,d, *where c; is the intracellular chlorophyll a concentration and d is the equivalent cell diameter) and the efficiency factor for absorption (a), or the chlorophyll* a*-specific absorption coefficient (b).*

the sample, which is received by the detector, and absorbance (D) (also referred to as optical density) is defined as the logarithm of the reciprocal of transmittance,

$$T = \Phi/\Phi_0 \tag{7.2}$$

$$D = \log_{10} I/T = \log_{10} T \tag{7.3}$$

where Φ_0 = the incident flux and Φ = the transmitted flux. For a homogeneous pigment solution the absorbance depends on the concentration of the pigment and the pathlength (the Beer-Lambert Law).

$$\mathrm{D} = 2.303a^*Cl \tag{7.4}$$

where a* is the $\log_e$ specific absorption coefficient for a pigment *solution* ($m^2.g^{-1}$), C is the pigment concentration ($g.m^{-3}$), and l is the pathlength (m). The Beer-Lambert law only holds for pigment solutions and is not applicable to cell suspensions that scatter light.

Absorptance is the appropriate measurement of how much light a cell suspension absorbs and should not be confused with absorbance.

Although current opinion favours the use of the term absorbance rather than the older expression of optical density, the use of the latter would remove much confusion. Light attenuation (scattering and absorption) by unicellular plants is dominated by scattering processes.

Of the total radiant flux incident on a cell, some is absorbed and some is lost by purely physical scattering processes. For a multicellular photosynthetic structure, scattering is normally partitioned into a reflected and a transmitted component and the total flux absorbed (Φ_a) is equal to the incident flux (Φ_0) minus the reflected (Φ_r) and transmitted fluxes (Φ_t),

$$\Phi_a = \Phi_0 - (\Phi_r + \Phi_t) = \Phi_0 - \Phi_s \tag{7.5}$$

where Φ_s is the scattered flux. The *total* flux absorbed, reflected, or transmitted is extremely difficult to measure. Instead, the fractions of the incident light absorbed (absorptance = α), reflected (reflectance = R), or transmitted (transmittance = T) are determined by

$$\alpha = \Phi_a/\Phi_0$$
$$R = \Phi_r/\Phi_0 \qquad (7.6)$$
$$T = \Phi_t/\Phi_0$$

Dividing Eq. 7.5 by Φ_0 and noting the identities in Eq. 7.6 leads to the following expressions for absorptance:

$$\alpha = 1 - (R + T) = 1 - \Phi_s/\Phi_0 \qquad (7.7)$$

Arranging the optical configuration of a spectrophotometer to collect all of the scattered light allows the absorptance (a) to be estimated from the absorbance (*D*), as follows:

$$D = -\log_{10} (1 - \alpha) \qquad (7.8)$$

This equation shows quite clearly the difference between absorb-ance (*D*) and absorptance (α). It should be stressed that this relationship can be used to convert absorbance measurements made on a spectrophotometer into true absorption measurements only if scattering is fully accounted for.

The parameter used extensively for characterizing the absorption of a cellular suspension is the absorption coefficient (α). The absorption coefficient is expressed as an exponential function of the absorptance (*a*) and the pathlength through the suspension.

$$a = -(1/l) \log_e(1 - \alpha) \qquad (7.9)$$

where *a* is the absorption coefficient (m^{-1}) and 1 is the pathlength (m). This relationship is a single scattering approximation and is only valid if multiple scattering does not occur within the suspension. Rearranging Eqs. 7.7 and 7.8 allows the absorption coefficient to be determined from the absorbance

$$a = 2.303\ D/l \qquad (7.10)$$

It is often desirable to know the absorption per unit mass, which is the specific absorption coefficient designated a^*. For example, when expressed per unit mass of chlorophyll *a*, the chlorophyll a-specific absorption coefficient is

$$a^* = a/C \qquad (7.11)$$

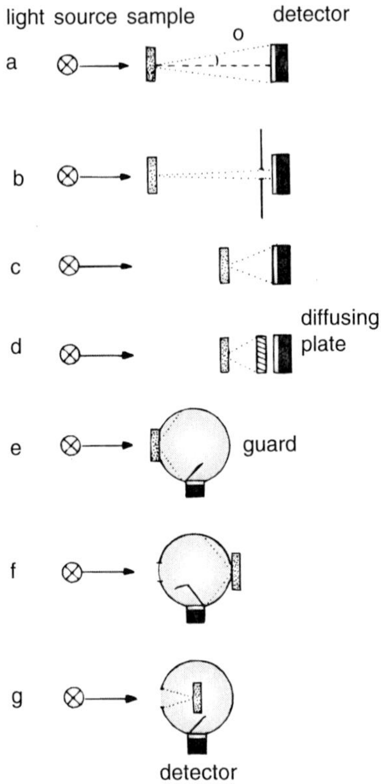

Figure 7.3: Experimental spectrophotometer configurations for measuring absorption, attenuation (scattering + absorption), and scattering.

where C is the chlorophyll *a* concentration ($g.m^{-3}$). Rather than normalizing to chlorophyll *a*, it is sometimes desirable to express absorption on a cell-specific basis. The absorption cross section and the efficiency factor for absorption can be obtained from determinations of the absorption coefficient and measurements of cell dimensions and numbers

$$sQ_a = a/N \tag{7.12}$$

where sQ_a is the absorption cross section (m^2. $cell^{-1}$), s is the geometric cross section (m^2 $cell^{-1}$), Q_a is the efficiency factor for absorption (dimensionless), and N is the cell concentration (cells m^{-3}). Substituting $a = a^*C$ into Eq. 7.11 and rearran-ging leads to

$$Q_a = a^*C/sN \tag{7.13}$$

which upon noting that the chlorophyll a concentration (C) equals the product of the cell concentration (N), cell volume (V, with units in $m^3.cell^{-1}$), and intracellular chlorophyll a concentration (C_i, with units g chlorophyll a m^{-3} cell volume) leads to

$$Q_a = a^*VC/s \tag{7.14}$$

Expressing the volume and surface area of a cell in terms of an equivalent spherical diameter d by using the geometric formulae V = $\pi d^3/6$ and $s = \pi d2/4$ allows Eq. 7.13 to be rewritten as

$$Q_a = (2/3)a^*C_i d \tag{6.15}$$

The efficiency factor for absorption (Q_a) varies from 0 for a particle that does not absorb light to 1.0 for a highly pigmented particle that absorbs

all the light incident on its geometric cross-sectional area. Curvilinearity in a plot of Q_a versus $C_i d$ arises from an inverse relation between a^* and $C_i d$. The decrease of a^* at large $C_i d$ is due to intracellular selfshading and comprises the phenomena known as the package effect.

Although measuring absorption requires that all scattered photons be collected, measuring attenuation requires that all scattered photons be excluded from the detector.

By reducing the collecting half angle to < 1°, scattered photons will be excluded from the detector and only light that has been transmitted through the suspension will be measured.

The exclusion of the scattered photons from the collecting angle of the photomultiplier results in a high absorbance reading and a conventional spectrophotometer with this configuration is really measuring attenuated (i.e., scattered and absorbed) light.

Similar expressions to those used for determining the absorption coefficients can be used to specify volume and specific attenuation coefficients (c, c*), the attenuation cross section (sQ_c and an efficiency factor for attenuation (Q_c).

Scattering can be obtained from absorption and attenuation measurements by difference, and comparable parameters can be derived. The efficiency factor for attenuation (Q_j is the sum of the absorption and scattering components.

Because of the small extent to which microalgal cells backscatter light, it is more difficult to measure backscattering than absorption, attenuation, or total scattering.

Measurements of backscattering together with total scattering can be used to determine forward scattering coefficients.

THEORETICAL TREATMENT OF THE OPTICAL PROPERTIES OF CELLS AND TISSUES

Efficiency factors for Q_c, Q_a, and Q_b can be predicted using Mie theory, although this involves very complex computations. Instead, the anomalous diffraction approximation of Hulst is often used.

This approximation appears to be appropriate for homogeneous particles or cells with refractive indices up to approximately twice that of the surrounding medium. Expressions for the efficiency factors for attenuation (Q_c) and absorption (Q_a) are given by

$$Q_c = 2.4\exp(-\rho\tan\xi)[\cos\xi\sin(\rho-\xi)/\rho + (\cos\xi)^2\cos(\rho-2\xi)] + 4(\cos\xi)\cos 2\xi/\rho \quad (7.16)$$

$$Q_a = 1 + [\exp(-2\tan\xi)(2\tan\xi+1) - 1]/2\tan^2\xi \quad (7.17)$$

$$Q_b = Q_c - Q_a \quad (7.18)$$

where $\rho = (4\pi\ d/\lambda)\ (m - 1)$ is the size parameter of the particle with respect to wavelength (λ), diameter (d) and the real part of the refractive index relative to that of the surrounding medium (m) and $\tan\xi = m'\ (m - 1)$, where m' is the imaginary part of the refractive index.

The expression for Q_a can be modified so that it is more amenable for many experimental requirements by introducing the parameter $\rho' = 4\pi\ dm'/\lambda$ (or $2\ \rho\ \tan\xi$). Equation 7.17 then becomes

$$Q_a = 1+2\ [\exp\ (-\rho')+1]/\rho'+[\exp(-\rho')-1]/(\rho)^2 \qquad (7.19)$$

The parameter ρ′ can be expressed in terms of the absorption coefficient of cell material as follows:

$$\rho' = a_m d \qquad (7.20)$$

where $a_m = 4\pi\ m'/\lambda$ is the absorption coefficient for cell material (m^{-1}) and d is the cell diameter (m). Although these expressions have been used extensively in many recent studies on algae, they strictly refer to homogenous spherical particles, and deviations from theoretical predic-tions may be expected.

Also they cannot be applied to situations where multiple scattering occurs. Theoretical descriptions (Eqs. 7.16-7.19) of the optical characteristics of particles with diameters of 1-20 μm (in the range that is relevant to most microalgal cells) indicate that absorption and scattering is dependent on cell size.

Most of the scattering occurs within a small cone in the forward (0°) direction and backscattering (180°) is often less than 1% of the total attenuated light.

Small particles with diameters that are considerably less than the wavelength of light exhibit scattering charact-eristics with a pronounced wavelength dependence, where scattering is proportional to the fourth power of the wavelength.

Although microalgal cells do not approach these dimensions, there is some evidence that very small species (< 2 μm diam) may exhibit wavelength-dependent scatte-ring, with greater scattering at short wavelengths. The optical characteristics of suspended cells are called *inherent* optical properties, because their magnitude depends only on the characteristics of the cells themselves.

In contrast, vertical attenuation coefficients for light penetration in water bodies are often referred to as *apparent* optical properties, because they are strictly a property of the radiation field.

However, the two are often related as the apparent

optical properties are largely dependent on the *inherent* optical properties of the aquatic medium.

SPECTROPHOTOMETRIC TECHNIQUES FOR MEASURING THE OPTICAL PROPERTIES OF CELLS AND TISSUES

The conventional spectrophotometer configuration shows the relative positions of the light source, sample cell, and detector. In most spectrophotometers, there are two cell positions, one for the reference and the other for sample cuvette, and the light beam is normally split so that it is alternately incident on either cuvette.

The detector is normally a photomultiplier, preferably in an end on configur-ation. The collecting cone of light received by the detector, defined by the half angle, is small, and the sensor only responds to transmitted light within a few degrees of the forward (0°) direction.

Clearly, radiant flux that is scattered at wide (> 10°) angles will not be detected. Erroneously high values for the absorbance in cell suspensions that scatter light can be expected as this instrument only measures the transmitted flux (Φ) that *reaches* the detector.

The amount of light that reaches the detector can be increased by increasing the half angle. Conversely, reducing the half angle to ~0.2° eliminates most (> 95%) of the scattered light and the detector will only measure the transmitted flux in the forward direction.

This approach allows estimation of the scattering characteristics of cell suspensions. A major problem with studies on the optical properties of plants is to fully account for scattering losses during absorption measurements.

Various methods have been utilized to overcome the difficulties of measuring the optical properties of cell suspensions or multicellular tissues using commercial spectrophotometers. Perhaps the simplest way to improve the collection of scattered light is by reducing the distance between the detector and the sample.

Alternatively, opal glass diffusers have been used, or the samples have been concentrated on glass fiber filters, so that the filter itself acts as a diffuser, substituting for the opal glass. Both procedures effectively increase the collecting angle of the detector.

Radiant flux that is scattered by the sample at wide angles and would normally be lost is collected by the diffuser and reaches the detector. Both the filter and opal glass techniques have, however, been criticized because they are thought to enhance absorption, leading to artificially high absorption coefficients.

Additional absorption enhancement phenomena are also possible because of multiple reflections between particles within the concentrated pigment layer. At high cell concentrations, the absorption per unit pigment may even be reduced in comparison to the equivalent cell suspension. Samples sandwiched between two filters may exhibit between two- and sixfold increases in absorption.

Although empirical correction factors can be applied to account for these increases, there is as yet no quantitative description to enable these techniques to be more applicable. Bannister (1988) has responded to some of the criticisms made by Maske and Hardt (1987) by showing that predicted errors associated with the use of the opal glass technique are generally small (± 10%).

Errors associated with the use of diffusers can be related to inherent differences in the scattering and absorption characteristics of cell suspensions. For instance, particles that scatter predominantly at narrow angles may show little absorption enhancement in comparison to those that scatter at wide angles, because of the reduced possibility of significant increases in total internal reflections within the cuvette at angles of incidence close to the normal.

Errors could be influenced by cell size, cell concentration, or pigment content, which argues for more detailed information on the scattering characteristics of cell suspensions.

Methodological differences, such as the type of measuring cuvette used or the relative geometrics of the sample, diffuser, and detector positions may alter the measurements. Difficulties may also arise because the scattering characteristics of the reference cell (generally water) do not match that of the sample cell suspension.

Although this may be overcome to some extent by the use of bleached cells or latex spheres of the appropriate dimensions, it remains uncertain to what extent these will match the characteristics of cell suspensions.

Obviously, there are difficulties in the quantitative description of the absorption characteristics of cell suspensions using diffuser techniques. Also, none of these methods account for backscattering or wide (> 50°) angle losses, although reflection losses at the walls of the cuvette should be accounted for in dual-beam instruments.

An alternative technique, which should theoretically ensure that *all* of the scattered photons are collected, involves the use of an integrating sphere.

Typically, this comprises a hollow sphere, although other shapes have been used, coated on the inside with a highly reflective (> 98%, X = 400-700 nm) white "paint," generally $BaSO_4$, although formerly spheres were coated with MgO.$BaSO_4$ suspensions are commercially available (Eastman-Kodak, white reflectance paint), although a 99-to-1, weight/weight mixture of $BaSO_4$ and polyvinyl alcohol can be used.

The white coating ensures that all photons entering the sphere are diffusely reflected with minimal energy losses. A sensor (either a photodiode or a photomultiplier) is used to measure the irradiance within the sphere. A baffle covers the sensor, so that only diffuse light reflected from the wall of the sphere is measured.

Basically, there are two types of sphere, the Taylor-type and the Ulbricht sphere. In the Taylor-type sphere, reflectance (i.e., backscattering by algal suspensions) and transmittance are measured as separate components of the total attenuated light. With the sample at the front port of the sphere, only transmitted photons are measured, whereas reflected (backscattered) photons are measured with the sample at the rear port. The measurements are calibrated with reference to the appropriate absorption/ reflectance standards.

Even though transmittance and reflectance measurements are used for characterizing the optical properties of macroalgae, reflectance (*backscattering*) *measurements* are generally *omitted* from determin-ations made on microalgal suspensions. Backscattering by algal suspensions is difficult to measure because reflection from the surface of the measuring cuvette may exceed backscatter by the algal suspension.

Conventionally, measurements involving microalgae are recorded in the absorbance mode, whereas measurements on macrophytes are recorded in the transmittance mode. For macrophytes, absorptance determinations are reported directly as the fraction of the incident light absorbed, whereas absorption by algal suspensions is usually quoted in terms of the absorption coefficient (a).

In the Ulbricht sphere, the sample is placed in the geometric center. With this configuration, the absorptance can be measured directly and theoretically all scattering losses can be accounted for. As far as we are aware, this type of instrument is not commercially available and custom-built models allow the measurement of absorptance and scattering, not absorbance.

With the sample in the beam, the sensor receives a fixed proportion of the light that is scattered from the sample and a modified form of Eq. 7.7 can be used with a small correction for the component of the diffuse radiation absorbed by the sample while it is inside the sphere. Absorptance can be calculated from

$$\alpha = 1 - \frac{\text{detector response with the sample in the beam}}{\text{detector response with sample out of the beam}} \quad (7.21)$$

where the denominator co rrects for the absorption of diffuse radiation within the sphere. Absorption coefficients can be calculated from Eq. 7.7.

In recent developments of the Ulbricht sphere for use with terrestrial plants, the sample has been illuminated with diffuse light, although there are no published accounts of such measurements being made on algae.

Although the integrating sphere should account for all scattered light, potential operating errors caused by often unavoidable deficiencies in sphere construction may be encountered.

There is little information on the use and construction of integrating spheres or of the factors that influence their performance in the phycological literature.

Because of the importance of accuracy in optical measurements, particularly for determinations of photosynthetic efficiency, integrating spheres are considered here in more detail. Full descriptions of the performance of various types of integrating spheres are given in the following references.

We assume that errors associated with the measurement of the *actual* flux attenuated by the sample are minimal. These may arise if the measuring beam has a larger area than the sample or if back reflection causes losses within a few degrees of the incoming flux.

This discussion is restricted to aspects of sphere construction and performance that influence the accuracy of reflectance measurements. Considering first a sphere with no internal mountings, the detector response will depend on the total flux (mol.s^{-1}) incident on the sphere wall (Φ_w). Φ_w is the product of the incoming flux (Φ_i), the reflectance or transmittance of the sample or standard, depending on the configu-ration used (see above), and the efficiency with which the sphere retains the incoming flux, often called the throughput (t), Φ_w/Φ_i . The throughput takes into account errors associated with sphere construction, including the reflectance of the inner wall. For reflectance measurements,

$$\Phi_w^{st} = \Phi_i R_{st}\, t_{st} \qquad (7.22)$$

and

$$\Phi_w^{\,s} = \Phi_i R_s t_s \tag{7.23}$$

where R is the reflectance and the symbols s and st refer to the sample and standard, respectively. Optimization of sphere design is most easily carried out in terms of reflectance, rather than scattering, as reflectance standards are readily available. If the measurements are carried out by substitution of the sample for the standard, $t_s \neq t_{st}$.

This is due to differences in reflectance between the sample and the standard and because the reflectance of all portions of the sphere wall will not be the same. This error increases as the reflectance of the sample deviates increasingly from that of the standard. The error, associated with this can be obtained from

$$t_s/t_{st} = 1 + x \tag{7.24}$$

The throughput (t_s/t_{st}) can be calculated using equation 7.25. Direct comparison of the samples and standards, for instance, in dual beam spectrophotometers will result in lower errors, although these may not be insignificant as the samples/standards used are flat, so that the effective sphere surface deviates somewhat from perfect sphericity.

The efficiency of the sphere (throughput) is a function of the reflectance of the sphere coating and sphere geometry, particularly the number and size of ports in the sphere wall. For a particular sphere the efficiency or throughput, can be determined from the following:

$$t = f_e R_c/[1 - R_c(1 - f_t)] \tag{7.25}$$

where f_e is the area of the entrance port divided by the total surface area of the sphere, f_t is the total area of all ports divided by the surface area of the sphere, and R_c is the reflectance of the sphere coating.

Losses can be significant in large spheres because many reflections are required before the flux reaches the detector. Small spheres are more efficient and provide the highest throughput, although this will be associated with an increase in the error (x), as the percentage of port area to

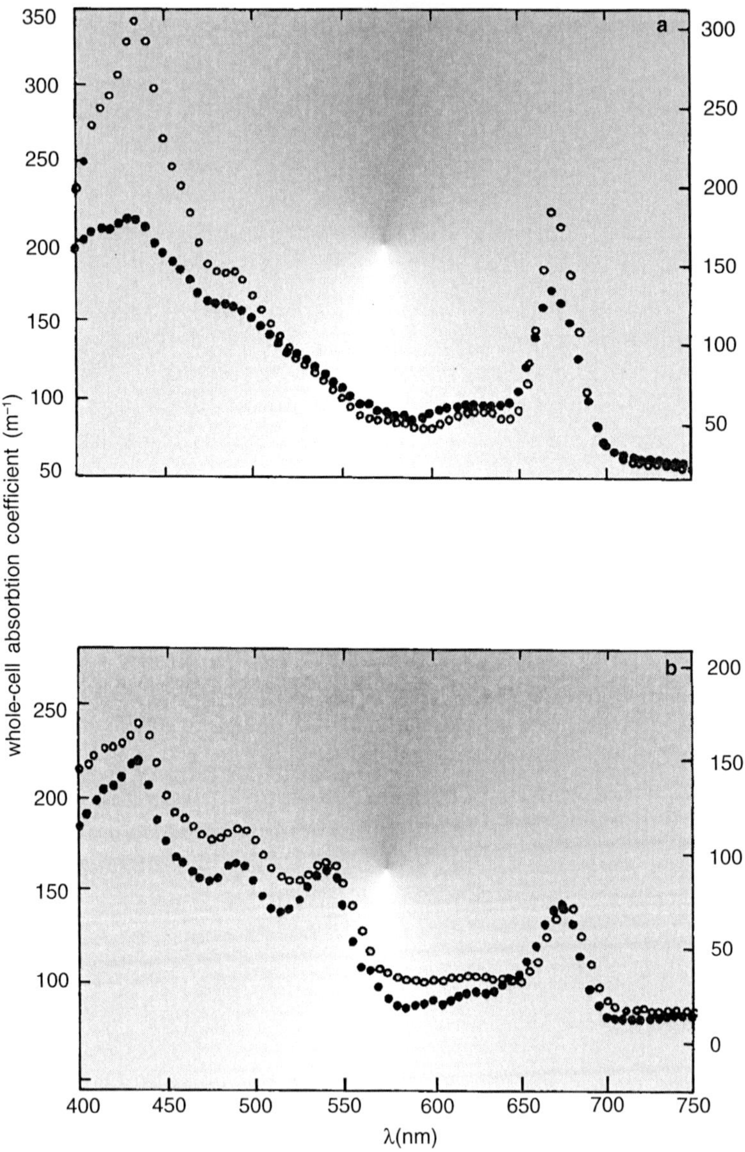

Figure 7.4: Demonstration of the package effect in a large Thalassiosira species (a) and a small Synechococcus species (b), using measurements of intact (0) and disrupted (0) cell absorption spectra. Note the increase in absorption after cell disruption is more pronounced in the larger =5-μm-diam Thalassiosira sp. than in the smaller =1.5-μm-diam Synechococcus sp..

internal surface area will be higher. Consequently, in the design of an integrating sphere, the efficiency should be as large as possible and the error should be small (maximizing t and minimizing x).

To do this, the reflectance of the internal coating should be as high as possible and the ratio of the size of the sample and entrance ports relative to the total surface area of the sphere should be as small as possible.

In contrast, detector port size has little effect on efficiency. Therefore, the appropriate sphere size represents a compromise between a requirement for a large sphere to minimize x and a small sphere to maximize t. Another important consideration is the positioning and type (photodiode or photomultiplier) of detector to be used.

For instance, the detector response should be the same irrespective of the angular distribution of the flux within the sphere. A convenient test uses varying concentrations of a scattering suspension in the sample compartment.

If only one detector is used, it should be positioned close to the entrance port in the upper portion of the sphere. However, positioning may vary due to differences in the scattering characteristics of the sample and the sphere configuration used.

Alternatively, a blank with an angular dependence of scattering that is similar to that of the sample could be used, although this requires more detailed information on the scattering characteristics of algal cells and tissues. Increasing the size of the detector could improve the measur-ements but has obvious limitations, because a flat (single) detector will decrease the sphericity of the sphere.

To overcome this problem several small sensors could be positioned at various points on the sphere wall, although this has not been used extensively. The choice of detector depends on the value of Φ_w. With a low value for Φ_w, a photomultiplier may be required, whereas a photodiode may be acceptable if the value of Φ_w is high.

The flux reaching the sphere wall can be calculated from

geometric considerations using the sphere efficiency or throughput, from the following expression:

$$\Phi_w = \Phi_i R\ [tA_d\ (d_e^{2/4} + D^2)] \quad (7.26)$$

where A_d is the area of the detector, d, is the entrance port diameter, and D is the distance from the entrance port to the detector. The range of expected fluxes can be determined using either R_{st} (maximum) or R_s (minimum).

Additional complications in the use of integrating spheres may arise when the sample is placed within the sphere or because of the use of baffles to shield the detector. This results in blockage effects and the formation of shadows or areas of reduced reflectance on the sphere wall.

Absorption/reflection of the internal flux by the sample can be corrected by recording the detector response after moving the sample to a position to one side of the incoming flux. The internally located sample also alters the radiation distribution within the sphere, resulting in areas of high reflectance on the sphere wall.

The influence of the sample on the internal flux depends on sample size and the reflecting and absorbing properties of the sample. Generally, these effects can be minimized if the sphere diameter is at least 1.5 times the largest dimension of any device mounted or located within the sphere.

Commercially available integrating spheres are generally of the Taylor type, in which the samples are located externally, so that blockage effects should be minimal. However, samples for use with Taylor spheres should be abutted as closely as possible to the inner wall and preferably the ports should have knife-edge openings, in order to maximize the collection of scattered light at wide angles.

Even if these recommendations are followed, the radiant flux scattered at extremely wide angles (~100-180°) will not be captured in the Taylor sphere. The significance of losses at wide angles will depend on the volume-scattering function of the material used. Scattering losses through the side walls of cuvettes can be reduced, if narrow pathlength vessels are used.

Notwithstanding these reservations, it would seem that the integrating sphere is the most appropriate instrument for measuring the optical properties of algae in the absence of complete (4π) angular measurements of scattering. Integrating spheres can now be custom built to suit particular requirements.

The Ulbricht sphere, in particular, seems ideally suited for measurements on microalgal suspensions, because it accounts for all scattering losses, even those at very wide angles. This sphere configuration has the added advantage that total scattering determinations, including the back-scattered flux, can be conveniently and more accurately made without the requirement for separate measur-ements of absorption and scattering.

Total scattering measurements in microalgal suspensions are normally determined from separate measurements of absorption (ignoring back scattering) and attenuation. Conventional spectrophot-ometers can be modified to measure attenuated light by abutting narrow (<< 1 mm) knife-edge slits against the front of the photomultiplier housing, with slit width:, chosen to reduce the collecting half angle to < 0.2°.

For most cells, this should exclude more than 95% of the scattered light, so that the attenuation measurements will be underestimated by less than 5%. Further reduction in the slit widths and collecting angle is not practical. The components of the scattered flux (reflectance and transmittance) within multicellular tissues can be determined with either a Taylor or Ulbricht sphere.

With the Taylor sphere, the samples are located in turn at the forward and rear ports for measurements of transmittance and reflectance, respectively.

Alternatively, in the Ulbricht sphere, total scattering measurements are made initially and then reflectance determinations are made by placing a highly absorbing backing behind the sample, so that the transmitted flux is eliminated and the flux measured in the sphere is due to only the reflectance component.

Transmittance is determined by difference. In theory, similar techniques involving the use of either integrating sphere are appropriate for the measurement of the back-scattered flux from unicellular suspensions. In practice, these measurements are difficult because of the low back-scattered signal obtained with most algal cultures.

With the Taylor sphere, there is also the problem of losses through the side walls of the cuvette. Angular measurements provide additional information on the optical characteristics of cells. The angular distribution of the scattered flux can be determined at regular intervals and integrated over π to 2π (back scattered), $-\pi$ to π (forward scattered) and 0 to 4π (total scattered) radians, using a rotating detector on a calibrated turntable.

These measurements are rarely made, largely because the forward-scattered flux predominates and is of an extremely high radiance in comparison to scattering at other angles.

First, it is physically very difficult to measure scattering accurately at narrow angles within a few degrees of the forward direction, and, second, the detector response has to be accurate over six-orders-of-magnitude variation in radia-nce.

New techniques using diffraction gratings and optical fibers in conjunction with photon-counting detectors, should give more accurate estimates of narrow-angle scattering by unicellular algae.

Absorption and scattering measurements made on cell suspensions provide optical parameters based on an average cell or group of cells in that population; they give no information on the optical characteristics of individual cells or of the variation within that population.

Recently, a microspectrophotometric technique was described for measuring the efficiency factors for absorption

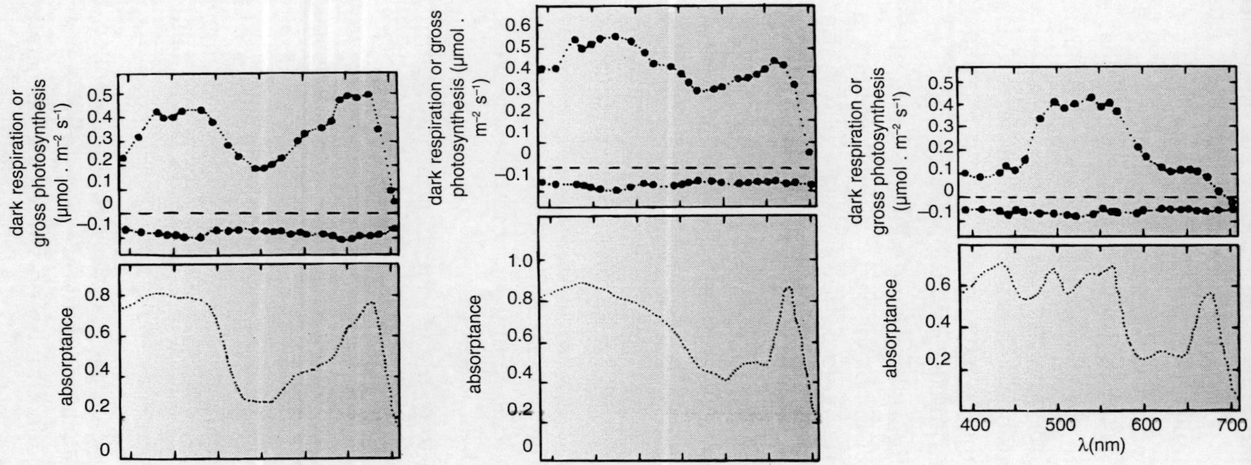

Figure 7.5: Photosynthetic action and absorption spectra of the macroalgae Ulva lactuca (a), Laminaria saccharina (b), and Delesseria sanguinea (c).

by individual particles or cells, allowing the identification of the major components that contribute to light attenuation in natural samples.

Problems with this technique include (1) the limited depth of field associated with microscope optical systems, which results in the illumination of only the portion of the sample within the plane of focus, (2) a tendency for cells in sample preparations to align along a preferred orientation, which may bias absorption characteristics, and (3) uncertainty in the correction for scattering.

Localized light-scattering measurements of individual phytoplankton cells has recently been described, and these instruments are likely to reveal more information on the optical characteristics of unicellular species.

Assessment of the Package Effect

A consequence of the localization of light-absorbing pigments within cells or organelles is to reduce their absorption per unit pigment in comparison to the same quantity of pigment dispersed in solution. This effect is referred to as the *package effect* (also known as the *sieve effect)* and results in a reduction in absorption at the absorption maxima with little change at those wavelengths that are only weakly absorbed.

For unicellular algae, the magnitude of the package effect depends on cell size and intracellular pigment content. Large cells, or those with a high pigment content, have a greater package effect than small cells or those with a lower pigment content.

Changes in the magnitude of the package effect often produce variations in the chlorophyll a-specific absorption coefficient (a*), which is a measure of the amount of light absorbed per unit chlorophyll a.

Although the presence of accessory pigments can modify the value of a*, low values are generally indicative of a large package effect and high values are associated with a small package effect.

The general features of the package effect in unicellular species have been identified, and experimental observations have largely confirmed theoretical predictions.

However, the experimental assessment of the magnitude of the package effect is not without difficulties in the estimation of scattering losses. There is as yet no method to quantify the package effect in multicellular tissues, although this has been estimated using Kubelka-Munk theory.

Indirect evidence indicates that the flattening of the absorption spectrum in multicellular tissues is due to enhanced absorption of wavelengths that are weakly absorbed and is not due to the package effect, but this requires further investigation.

There may be benefits associated with the enclosure of light-absorbing pigments within organelles. There is now good evidence that variations in the magnitude of the package effect in thin multicellular tissues resulting from changes in chloroplast orientation can have a considerable effect on light absorption and may reduce the possibility of photoinhibitory damage.

Chloroplast aggregation in response to high light has also been observed in some unicellular species, where it may serve a similar function. Chloroplast movements and orientation changes are also common in more complex multicellular tissues, where they may modify light gradients through photosynthetic tissue.

The first estimates of the package effect in unicellular species used Mie theory to calculate the in vitro absorption spectra from in vivo measurements using Eqs. 7.16-7.17. However, uncertainty in predicting the optical characteristics of cells based on theoretical models that do not account for inhomogeneities in intracellular pigment distribution argues for an experimental approach to this problem.

A technique is required to remove quantitatively all of the pigment without altering its in vivo absorption characteristics.

Extraction of the light-absorbing pigment by organic solvents may disrupt macromolecular interactions between chlorophyll and other organic molecules and will alter in vivo absorption characteristics, making organic solvents unsuitable extractants for estimating the package effect.

One technique to assess the package effect involves the disruption of intact cells by sonication or high-pressure treatments at low temperatures. These treatments break down cell structures, leaving predominantly thylakoid fragments.

Cell disruption by high pressure in an X-Press (L.K.B. Biotec) proved particularly useful with recalcitrant cells that were not easily fragmented by sonication and has the added advantage of being carried out at subzero temperatures (–40°C) at which pigment breakdown should be minimal.

However, good agreement was found between the two techniques with cells that were more easily disrupted. Pigment breakdown can be prevented by sonicating cells under an inert atmosphere. Another technique involves solubilization of thylakoid membranes using the nonionic detergent Triton X-100.

This technique does, however, produce spectral shifts in absorption in the red region of the spectrum. However, these shifts appear to be insensitive to the concentration of detergent used, and the characteristic shape of the in vivo absorption spectra was retained in the blue region.

Although these techniques can give an experimental assessment of the overall significance of the package effect, they cannot resolve the separate influences of cell size, chloroplast size or numbers, or variations in thylakoid structure.

Indirect estimates by Berner et al. suggest that the optical properties of the thylakoids have the greatest influence on the magnitude of the package effect.

However, quantification of the package effect using these techniques is presently hampered by an inability to ascribe attenuation measurements at X = 750 nm to either scattering or absorption.

Conventionally, the attenuation at X = 750 nm is ascribed to scattering, and a flat baseline correction is applied to the absorption spectra between 400 and 700 nm. However, this apparent absorption is found even in optical configurations where all of the scattered light should, on the basis of theoretical predictions, have been collected.

Further improvements in the techniques used for assessing the magnitude of the package effect are needed. In addition, more detailed experimental information on the absorption and scattering properties of algal cells and tissues is required.

As yet, there are no experimental techniques for measuring the package effect in multicellular tissues and present theoretical treatments have too many constraints to be of general practical use.

THEORY AND MEASUREMENT OF ACTION SPECTRA

An effective means of utilizing the *available* light would seem to be a prerequisite for survival in the aquatic environment.

Many species have to contend with considerable spectral variations in light quality on time scales of minutes to days due to water movements, the extent of submergence and/or because of variations in the optical properties of water.

Although the distribution of many plants is often correla-ted with marked differences in light quality, a causative explanation for the distribution of algae based on differences in light quality is currently contentious.

Evaluation of the significance of spectral variations in light quality on photosynthetic performance and the effectiveness of different combinations of accessory pigments can be assessed by measurements of action spectra.

These are determined from measurements of photosynthetic rate at limiting light levels over narrowly defined spectral bands (25 nm or less) in the range 300-750 nm. Under these conditions, the rate of photosynthesis (*P*) at a particular wavelength will be determined by the product of the photon yield on an absorbed light basis (ϕ_m), the incident irradiance (*E*), and the absorptance (α), which is a measure of the amount of light absorbed,

$$P(\lambda) = \phi_m (\lambda) E(\lambda)\ \alpha(\lambda) \tag{7.26}$$

If the photon yield, ϕ_m, is invariant, the action spectrum should have the same shape as the absorptance spectrum. Differences between the action spectrum and the absorption spectrum will reflect differences in the ability of individual pigments to utilize the absorbed light in photosynthetic reactions.

Accessory pigments that exhibit little or no transfer of excitation energy to the chlorophyll a pigment-protein complexes will have a low $\phi_m(\lambda)$, and this will result in a low photosynthetic rate.

With macrophyte tissues, the photosynthetic rate is generally expressed on a unit area basis and *P* is expressed in units of micromoles of O_2 per square meter per second.

As *E* is expressed in micromoles of photons per square meter per second and a is dimensionless, ϕ_m is expressed in moles of O_2 per mol photon. With microalgal suspensions, *P* is generally expressed on a unit chlorophyll (or biomass) basis and the rate of photosynthesis at any given wavelength is given by

$$P^{chl}(\lambda) = \phi_m(\lambda) \mathrm{E}(\lambda) a^*(\lambda) \tag{7.27}$$

where a^* is the in vivo chlorophyll a-specific absorption coefficient. A better way to examine variations in the value of $\phi_m(\lambda)$ attributable to various accessory pigments is to plot the photon yield against wavelength. In the past, single measurements of photosynthesis and absorbed light [E (λ) α (λ)] were used to estimate ϕ_m.

In view of the difficulty of making photosynthesis measurements at limiting light levels, ϕ_m should strictly be determi-ned from the slope of P(X) versus E(X) α (λ). Measurements of ϕ_m should also be made at values of E above the light compensation point, where transitory respiration phenomena (such as those associated with the Kok effect) are absent.

The irradiances employed by some investigators may not always be above the light compensation point, particularly in the blue part of the spectrum and may not give an accurate assessment of the role of individual pigments in light utilization.

Xenon arc sources are now widely available and give the necessary output and light quality required for action spectra determinations at short wavelengths.

The measurement of photosynthetic action spectra requi-res the determination of photosynthesis rates at discrete wavelengths using O_2, CO_2, or 14C exchange. In the past, manometric techniques were used to determine action spectra based on net O_2 exchange, but these have been superseded by O_2 electrodes.

Action spectra for net CO_2 exchange have, as for as we know, been restricted to measurements made on terrestrial plants.

Although the ^{14}C technique has been used in laboratory studies, its usefulness is particularly evident for "field" measurements of action spectra on dilute algal suspensions where O_2 exchange techniques are of insufficient precision.

Isolation of the spectral bandwidths can now be achieved with a wide range of commercially available narrow-bandpass interference filters, although high-intensity monochromators are to be preferred.

In general, the action spectra of multicellular green and brown algae are similar to those reported for a number of terrestrial vascular plants, although measurements on green unicellular species exhibit a lower absorption in the green region of the spectrum.

In contrast to the green and brown algae, the action spectrum of the red algae shows a marked peak around 500-600 run, with little photosynthesis in either the blue or red ends of the spectrum. Cryptomonads exhibit similar responses to those shown for the red algae but may have higher photosynthesis rates in the blue and red spectral regions.

It is also evident that near-ultraviolet wavelengths should not be ignored in assessing the photosynthetic performance of algae.

Superficial agreement is usually observed between action and absorptance spectra in species of the Chlorophyta, Bacilliarophyta, and Pyrrophyta.

Apart from the data of Lewis et al. (1987), all these species show high absorption and photosynthesis in the blue region of the spectrum, and this discrepancy may be related to methodological problems.

However, in phycobili protein-containing phytoplankton (*Rhodophyta*, *Cryptophyta*, and *Cyanobacteria*), the action spectrum largely reflects light that is absorbed by the bilipigments (*Phycoerythrin* and *Phycoc-yanin*) in the 500-600 nm waveband, and low photosynthesis rates are found in the blue and red spectral regions.

Current opinion largely favours the interpretation that spectral variations in ϕ_m are a result of alterations in the distribution of excitation energy between PSI and PS2, and that optimal photosynthetic performance can only be achieved when these are balanced.

The well-known red-drop, for instance, at wavelengths $>$ 680 nm is ascribed to a deficiency in light absorbed by PS2. Although the drop in the blue is often related to absorption by nonphotosynthetic cell components or photoinduced damage, this could also be due to a reduction in the amount of light absorbed by PS2.

Bilipigments transfer excitation energy exclusively to PS2, whereas most of the chlorophyll in phycobilin containing species is associated with PS1. Light absorbed by chlorophyll in the blue and red spectral regions is largely ineffective in photosynthesis due to overexcitation of PSI, resulting in a mismatch between the absorptance and action spectra. Evidence from laboratory and field measurements suggest inefficiencies in energy transfer to PS2 by phycobiliproteins under some conditions.

However, ascribing differences in absorptance and action spectra based solely on balanced excitation of PS2 and PSI ignores internal controls that can regulate the distribution of energy between the two photosystems via State 1-State 2 transitions or spillover.

As energy transfer can only occur from PS2 to PS1, all action spectra that are determined without supplementary light may be biased toward the absorption spectrum of PS2 and may be a poor guide to the ability of a plant to utilize the mixture of wavelengths that are available under natural conditions.

It is evident that the addition of light, predominantly absorbed by PS2, can result in the enhancement of photosynthesis in the blue or red regions of the spectrum, indicating that many or all of the accessory pigments are photosynthetically competent.

Action spectra may be used, not only for examining which pigments transfer light energy to chlorophyll a (in which case supplementary light should be used) but also for measuring the ability of a species to photosynthesize in light of different spectral qualities (in which case they should be given in isolation).

Although some enhancement is likely to occur under natural conditions, it is uncertain whether the available wavelengths would result in the balanced operation of PSI and PS2.

Measured and calculated responses of macrophytes to representative broad-band underwater light fields provides no evidence for enhancement under commonly occurring spectral regimes, consistent with data for terrestrial vascular plants.

As a general protocol, however, action spectra should be measured both in the presence and in the absence of supplementary light. As an alternative to O_2 evolution (or

CO_2-exchange), in vivo fluorescence excitation spectra may be more conveniently and readily measurable, particularly under field conditions.

If the fraction of open-to-total PS2 reaction centers is maintained at a constant level, fluorescence and O_2-evolution spectra should, theoretically, have similar characteristics.

Recent studies have demonstrated good agreement between fluorescence and O_2 measurements, using a modulated fluorescence technique and a strong background light to maintain the fraction of open-to-total PS2 reaction centers constant.

There may, however, be problems in using this technique with populations dominated by bilipigment-containing organisms, where PS2 fluorescence measurements may underestimate photosynthetic performance.

Also, there are problems in extending this technique to measurements of natural phytoplankton populations, which require further examination.

Chapter 8

FACTORS AFFECTING PHOTOSYNTHESIS

Earlier investigators of the effects of various conditions upon the rate of photosynthesis attempted to distinguish among *minimum, optimum,* and *maximum* values for each factor in relation to photosynthesis.

In evaluating the effect of temperature upon photosynthesis, for example, it was generally considered that there was a minimum temperature below which on photosynthesis occurred, an optimum at which the process takes place most rapidly, and a maximum above which photosynthesis ceases.

Advocates of this point of view, however, soon found themselves confronted with the anomalous situation of a fluctuating "optimum."

The "optimum" carbon dioxide concentration was found to be greater at high light intensities than at low ones, the "optimum" temperature was found to vary with the light intensity, and the "optimum" light intensity was different for plants well supplied with water than for those which were inadequately supplied.

The first important step in the classification of this problem of the influence of various factors upon photosynthesis was taken when Blackman (1905) enunciated the "principle of limiting factors."

This principle is essentially an elaboration of Liebig's "law of the minimum" and was stated by its author as follows: "When a process is conditio-ned as to its rapidity by a number of separate factors, the rate of the process is. limited by the pace of the 'slowest' factor".

The explanation of this principle can best be presented in terms of the illustration given by Blackman Assume the intensity of light to be just great enough to permit a leaf to utilize 5 mg. of carbon dioxide per hour in photosynthesis.

If only 1 mg. of carbon dioxide can enter the leaf in an hour, the rate of photosynthesis is limited by the carbon dioxide factor. As the carbon dioxide supply is increased the rate of photosynthesis is also increased until 5 mg. of carbon dioxide enter the leaf per hour.

Any further increase in the supply of carbon dioxide will have no influence upon the rate of photosynthesis, unless a sufficient concent-ration is present to bring about retarding effects, because insufficient light energy is available to permit its utilization.

Light has now become the limiting factor and further increase in the rate of photosynthesis can be brought about only by an increase in the intensity of light. These results are indicated graphically as ABC in Figure elsewhere in this chapter.

This theory assumes a progressive increase in the rate of the process with a quantitative increase in the limiting factor (in this example, carbon dioxide) until the point is reached at which some other factor becomes limiting (in this example, light intensity).

At this point the increase stops abruptly, and the rate of photosy-nthesis becomes constant. According to this concept, when the magnitude of photosynthesis is limited by one of a set of factors, only a shift in that factor toward a condition more favourable for the process will result in an increase in the rate of photosynthesis.

If the light intensity is sufficient to permit the leaf to utilize 10 mg. of carbon dioxide per hour, then the rate of photosynthesis will rise with increase in the carbon dioxide concentration to a value about twice as great as that at

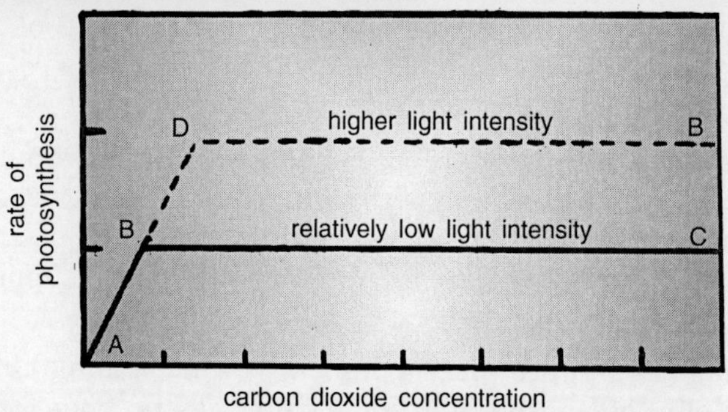

Figure. 8.1: Diagram to illustrate Blackman's interpretation of the principle of limiting factors.

which the maximum rate of photosynthesis was attained at the lower light intensity.

The results under these conditions can be indicated graphically by ADE. Light and carbon dioxide are not the only factors which can be limiting in the photosynthetic process. Theoretically, as examples given later in the chapter will show, any of the factors which influence this process can, under certain conditions, become, limiting.

Most subsequent workers have been unable to accept the principle of limiting factors in quite the simple form in which it was first proposed by Blackman.

Most investigators have found that, when the rate of increase of photosynthesis is plotted along the ordinate with the quantitative variations in some one factor as the abscissa, the resulting curve is not found to show an abrupt transition to the horizontal as postulated by Blackman's formulation of this principle, but shows instead a gradual transition to a position approximately parallel to the abscissa.

Within this transition region it is evident that in rease in either of the two factors involved will result in an increase in the rate of photosynthesis.

The explanation for the occurrence of this gradual transition in the direction of the curve, rather than the abrupt change postulated by the original Blackman theory, results at least in part from the fact that the seat of the photosynthesis is in the chloroplasts of which there are millions in even a small leaf.

Patently it is impossible that each and every chloroplast will be subjected to exactly the same conditions at exactly the same time. All of the chloroplasts are not equally exposed to light; neither are all of then equally well supplied with carbon dioxide.

As a factor approaches a limiting value it may check the rate of photosynthesis in some chloroplasts sooner than in others. It is quite possible therefore for light to be the limiting factor for some chloroplasts, while carbon dioxide is simultaneously the limiting factor for other chloroplasts.

Similar comments apply to most of the other factors influencing photosynthesis. Hence the rate of photosynthesis, as measured in terms of entire organs, will exhibit only a gradual change when factors affecting the process are modified, and there exist well-defined regions in curves such as those shown in Figure elsewhere in this chapter, in which two or even more factors may be considered to act simultaneously as limiting factors.

It should be clearly understood that in speaking of "limiting factors" as applied to physiological processes, it is not their absolute magnitude which is significant, but their relative magnitude in proportion to the amounts actually required in the process.

The quantitatively smallest factor does not necessarily condition the rate of the process, since it may be necessary only in traces, while larger amounts of some other material, or a greater intensity of some other factor may be necessary.

To illustrate, suppose that we assume ten units of *a*, two units of *b*, and one unit of *c* are necessary for the formation of one unit of *d*. If we suppose that only five units of *a* are available, none of *d* can be formed regardless of the quantities of *b* and *c* available. Although *c* may be in absolute minimum, *a* is in relative minimum and thus acts as the limiting factor.

For this reason many authorities consider it to be more satisfactory to speak of the "relatively limiting factor," "factor in relative minimum," or "most significant factor," rather than of the "limiting factor." One other qualification of the theory of limiting factors not envisaged in the original Blackman formulation should also be mentioned.

When present in a high enough intensity or concentration, most of the factors influencing the rate of photosynthesis exert a depressing or inhibitory effect on the process. The modifications which have been imposed upon the original concept of limiting factors do not invalidate this principle as a good approximation to the facts, nor do they destroy its value as a point of view from which to interpret the influence of various factors upon the rate of photosynthesis.

The nificant fact is that the rate of the process, except in relately narrow transition regions, is usually determined in the ±in by the least favourable factor, which may for convenice be spoken of either at the limiting factor or as the factor relative minimum.

THE ROLE OF CARBON DIOXIDE

All of the carbon dioxide used by green plants reaches the chloroplasts as dissolved carbon dioxide, carbonic acid, or one of the salts of the latter.

In land plants the atmosphere is the only important source of carbon dioxide. Carbon dioxide released in respiration may be utilized in photosynthesis without leaving the plant, but under conditions favourable for photosynthesis this does not constitute a very large fraction of the total used.

Submersed water plants use carbonates and bicarbonates as well as dissolved carbon dioxide and carbonic acid as substrates of photosynthesis.

The atmosphere is composed chiefly of two gases, nitrogen (about 78 per cent) and oxygen (about 21 per cent), but also contains, in addition to a variable but never large amount of water-vapor, small quantities of other gases. One of its minor constituents, carbon dioxide, which constitutes on the average only about 0.03 per cent by volume of the atmosphere, plays a role of the greatest significance in the biological world.

As a result of the photosynthetic activity of green plants, the carbon dioxide from the air becomes chemically bound for periods of indefinite length in the organic molecules which are the basis of all life.

In view of its important biological role, the proportion of carbon dioxide in the atmosphere seems precariously small. The absolute amount present, however, is enormous. Estimates, necessarily very approximate, place the total quantity of carbon dioxide in the atmosphere at about 2×10^{15} kg.

According to Schroeder (1919), the quantity of carbon dioxide used annually in photosynthesis by land plants is about 6×10^{13} kg. This is only about one-thirtieth the amount actually present in the atmosphere.

Sources of the Atmospheric Carbon Dioxide

While green plants are continually removing carbon dioxide from the atmosphere, other processes are continually replenishing the atmospheric reservoir with this gas. Carbon dioxide is continually being returned to the atmosphere as a product of the respiration of plants and animals.

Plants are more important producers of carbon dioxide than animals. Carbon dioxide is released into the atmosphere as a result of the respiration of both green and non-green plants. The relatively great importance of the latter group of organisms as generators of this gas is not always appreciated.

The organic residues of plants and animals are decomposed as a result of the activities of bacteria and fungi. During such decay processes the carbon of these residues is mostly released in the form of carbon dioxide as a result of the metabolic activities of these organisms and escapes into the air.

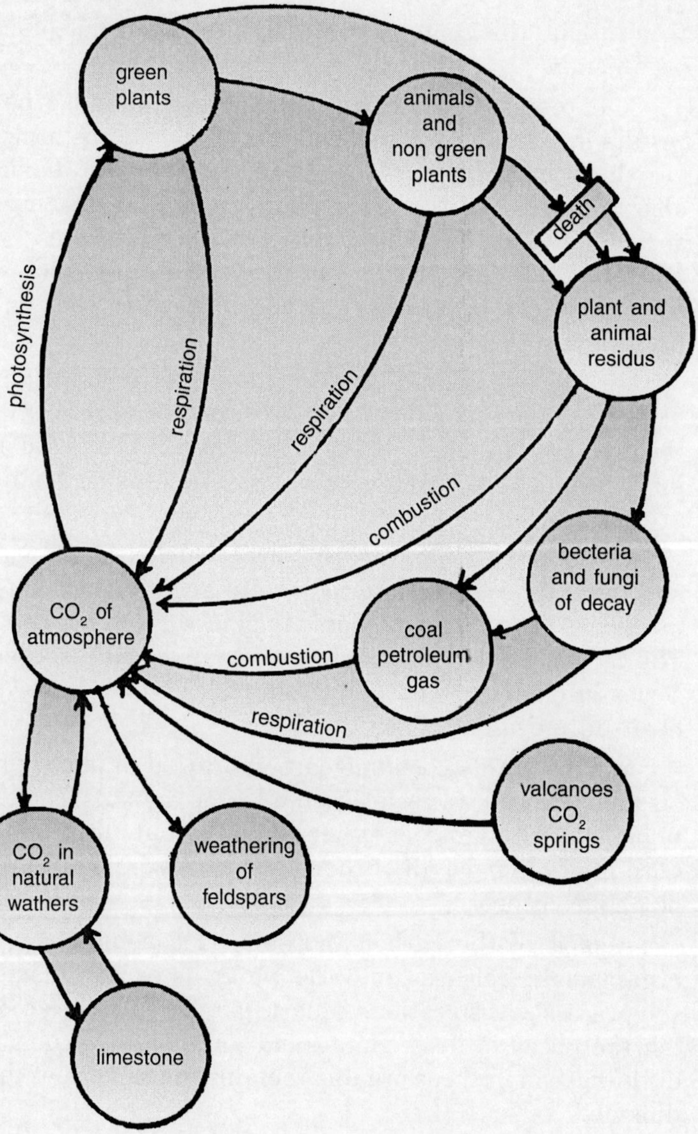

Figure 8.2: The carbon cycle.

The evolution of carbon dioxide gas from soils is often very considerable and is frequently referred to as "soil respiration"; this represents largely the respiration of microorganisms.

The respiration of the soil bacteria alone probably results in a greater return of carbon dioxide to the atmosphere than the respiration of all animals Carbon dioxide is also released into the atmosphere from volcanos, mineral springs, and in the combustion of coal, oil, gasoline, wood, and other fuel materials, but the total annual increment from these sources is very small relative to the amount present in the atmosphere.

On the other hand, the weathering of certain igneous locks (feldspars) combines carbon dioxide and thus reduces the quantity of this gas in the atmosphere. Oceans are much more important reservoirs of carbon dioxide than the atmosphere.

The oceans occupy nearly three fourths of the earth's surface and are estimated to contain about eighth times as much carbon in forms available to plants as the atmosphere. The carbon dioxide in ocean waters in involved in a complex series of chemical and biological cycles which have never been fully evaluated.

Marine plants consume carbon dioxide in photosynthesis and release it in respiration. Marine animals feed either upon marine plants or other animals, but ultimately, as with land animals, all of their food comes from the process of photosynthesis.

A part of the carbon in the food consumed by such organisms is released into the water as carbon dioxide in the process of respiration. Aquatic microorganisms accomplish the decay of dead plants and animals, releasing most of the carbon in these organic remains in the form of carbon dioxide.

Complex equllibria Between the dissolved carbon dioxide, carbonates and bicarbonates also exist. Large quantities of carbonates are tied up by certain marine

Table 8.1: Diffusion of carbon dioxide through multiperforate septa. Pores 0.380 mm in diameter; septa I cm. from sodium hydroxide solution.

Septum	*Area of tube, cm.²*	*Distance apart of pores in diameters*	*Diffusion CO_2 through septum, cc. per hour*	*Diffusion CO_2 through open tube, cc. per hour*	*Per cent of septum area occupied by pores*	*Diffusion through pores as per cent of diffusion through open tube*
1	9.347	2.63	0.433	0.771	11.34	56.1
2	9.186	5.26	0.401	0.775	2.82	51.7
3	9.456	7.80	0.312	0.768	1.25	40.6
4	9.511	10.52	0.241	0.767	0.70	31.4
5	9.186	13.10	0.156	0.744	0.45	20.9
6	9.347	15.70	0.106	0.740	0.31	14.0

animals in the formation of shells. Other marine animals precipitate large quantities of carbon dioxide in chemically combined form as the calcium carbonate of calcareous rocks.

The conversion of bicarbonates into carbonates results in the release of carbonic acid and thus increases the available carbon dioxide content of the water. Eventually such rocks (limestones, etc.) may be raised above sea level, and the carbon dioxide tied up in the form of carbonates again is released to the atmosphere or dissolved in running water during dissolution of the rock.

Similar although not quite such complex cycles of carbon dioxide exist in the bodies of fresh water. There is also a constant exchange of carbon dioxide between the oceans and the atmosphere.

In fact, on theoretical grounds, there is good reason to suppose that the carbon dioxide concentration of the atmosphere is more or less effectively maintained in dynamic equilibrium with that of the oceans.

Carbon dioxide probably escapes from the oceans whenever its atmospheric concentration falls below the usual value, and dissolves in the oceans whenever a contrary shift in atmospheric carbon dioxide concentration occurs.

The maintenance of such a large-scale dynamic equilibrium between the oceans and the atmosphere is probably the principal factor accounting for the constancy of the carbon dioxide concentration of the atmosphere. The cycle of carbon in nature is shown diagram-matically in Figure elsewhere in this chapter.

The Entrance of Carbon Dioxide

Although the bulk of the carbon dioxide entering the leaves of land plants undoubtedly passes in through the stomates, substantial amounts may diffuse directly into the epidermal cells in some species.

For example, a considerable proportion of the carbon dioxide used in photosynthesis is certain species which have stomates only in the lower epidermis, such as coleus, begonia, and avocado, passes into the leaves through the upper epidermis.

By the use of carbon dioxide made with the radioactive C^{14} isotope, Dugger (1950) has also shown that this gas can pass into the leaves of coleus and hydrangea through their upper, unstomated surfaces. All entrance of carbon dioxide, bicarbonates, or carbonates onto the leaves of submersed hydrophytes, occurs directly brought the epidermis. The rate of entrance of carbon dioxide through stomates is very considerable in proportion to the aggregate area of the stomatal pores.

Under conditions favorable for photosynthesis Brown and Escombe (1900) found that carbon dioxide would diffuse into a catalpa leaf from the atmosphere at the rate of 0.07 cc. per $cm.^2$ of leaf surface per hour.

Since the stomata's in this leaf occupy only 0.9 per cent of the surface, diffusion of carbon dioxide gas through them took place at a rate of 7.77 cc. per $cm.^2$ of stomatal aperture per hour. (The assumption vas made that all carbon dioxide entered through the tomata's.) Under the same conditions a normal secution of odium hydroxide absorbs from the atmosphere, even in rapidly moving air, only 0.177 cc. of carbon dioxide per $cm.^2$ per hour.

In other words, carbon dioxide gas diffuse through the stornata's at a rate approximately fifty times as fast as it diffuses into an efficient absorbing surface. The extremely rapid rate of diffusion of carbon dioxide gas through the stomata's can be interpreted in the light of principles of diffusion of gases through small openings.

Table elsewhere in this chapter condensed from the work of Brown and Escombe, indicates that these same principles hold, in general, for carbon dioxide as well as water-vapor. The most important principle illustrated, that the rate of diffusion does not decrease proportionately with reduction in he aggregate area of pores, is shown in the last two columns or septum 4 (pores 10.52 diameters apart),

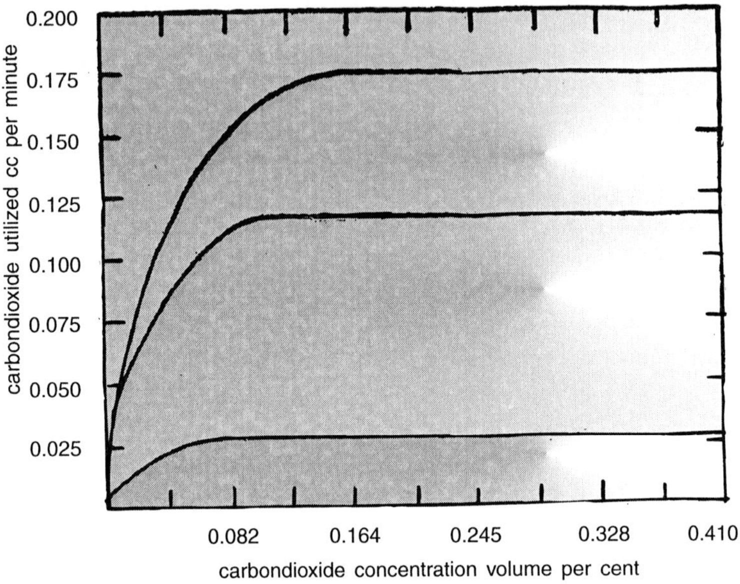

Figure 8.3: Relation between different carbon dioxide concentrations and rate of photosynthesis in wheat at three different light intensities.

for example, the diffusion is 31.4 per cent of that from, the open tube, although only 0.70 per cent of the septum surface is occupied by the apertures.

Effects of Variations in the Atmospheric Concentration of Carbon Dioxide upon the Rate of Photosynthesis. Although the average carbon dioxide content of the atmosphere is 0.03 per cent, the actual range in plant habitats is from about half to several times this value Lower than average values are not infrequent in relatively quiet air in zones in which high rates of photosynthesis prevail.

In a field of corn, for example, the carbon dioxide content of the air surrounding the plants may become measurably less than the average atmospheric value luring daylight hours whenever high rates of photosynthesis occur. Similarly, in the atmosphere on the level with the crowns of trees in a dense forest the carbon dioxide content is sometimes *considerably* less than the average *atmospheric*

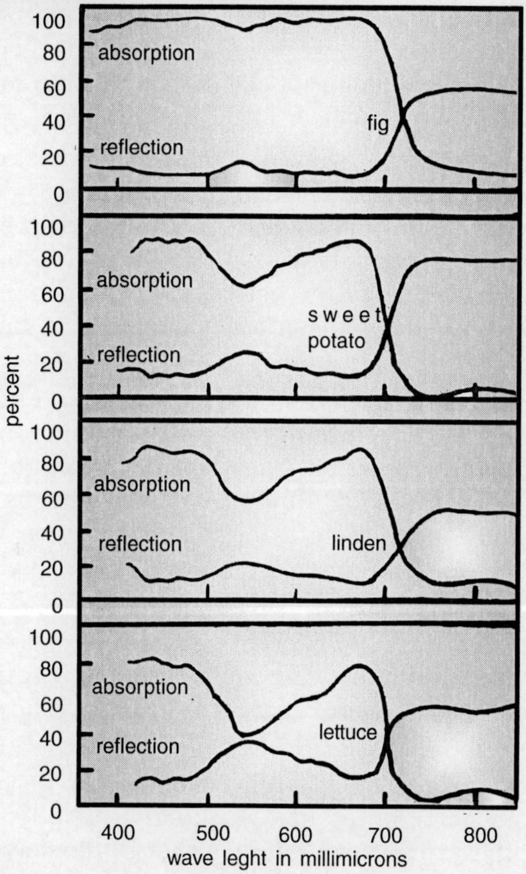

Figure 8.4: Absorption and reflection spectra of leaves of four species.

value during hours when rapid photosynthesis is in progress.

In a tightly closed greenhouse the carbon dioxide content of the air may decrease materially during the course of a bright day. Investigations of Lundegardh (1931) and others indicate that a considerable part of the carbon dioxide utilized by plants in many habitats is released locally as a result of "*soil respiration*," i.e., in the respiration of soil *microrganisms*.

Such a release of carbon dioxide is especially pronounced in wellfertilized soils, soils rich in organic matter, and in many forest soils. "Soil respiration," when marked, may result in a local enrichment of the carbon dioxide concentration in the air stratum close to the surface of the ground.

Such a rise in carbon dioxide content is greatest during the night hours when the offsetting effect of photosynthesis in low-growing plants is absent. On a well-fertilized field the formation of carbon dioxide as a result of "soil respiration" during a 24-hr. period may equal or exceed the consumption in photosynthesis during the day-light hours.

The carbon dioxide content of the air is also influenced by fogs and mists. The quantity present per unit volume of air is measurably higher on foggy mornings than on clear mornings, and rates of apparent photosynthesis are correspondingly increase in a foggy as contrasted with a clear atmosphere if no other condition are limiting.

Although it is customary to express atmospheric concentrations of carbon dioxide as percentage by volume, such units are valid only when all of the concentrations to be compared are at approximately the same atmospheric pressure.

The rate of diffusion of carbon dioxide into a leaf is a function of its partial pressure which varies directly as the total atmospheric pressure. Hence, although the percentage of carbon dioxide in the atmosphere is about 0.03 per cent both at sea level and, for example, at an altitude of 15,000 feet, its partial pressure is very different.

At sea level the partial pressure of this gas is about 0.23 mm. Hg; at 15,000 feet altitude, about 0.13 mm. Hg. In terms of fundamental units, therefore, the effective concentration of carbon dioxide varies considerably with altitude, and this may be a factor to be taken into consideration when photosynthetic rates or development of plants at different altitudes is being compared.

In general, at least over relatively short periods, with increase in the concentration of atmospheric carbon dioxide,

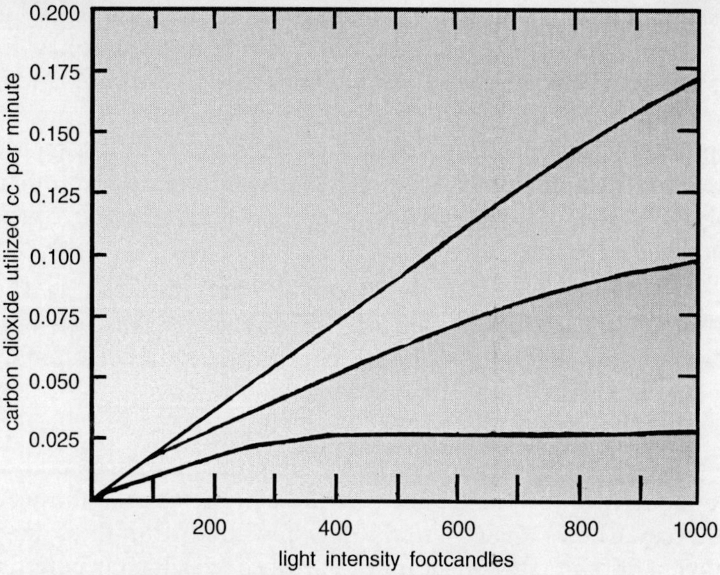

Figure 8.5: Relation between different light intensities and rate of photosynthesis of wheat plants at three different carbon dioxide concentrations.

there is an increase in the rate of photosynthesis until some other factor, most commonly light, becomes limiting.

The results of an experiment on the relation of carbon dioxide concentration to the rate of photosynthesis are shown in Figure elsewhere in this chapter in which, it should be noted, the highest light intensity used was my about 10 per cent of noonday summer sunlight. If no other factor is limiting, the rate of photosynthesis rises in most species, at least for a while, with increase in the carbon dioxide concentration up to, at a minimum, 15-20 times the usual atmospheric concentration.

Relatively high concentrations of carbon dioxide, in general, retard photosynthesis. The concentration at which such depressant effects are initiated varies with the kind of plant, stage of development of the photosynthetic tissue, length of exposure to carbon dioxide, and other prevailing environmental conditions.

In the leaves of *Hydrangea otaksa,* for example, the

rate of photosynthesis, although considerably retarded, is not entirely inhibited in short time experiments at concentrations as great as 20 per cent carbon dioxide. Under natural conditions during summer months in moist, emperate regions the carbon dioxide concentration of the atmosphere is most frequently the limiting factor in photosynthesis for all photosynthetic tissues which are well exposed of light.

There seems to be little doubt that increase in the atmospheric concentration of this gas to at least several times is average value of 0.03 per cent has a continuously favourable effect on photosynthesis, as long as no other factors are limiting.

There is evidence, however, that only slightly higher concentrations of carbon dioxide which favor enhanced photosynthesis over periods of a few hours or days may have a detrimental effect on the process over longer periods.

Thomas and Hill (1949), for example, found that tomato plants exposed o ten times the atmospheric concentration of carbon dioxide luring daylight hours showed detrimental effects within less ban 2 weeks.

THE ROLE OF LIGHT

The energy stored by green plants in the molecules of carbohydrates during photosynthesis can be supplied only by light. Any source of radiant energy which includes wave lengths within the range of the visible spectrum will induce photosynthesis, provided its intensity is sufficiently great.

Although a few of the longer wave lengths of ultraviolet apparently are effective in photosynthesis, and some of the shorter wave lengths of infrared can be used by sulphur bacteria, in general this process can occur only in the visible part of the spectrum.

Under natural conditions sunlight, either direct or reflected front the sky or other objects, is the only source of radiant energy including wave lengths which can be used in photosynthesis. Photosynthesis will occur under electric

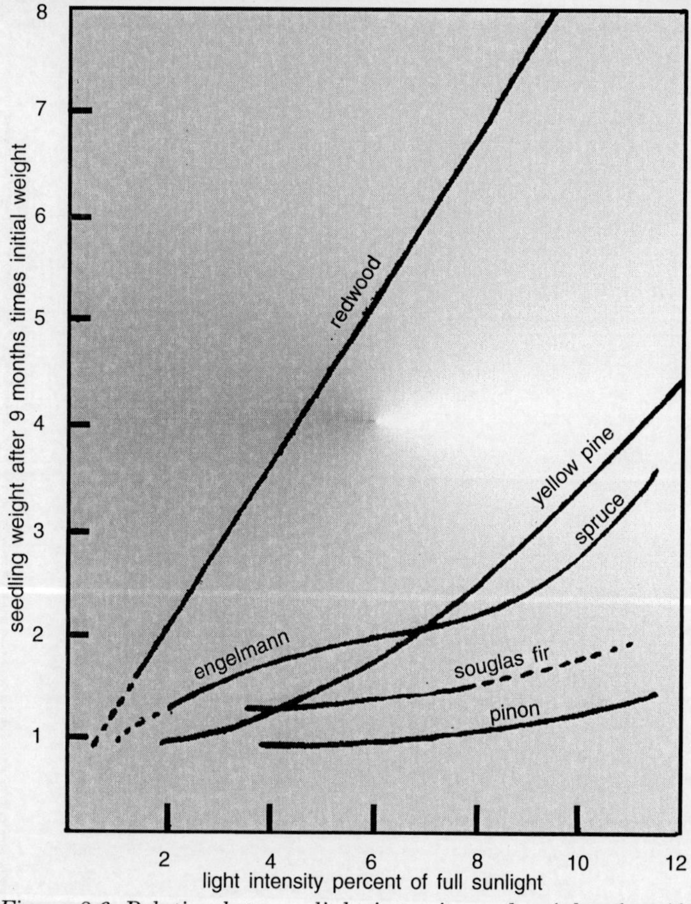

Figure 8.6: Relation between light intensity and weight of conifer seedlings after 9 months.

lights or other artificial sources of illumination if of sufficient intensity.

Such light sources are often used in experimental work on photosynthesis and to some extent in greenhouses as supplementary sources of illumination. Light, like all forms of radiant energy, varies in intensity adiance), quality, and duration and the influence of this for upon photosynthesis will be discussed under these three fidings.

Before the various effects of light upon photosynthesis

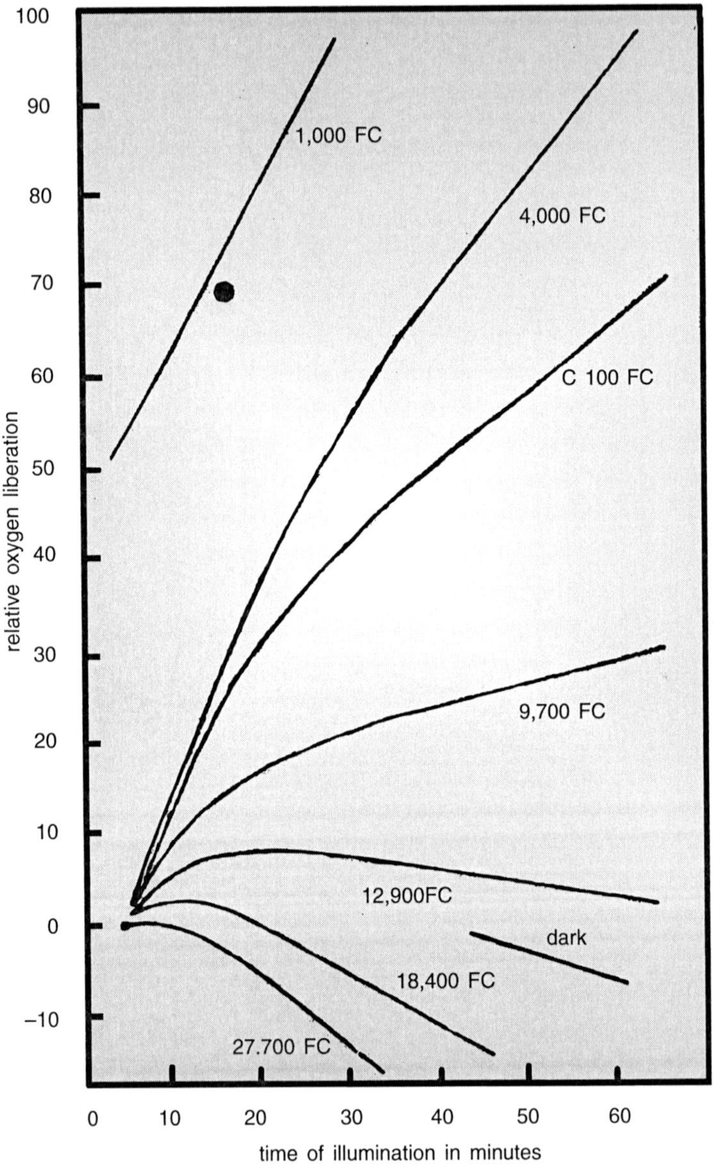

Figure 8.7: Relation between light intensity in foot-candles and oxygen liberation by Chlorella. Oxygen consumption (photoxidation) occurs under the higher intensities.

are considered, however, it will be desirable to analyze the physics relations between leaves and incident

The Optical Properties of Leaves

Of the visible light which falls on leaves, as with radiant energy generally, a part reflected, a part is transmitted through the leaf, and a part is orbed by the leaf. The proportion of the *visible light* incident upon a leaf which is absorbed varies considerably according to the kind of leaf and the intensity of light, but it is frequently in the neighborhood of 80 per cent and probably often higher.

A clear distinction should be drawn between the proportion of visible light absorbed by a leaf and the proportion of the total incident radiant energy absorbed, the latter being in the neighborhood of 50 per cent for many kinds of leaves.

For any given kind of leaf the proportions of incident light reflected, transmitted, and absorbed vary considerably according to wave length. In general a larger proportion of the incident light is absorbed by thick than by thin leaves.

For normally green leaves maximum reflection in the range of visible light occurs in the extreme long red with a secondary, but less pronounced, maximum in the green. Conversely, maximum absorption is in the blue-violet and orange-short red regions, corresponding approximately with the prominent absorption bands of the chlorophylls.

Reflection of infrared by leaves is about 50-60 per cent in the wave length range of 760-1100 mμ.

Effects of Variations in the Intensity of Light upon the Rate of Photosynthesis. In general, with increase in light intensity there is an increase in the rate of photosynthesis until some other factor, in this example, the carbon dioxide concentration, becomes limiting.

At relatively low light intensities, as long as carbon dioxide is not the limiting factor, the rate of photosynthesis as approximately proportional to the light intensity. For the maximum concentration of carbon dioxide indicated in

Figure elsewhere in this chapter (0.11 per cent), the maximum light intensity used was not great enough for the carbon dioxide factor to have become limiting.

It should also be noted that the maximum light intensity employed-1000 footcandles-is much inferior in intensity to usual summer sunlight, which at noon on a clear day usually is equivalent to 8,00010,000 foot-candles.

At usual atmospheric carbon dioxide concentrations, maximum photosynthetic rates are attained when leaves are exposed to light intensities considerably less than the maximum sunlight intensity. In apple leaves, for example, peak photosynthetic rates are reached at light intensities one-fourth to one-third full sunlight.

Similarly in maize leaves maximum rates are attained at about one-fourth the peak intensity of summer sunlight and in loblolly pine (*Pinus taeda*) needles about one-third full sunlight. On the other band, in pronounced shade species, the highest rates of photosynthesis under otherwise favourable natural conditions are reached at sit intensities no higher than 1000 foot-candles.

Results such as those discussed above will be obtained only when a single leaf or a small plant, in which there is little or no shading of one part by another, is used as the experimental material. When the effect of light on photosynthesis is considered in terms of an entire tree, however, a different relation holds.

Thus Heirecke and Childers (1937) showed that the rate of photosynthesis for an entire apple tree increased progressively with increase in light intensity up to or nearly that of full sunlight.

This is undoubtedly because many of the interior leaves on a large tree are heavily shaded. Although, in general, maximum rates of photosynthesis are attained in, the leaves of most (probably all) species at light intensities considerably below that of full sunlight, these investigators showed that many of the interior leaves of an apple tree receive as little as 1 per cent or less of the sunlight received by

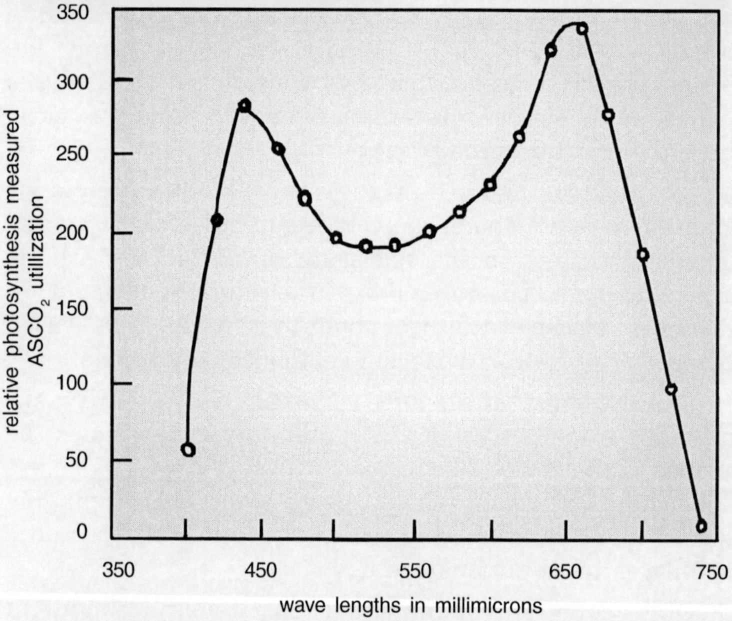

Figure 8.8: Relative rates of photosynthesis of wheat in different wave lengths of light of equal intensity.

peripheral leaves. Even in full sunlight, therefore, many of the leaves on an apple tree do not photosynthesize at their maximum capacity.

The lower the light intensify the greater the proportion of the leaves of which this will be true. Hence the greater the intensity of the incident light, the greater the average rate of photosynthesis per unit of lead area.

The total photosynthesis per tree, therefore, increases progressively with increased illumination up to or at least close to the maximum possible sunlight intensity.

Internal shading effects on the rate of photosynthesis have been demonstrated experimentally for such diverse plants as he loblolly pine (*Pinustaeda*) by Kramer and Clark (1947) nd the hornwort (*Ceratophyllum demersum*)—a *submersed quatic*—by Meyer (1939) and doubtless occur in many other rinds of plants with densely arranged foliage.

Similar effects exist in compact stands of plants such

as fields of some crop pecies. Mutual shading of the plants in plots of alfalfa is efficiently marked so that the photosynthetic rate of such dots considered as a unit is highest at peak light intensities, or at intensities close thereto, as in an apple tree.

In fields of maize, on the other hand, the plants apparently do not shade each other sufficiently to have any appreciable effect on the aggregate rate of photosynthesis on bright days. The intensity of the sunlight incident on the earth's surface varies from hour to hour and from season to season, as well as with meteorological conditions.

Clouds, fogs, dust, and atmospheric humidity, all influence the intensity of the radiation which reaches the surface of the earth. The exposure and pitch of a slope are also factors influencing the intensity of the light impinging upon a given location, and are particularly of importance in hilly or mountainous country.

Other conditions being equal the intensity of sunlight also increases with increase in altitude in aquatic habitats light intensity decreases with depth below the surface of the water. Most variations in the intensity of natural light are accompanied by variations in light quality of greater or lesser magnitude.

Usually, however, under out-of-doors conditions, variations in the intensity component of light are of greater physiological influence than the accompanying variations in the quality component.

Ecologically one of the most important factors causing different species of plants to be exposed to differences in light intensity is the effect of taller plants in shading those of lesser stature.

Some species thrive and photosynthesize efficiently only in fully exposed locations; others can complete their normal life cycle in intensely shaded habitats.

Even under a tree with a rather open crown the light intensity is only one-tenth to one-twentieth that of full sunlight. Hence light is usually the limiting factor for photosynthesis in most species of plants when growing in the shade of trees.

Species which normally grow in deep shade are often exceptions to this statement. On cloudy days light is also usually the limiting factor in photosynthesis. Because of the prevatlence of cloudy weather in many regions during the winter, plants under glass often photosynt-hesize at very low rates during those months.

The short length of the daylight period also contributes to low daily rates of photosynthesis during the winter season. A number of studies have been made of the minimum light intensities at which various species of plants are just barely able to survive.

Unless foods have previously accutmulated, the minimum light intensity at which a plant will remain alive for indefinite periods during its normally active seasons must permit sufficient photosynthesis to compensate for both day and night respiration, and in all probability must also allow for some assimilation.

Bates and Roeser (1928) studied the effects of low light intensities upon the growth of a number of species of evergreens native to the western United States. The seedlings were exposed to a 200 watt, blue tungsten lamp for 10 hours a day.

Differences in light intensity were obtained by growing the seedlings at different distances from the source of illumination. Their results (Figure elsewhere in this chapter show that redwood seedlings were able to maintain their initial dry weight in a light intensity less than 1 per cent of full sunlight, while pinon pine required about 6 per cent, and the other three species were intermediate in their requirement.

Extremely high light intensities exert an inhibitory effect on photosynthesis, a phenomenon called *solarization*. Holman (1930) showed that bean leaves exposed to an illumination of 6800 foot-candles accumulated starch readily, but that little starch was synthesized at twice this illumination value. This effect is exerted upon the photosynthetic mechanism itself and not on the process of starch synthesis. Solarization effects appear to result principally, and protbably entirely, from the phenomenon of *photo-oxidation,* in which leaves consume oxygen in the light, and use it in the oxidation of certain cell constituents, carbon dioxide being released in the process.

The data shown graphically in Figure elsewhere in this chapter illustrate the occurrence of photo-oxidation in *Chlorella,* but the existence of this phenomenon has also

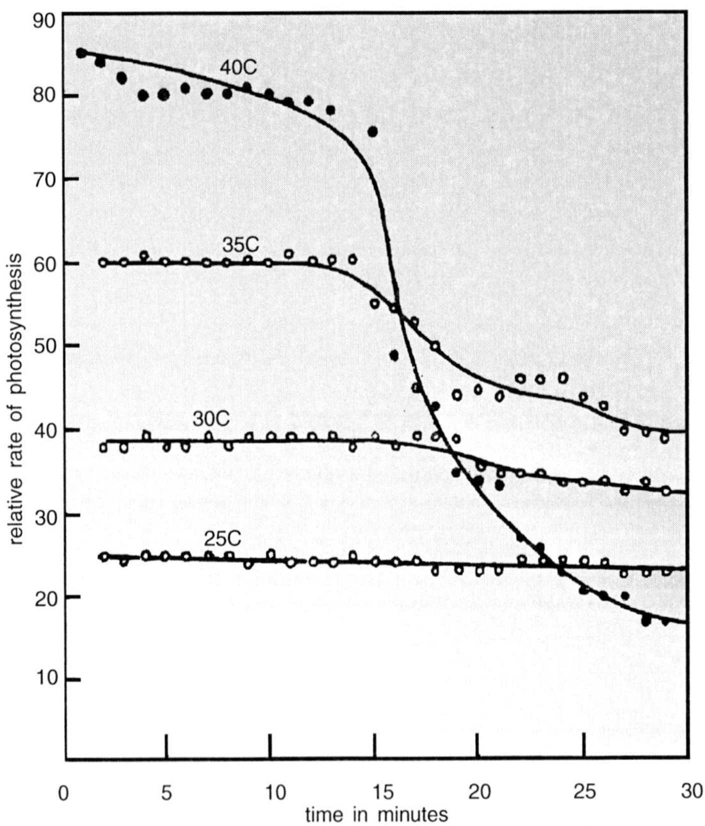

Figure 8.9: Relative rates of apparent photosynthesis in waterweed. (Anacharis canadensis) at different temperatures over a period of 30 minutes.

been demonstrated in other species. At lower light intensities a steady or nearly steady rate of photosynthesis is maintained by *Chlorella* but the higher the light intensity above 4000 foot-candles the more markedly the rate falls off with time.

At 27,700 footcandles, the highest intensity uses, oxygen consum-ption (photooxidation) sets in almost immediately. Photo-oxidation should not be confused with ordinary respiration as it is an entirely different process.

It operates through at least a part of the photosynthetic mechanism and may occur at a rate three or four times greater than respiration. In a sense photo-oxidation may be regarded as a variant of photosyn-thesis in which oxygen is used as the substrate instead of carbon dioxide.

Oxygen consumption at high light intensities results not merely from a superimposing of photooxidation upon photosynthesis but at least partly from an inactivation of the latter process by the former. Short periods of photo-oxidation are usually not harmful to leaves or other photosynthetic organs, but continuation of this process for more than a few hours commonly results in decolorization of chlorophylls and ultimately in death of the cells in which it is occurring.

Light may exert indirect as well as direct effects upon photosyn-thesis. Low light intensities favour stomatal closure and hence may sometimes check photosynthesis by restricting the entrance of carbon dioxide as well as by acting as a direct limiting factor.

Similarly high light intensities often cause increased rates of transpiration. Indirectly this causes a reduced water content of the leaf cells, which may in turn cause a diminished rate of photosynthesis.

A high light intensity also has the usual effect of raising leaf temperatures somewhat above the prevailing temperatures of the surrounding atmosphere and may thus influence photosynthesis indirectly by its effect on thermal conditions within leaves.

Very high light intensities also have a destructive effect upon chlorophyll and other cell constituents as mentioned in the preceding paragraph.

Effects of Different Light Qualities upon Photosynthesis

Hoover (1937) investigated the effect of different wave lengths of radiation upon the rate of photosynthesis of wheat plants. By the use of suitable filters he was able to irradiate the plants with narrow spectral bands.

All measurements were made with equal but low intensities of radiation incident upon the plants and under such conditions that no other factor was limiting for photosynthesis.

The results of his investigation indicate the occurrence of maximum photosynthesis at a wave length of 655 mμ in the red, and a secondary maximum of 440mμ in the blue. It is worthy of note that this curve does not show a very close agreement with the absorption spectrum of chlorophyll.

The results of all investigators on the relation between light quality and photosynthesis do not agree with those just described. Gabrielsen (1948), for example, found in several species, including wheat, that the highest rates of photosynthesis occurred in orange-red light, the next highest in greenyellow light, and the lowest in violet-blue light.

With *Ulva lactuca* (a *marine alga*), however, results were obtained similar to those of Hoover for wheat. It is not certain whether the differences in the effect of light quality on photosynthesis from one species to another which appear to exist are real or not.

It is possible that the relation between light quality and photosynthesis is not the same in all kinds of plants, and may even be different in two plants of the same species which have developed under different conditions.

On the other hand, the technical difficulties in this type of experimentation are considerable, and it is not clear just how much of the available data has been obtained under sufficiently critical conditions.

It is also possible, therefore, that the diverse results which have been recorded are more apparent than real, and are largely the outcome of the different experimental techniques which have been used.

There are a number of conditions under which plants growing in their natural habitats are exposed more or less continuously to light of a different quality from that of full sunlight at the earth's surface.

On cloudy days, for example, the intensity of light is not only less than on clear days, but it is proportionately richer in blue and green wave lengths. Light which has been filtered through the crown of a tree is usually proportionately richer in green rays than direct sunlight because of the greater proportionate absorption by leaves in the red and blue portions of the spectrum.

This effect upon light quality is most marked in hardw-ood forests in which the tree crowns form an almost continuous canopy.

The herbs, shrubs, and smaller trees growing in such forests are subjected to light which is not only of much lower intensity than full sunlight, but is also different in quality from the light impinging upon the forest canopy.

In habitats of submerged aquaties both the intensity and quality of the light are usually very different from the intensity and quality of the sunlight at the earth's surface. Pure water absorbs radiations in the red-orange portion of the spectrum much more effectively than in the blue-green region.

While the absorption coefficients of natural waters for various wave lengths of light vary somewhat depending upon the substances dissolved or dispersed in the water, in general shorter wave lengths penetrate to greater depths than longer wave lengths. Hence with increasing depth in either fresh or oceon water not only is the intensity of the light reduced, but its quality is greatly modified.

Aquatic plants growing at a depth of 20 meters, for example, will be exposed to light proportionately much richer in blue-green rays, although of lower intensity, than those at a depth of 1 meter. Alpine plants are also exposed to light of different composition than species at lower altitudes.

The atmosphere absorbs the shorter wave lengths of the sun's radiation more effectively than the longer ones. Because of the shorter column of atmosphere through which it passes, sunlight at high altitudes is therefore not only more intense than at lower elevations, but is also relatively richer in the shorter wave lengths of visible radiation and the ultraviolet.

Effects of Duration of the Light Period upon Photosynthesis

In general a plant will accomplish more photosynthesis in the course of a day if exposed to illumination of favorable intensity for ten or twelve hours than if suitable light conditions prevail for only four or five hours.

In arctic regions photosynthesis may occur continuously throughout the 24-hr. day of the summer months although the rate may vary cyclically throughout the day. A considerable capacity for sustained photosynthesis under continuous light is indicated by the results of Bobning (1949).

Leaves on young apple trees, exposed to a continuous illumination of about 3200 footcandles at 25°C, and the usual atmospheric concentration of carbon dioxide, were shown to photosynthesize at an undiminished rate for periods of at least 18 days.

Temperature Effects on Photosynthesis

The measurement of the effect of temperature upon photosynthesis in terrestrial plants is complicated by the fact that the leaf temperatures of such plants are seldom the same as atmospheric temperatures.

Whenever leaves are exposed to direct illumination,

which is almost invariably the situation when photosynthesis is occurring at a rapid rate, their temperatures exceed those of the surrounding atmosphere.

It is difficult, therefore, if not impossible, to maintain the temperature of the leaves of land plants at a desired value while they are exposed to light of any considerable intensity. Evaluation of the effect of the temtperature of leaves upon photosynthesis is possible only if the actual leaf temperature is measured.

For this reason many of the more critical studies of the effect to temperature upon photosynthesis have been made with submerged water plants, in which a close thermal equilibrium is maintained between the plant body and the surrounding water.

Temperature Limits of Photosynthesis

Photosynthesis 3n take place over a wide range of temperatures. It has been reported to occur in some species of conifers at temperatures slow as -35°C. and in some kinds of lichens at –20°C. reeland (1944) has shown that the photosynthetic rate may exceed the rate of respiration in several species of conifers at temperatures as low as—6°C.

Tropical plants cannot carry on photosynthesis at temperatures as low as those at which many temperate zone plants do. In most tropical species photosynthesis apparently will not occur at temperatures below about 5°C.

At the other end of the temperature range for photosynthesis stand the species of algae indigenous to hot springs which can survive 75°C. and probably carry on photosynthesis at temperatures close to this value.

Many semidesert and tropical species can withstand air tempera-tures of 55°C. and probably photosynthesize at temperatures not far below this. In most plants of temperate regions the range of temperat-ures within which photosynthesis occurs at a relatively rapid rate is about 10°-35°C.

The Effect of Temperature on the Rate of Photosynthesis. If neither carbon dioxide, not light, nor any other factor is

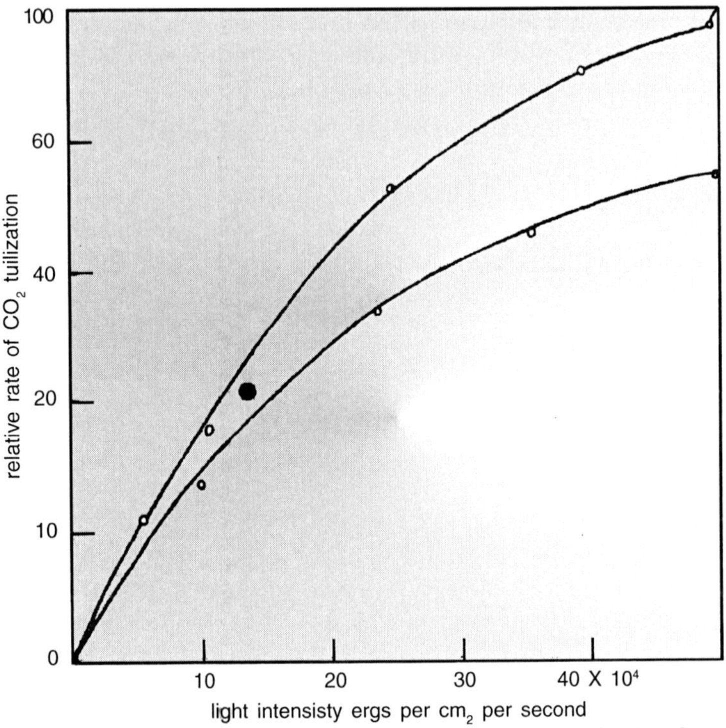

Figure 8.10: Comparative rates of photosynthesis in wheat at low, high oxygen concentrations under different light ini sities. (10 × 10^4 ergs per sec.-0.143 greal. per cm.^{2} min).

limiting, the rate of photosynthesis increases with rise in temperature up to a point which varies somewhat from one kind of a plant to another.

Further increase in temperature results in a rapid decline in the rate of photosynthesis, resulting primarily from injurious effects of higher temperatures on the protoplasm.

Furthermore, as first clearly shown by Matthaei (1905) for cherry laurel (*Prunus laurocerasus*) but since confirmed by other investigators for other species the rate of photosynthesis at all higher temperatures decreases with time.

The higher the temperature the sooner this decline in

rate sets in, and the more rapidly that it occurs. In the cherry laurel, for example, the rate of photosynthesis is essentially constant for a number of hours at temperatures of 23.7°C. and lower. At 30.5°C., however, the rate is measurably less after several hours than at the beginning of the photosynthetic period.

At 37.5°C, at which the highest initial photosynthetic rate is attained, the rate falls off still more rapidly, and within a few hours is markedly less than initially. Under such conditions, within a favorable temperature range (about 10° to 35°C.), the temperature coefficient of photosynthesis is about two.

The diminution in the rate of photosynthesis with time, particularly marked at higher temperatures, is evidence of the increasingly limiting effect of some internal factor, generally called the "*time factor*." The exact nature of this time factor s unknown, and it is possible that it may represent the composite influence of several internal conditions.

One of the more probable mechanisms of this effect is that of an inactivation of enzymes at higher temperatures. The temperature relations of enzymatic reactions are similar to those of the photosynt-hetic reaction, a fact which supports this view.

Other possible components of the time factor are the destructive effects of relatively high temperatures upon other constituents of the protoplasm than enzymes, the accumulation of he end products of the reaction which may exert a retarding affect on the rate of photosynthesis or failure of the diffusion of carbon dioxide toward the chloroplasts to keep pace with is use in photosynthesis, even though the external supply is not limiting.

Similar time factor effects are present in the temperature relations of other plant processes, such as respiration and growth. It should be emphasized again that the relation between photosynthesis and tempera-ture described above holds only when no other environmental

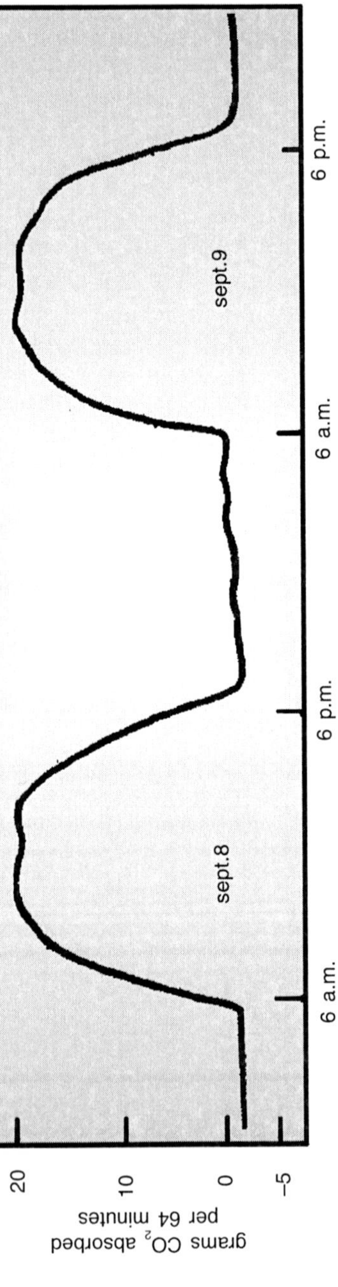

Figure 8.11: Daily variations in the rate of apparent photosynthesis of alfalfa.

factor is limiting. Such experiments on the overall temperature characteristics of the process must therefore be conducted with the plants exposed to an atmosphere in which the carbon dioxide concentration is considerably higher than the usual atmospheric concentration of 0.03 per cent.

In nature the maximum rate of photosynthesis which might be achieved under the prevailing temperature is often not realized because of the limiting effect of some other factor.

Temperature, within the ordinary physiological range for plants, has little effect on the rate of photosynthesis of plant: growing in deep shade or of plants exposed to the low light intensities of cloudy days. Under such conditions light is the limiting factor.

Similarly, on warm days, well-watered plants exposed to bright light often do not photosynthesize at the maximum rate possible under the prevailing temperature because carbon dioxide at atmospheric concentration is the limiting factor.

Thomas and Hill (1949), for example, found that temperature had very little influence on the rate of photosynthesis of alfalfa under field conditions within a range of 16.4° to 29°C. In other words the temperature coefficient of the process under such conditions is approximately one.

The Role of Water in Photosynthesis

Less than 1 per cent of the water absorbed by a plant is used in photosynthesis. It therefore seems probable that the indirect effects of the water factor upon photosynthesis are more pronounced than it; direct effect.

In other words, deficiency of water as a raw material is rarely if ever a limiting factor in photosynthesis, Nevertheless a reduction in the water content of leaves usually results in a decrease in the rate of photosynthesis as is illustrated by the results of Schneider and Childers (1941).

These investigators studied the effects of withholding water upon the rate of apparent photosynthesis in apple trees. When the soil was allowed to dry out gradually, starting from the field capacity, reduction in the rate of apparent photosynthesis (and transpiration) became evident within a few days at an air temperature of 26.7°C, and was pronounced before visible wilting took place.

When the soil water content had fallen to the permanent wilting percentage, and the leaves were distinctly wilted, apparent photosynt-hesis was 87 per cent less than the initial rate. Upon watering the soil the leaves regained turgitdity within a few hours, but the original rates of apparent photosynthesis were not reattained until 2-7 days had passed.

An important implication of this last observation is that the retarding effects of drought on photosynthesis linger for some .time after water has again become available in the soil.

Submersion of roots also has a pronounced retarding effect on apparent photosynthesis (and transpiration) in apple, usually becoming evident within 2-7 days after flooding the soil with water.

With continued water-logging of the soil around the roots, rates of apparent photosynthesis often become immeasurable. This effect is doubtless largely the result of a retardation in water absorption.

The influence of a reduction in the water content of leaves upon the rate of photosynthesis probably results from either r both of two principal causes:

(1) a reduction in the diffusive capacity of the stomates, and

(2) a decrease in the hydration r the chloroplasts and other parts of the protoplasm which in some manner diminishes the effectiveness of the photosynthetic mechanism.

Decrease in the water content of leaves unquestionably causes a reduction in the diffusive capacity of the stomates. Mitchell (1936) and others have observed, however, that in some plants relatively high rates of photosynthesis may prevail at times when the stomates appear to be closed. There are Several possible explanations for this apparently anomalous observation.

One is that stomates which appear closed to microscopic observations are not entirely closed to the passage of gases. A second is that reservoired carbon dioxide within the leaf cells may be used in photosynthesis while the stomates are closed or nearly so.

A third is that considerable amounts of carbon dioxide may enter the leaves of some species directly through the epidermis as described earlier.

The evidence in favour of the view that the decreased hydration of the protoplasm which accompanies a reduction in cell turgidity causes a decreased rate of photosynthesis comes chiefly from experiments with water plants.

Walter (1929), for example, has studied the effect upon their rate of photosynthesis of immersing plants of waterw-eed (*Anacharfs canadensis*) in sucrose solutions of various concentrations.

The greater the concentration of the sucrose solution the less the turgidity of the cells, the less the hydration of protoplasm and the slower the rate of photosynthesis.

In one experiment the rate of photosynthesis was appreciably retarded by immersion of the plants in an 0.3 molal solution and almost entirely stopped in an 0.7 molal solution of sucrose with an osmotic pressure of about 18 atm.

Plasmolysis of the cells occurred at a solution concentration of between 0.3 and 0.4 molal. The rate of respiration. on the other hand, was practically unaffected by sucrose solutions at any concentration up to and including 1.0 molal.

Since the waterweed is a submerged aquatic with thin leaves which bear no stomates, any reduction in the rate of photosy-nthesis resulting from a diminution in cell turgor most likely results from direct effects upon the hydration of the protoplasm of the photosynthesizing cells.

In general, it appears that the rate of photosynthesis is less affected by reduction in leaf water content than the rate of transpiration.

This is indicated by the results of Heinicke and Childers (1936) who determined the average rates of photosynthesis and transpiration over a one-week period in two apple trees, one of which was well watered while the other was growing in soil which was gradually drying out.

The rate of photosynthesis of the plant in the dry soil was about half as great as in the plant which was watered. The rate of transpiration, however, was only about one-fourth as great in the former plant as in the latter.

Effect of Oxygen Concentration on Photosynthesis

The photosynthetic organs of terrestrial plants are seldom exposed to oxygen concentrations which deviate appreciably from the usual atmospheric concentration of about 21 per cent.

Hence studies of the effect of oxygen concentration on the rate of photosynthesis are principally of theoretical interest.

In at least some, and probably all, plants, increase in the oxygen concentration results in a decrease in the rate of photosynthesis, and the normal atmospheric concentration is sufficiently high to induce a slower photosynthetic rate than obtains at lower oxygen concentrations.

For example, MeAlister and Myers (1940) showed that the rate of photosynthesis in young wheat plants was about 30-50 per cent higher in 0.5 per cent oxygen than in 20 per cent oxygen at a high light intensity and atmospheric carbon dioxide concentration.

This effect of oxygen is not merely a decrease in apparent photosynthesis resulting from an enhanced respiration rate at the higher oxygen concentration but is on the process of photosynthesis *per se*. Neither is this effect one of photo-oxidation offsetting photosynthesis, because the magnitude of the retardation in photosynthesis under relatively high concentrations of oxygen is too great to be accounted for in this way.

The only satisfactory explanation appears to be that oxygen actually exerts a direct inhibitory effect on photosynthesis, and the greater the concentration of oxygen the greater this effect.

Effects of Certain Chemical Compounds on Photosynthesis

Many different kinds of chemical compounds, upon absorption by plant cells, have effects-direct or indirect-upon the rate of photosyn-thesis. Especially noteworthy are the effects of certain substances which markedly influence the rate of photosynthesis when present only in minute quantities.

Among these are hydrocyanic acid, hydroxylamin, hydrogen sulphide, and certain compounds containing the iodoacetyl radical. Hydrocyanic acid, for example, has a pronounced retarding effect on the photosynthesis of *Chlorella at* a concentration of only 4×10^{-5} molar.

All of these substances appear to act as enzyme inhibitors and each of them appears to affect one specific enzyme system of the several which operate in the mechanism of photosynthesis.

This fact has been used to advantage by investigators of the chemical dynamics of photosynthesis, who have thereby been enabled to inhibit the process at different stages, and thus to differentiate more clearly among the several partial reactions of photosynthesis.

For example, the enzyme system which is sensitive to hydroxylamine participates only in the oxygen-releasing stage of photosynthesis.

Narcotics, of which chloroform, ether, and the urethans are examples, also exert retarding or inhibitory effects on photosynthesis when present in very low concentrations, unless the concentration is too high, in which case death of the cells may result, the effect of such substances is reversible.

Narcotic inhibition of photosynthesis does not appear to result from effects on specific enzymes, but from some more general influence, which is believed to be retated to their surface activity.

The Effects of Internal Factors on the Rate of Photosynthesis. In addition to the environmental factors which influence photosynthesis, the rate of the process is also influenced by certain factors within the plant.

In general, because of the experimental difficulties encountered in their investigation, the effects of such internal factors on photosynthesis are less well understood than those of external factors.

Some discussion of several of these factors is warranted, however, by the present of our knowledge.

Chlorophyll Content

In their extensive study of the relationship between chlorophyll content and photosynthesis Wilistatter and Stoll (1918) devised the *photosynthetic number* "Assimilationszahl") as an index to this relation. The phototsynthetic number is the number of grams of carbon dioxide absorbed per hour per gram of chlorophyll.

These two investigators studied the relation between chlorophyll content and photosynthesis in green-leaved and yellow-leaved varieties of the same species. In this experiment the leaves were exposed to strong light in an atmosphere of 5 per cent carbon dioxide at 25°C.

As shown in this table the rate of photosynthesis in greenved varieties is not much in excess of that in yellow-leaved varieties of the same species, and, when expressed in terms of the photosynthetic number, the yellow-leaved varieties are much more efficient per unit of chlorophyll present.

Other investigations by the same workers also seem to point to the conclusion that there is no proportional relationship between chlorophyll content and photosynthesis in the leaves of vascular ants. In other-words, it appears that the chlorophyll contact of the leaves is seldom the limiting factor in photosynthesis in such species even when all external conditions are favorable for the process.

Hydration of the Protoplasm

That the hydration of the protoplasm is an important internal factor influencing photosynthesis has already been shown in the discussion of the water actor in photosynthesis.

Leaf Anatomy

The rate of photosynthesis in any leaf is partly conditioned by the anatomy of that leaf. The size and distribution of the intercellular spaces, the relative proportions and distribution of palisade and spongy layers, the size, position, and structure of the stomates, the thickness of the cuticular and epidermal layers, the amount and position of clerenchyma, proportion and distribution of non-green nesophyll tissues, and the size, distribution and efficiency of he vascular system, all influence the rate of photosynthesis.

The effects of the structure of leaves upon the rate of photosynthesis result principally from influences upon the rate of entrance of carbon dioxide, upon the intensity of light penerating to chlorenchyma cells, upon the maintenance of the turgidity of the leaf cells, and upon the rate of translocation. A soluble carbohydrates out of the photosynthesizing cells.

Protoplasmic Factors

Evidence from various types of experiments, some of which has been presented on the foregoing pages, indicates conclusively that certain other conditions resident in the protoplasm of plant cells, other than chlorophyll content and hydration, influence the rate of photosynthesis.

The most important of such factors is undoubtedly the enzyme complement of the protoplasmic system. That a number of enzymes play a part in photosynthesis is beyond question. There is also little doubt that the proportions and quantities of these enzymes may vary in different kinds of photosynthetic cells, or in the same cell under different conditions, but until more is known of the physicochemical nature of the photosynthetic catalysts no discussion of them beyond these generalized statements is warranted.

Accumulation of the End Products of Photosynthesis

During photosynthesis the carbohydrates synthesized in the process, or in immediately following secondary reactions, accumulate **in** the photosynthesizing cells more rapidly than they are translocated toward other tissues.

Under at least some conditions accumulation of carbohydrates appears to exert a retarding effect upon photosynthesis. The results of Boysen-Jensen and Muller (1929), Kjar (1937), and others, however, appear to indicate that there is no consistent relationship between the concentration of carbohydrates in the leaf cells of intact plants and the rate of photosynthesis.

Daily Variations in the Rate of Photosynthesis

Thomas and Hill (1937) measured the daily variation in rates of apparent photosynthesis for small plots of alfalfa under conditions approximating a "*standard day.*" Well-watered plots of alfalfa 6 feet square were enclosed in transparent celluloid cabinets and air circulated through each cabinet at rates ranging up to several hundred cubic feet per minute.

The net consumption of carbon dioxide by the plants was ascert-ained by measuring the difference in the concentration of this gas in the inflowing and outflowing streams of air.

In general, as with the apple tree previously described, the rate of photosynthesis under these conditions showed a close correlation with the light intensity. Innumerable other types of daily periodicities of photosynthesis are possible.

The pattern of any such periodicity depends in part on the kind of plant and on the unit of plant material for which photosynthesis is measured-whether a single leaf, a small plant, a large plant, such as a tree, or a plot of vegetation. It will also obviously vary with the daily cycle of environmental conditions which not only differs in a general way from one climatic center to another, but also shows seasonal and daily variations within any climatic

Chapter 9

OXIDATION DURING PHOTOSYNTHESIS

Photosynthetic water cleavage into dioxygen and metabolically bound hydrogen is of central relevance for the bioenergetics of the exploitation of solar radiation as the unique energy source of the biosphere.

The key step of the overall process is water oxidation which takes place in system II via a four-step univalent redox reaction sequence.

The kinetic pattern of photosynt-hetic water oxidation has been resolved. It can be summarised by the scheme depicted in Figure elsewhere in this chapter.

Basically, three types of events can be distinguished:

1. generation of sufficiently oxidising redox equivalents (holes) by photooxidation of a special chlorophyll-a referred to as P680,
2. transfer of the holes via at least one redox group Z acting as oneelectron component, and
3. stepwise univalent electron abstraction from the manganese-containing catalytic site of water oxidation leading to oxygen evolution after the accumulation of four holes.

The functional groups participating in these reactions are incorp-orated into a protein complex containing at least seven polypeptides.

The exact location has not yet been clarified. In this

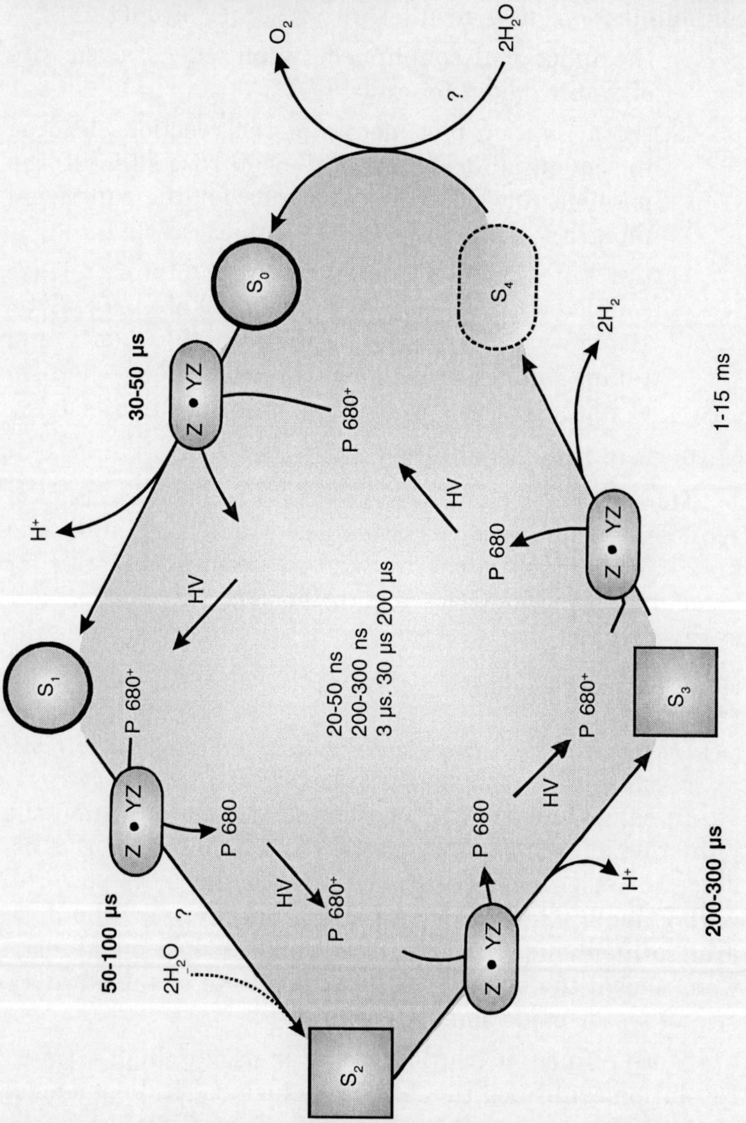

Figure 9.1: Functional scheme of photosynthetic water oxidation to dioxygen. Oxidised redox equivalents are produced by the P680° photoreaction within few picoseconds, typical half transfer times via intermediate redox component Z (predominantly in the ns time domain) to the catalytic site (SO JAB—1.5 me) are denoted inside and at the corners, respectively, of the scheme.

communication, new results are presented about:

(*i*) the functional coupling between the catalytic site of water oxidation and $P680^{+}$,

(*ii*) the activation parameters of the reactions leading to sequential oxidation of the catalytic site, (ill) the possible role of hydrogen bonds for the functional integrity of the system 11 complex, and

(*iv*) the kinetics and stoichiometry of proton release coupled with the stepwise -oxidation of the catalytic site of water oxidation. Based on these data and taking into account previous results the mechanism of photosynthetic water oxidation is discussed.

Materials and Methods

The preparation of thylakoids and PS II fragments from cyanob-acteria (*Synechococcus vulcanus* Copeland) and higher plants (spinach) as well as the equipments for measuring flashinduced absorption changes and oxygen evolution have been described in detail in previous reports.

RESULTS AND DISCUSSION

(A) *The reduction kinetics of* $P680^{+}$ *as an indicator of the functional coupling between the catalytic site and the reaction centre*

In samples with fully competent oxygen evolution the reduction of P680+ is dominated by kinetics in the ns-domain. Based on measurements with the most powerful ADRY-agent, 2-(3-chloro-4-trifluoromethyl) anilino-3, 5-dinitrothiophene (ANT2p), the $P680^{+}$ reduction kinetics were shown to depend. on the redox state of the catalytic site of water oxidation.

More refined measurements at markedly higher time -resolution confirmed this basic conclusion. The dependence of the ns-kinetics on the redox state S_1 was interpreted by -electrostatic effects on. the redox equilibrium between two components which are assumed to act as primary and secondary donor of $P680^{+}$.

Alternatively, the data could be also .explained by struc-

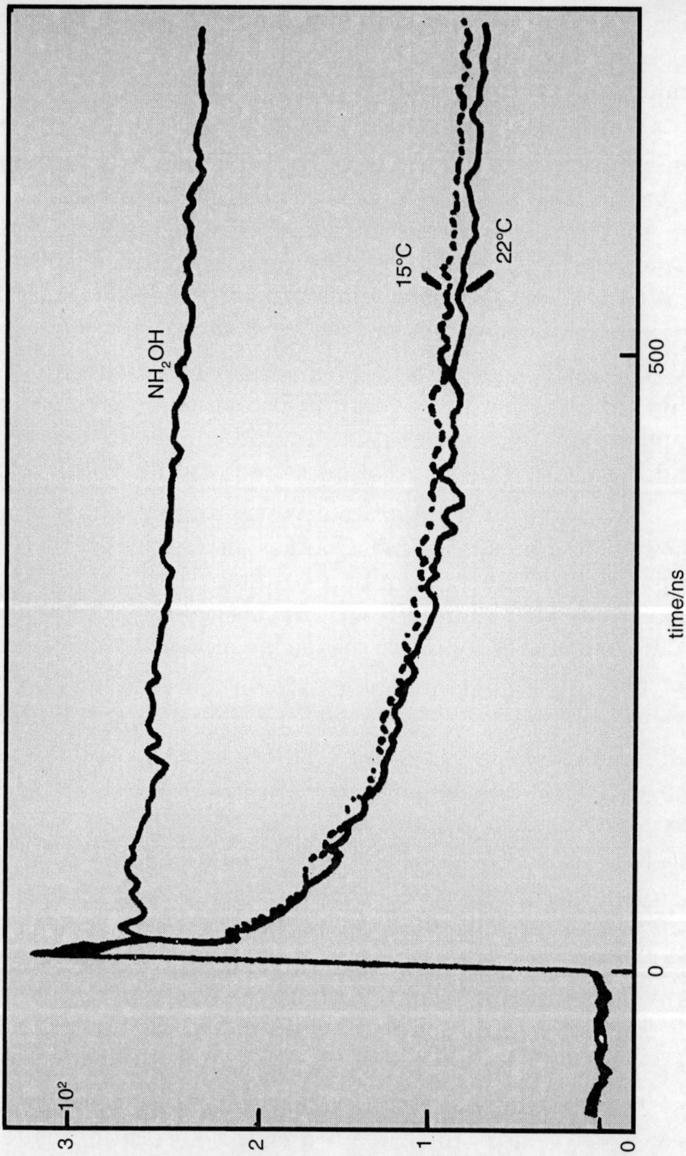

Figure 9.2: Absorption changes at 830 nm as a function of time in O_2, evolving PS II membrane fragments from spinach under repetitive flash excitation (1 Hz) at -1.5°C (dotted trace) and +22°C (full trace). For comparison there is depicted the trace obtained in the presence of 3mM NH_2OH.

tural changes of the states S_2 and S_3 that modify the electronic and nuclear coupling between $P680^+$ and its donor component referred to as Z in the literature.

In order to analyse this coupling more thoroughly, the temperature dependence of $P680^+$ reduction was measured by monitoring laser-flash-induced absorption changes at 830 nm in PS II membrane fragments from spinach. Figure elsewhere in this chapter shows traces obtained at +20°C and –1.5°C, respectively, under repetitive flash excitation on samples with intact oxygen evolution.

The results reveal almost identical relaxation kinetics. This indicates that the overall $P680^+$ reduction is practically independent of temperature in the physiological range under steady state population of redox states S_i (i=0,...3).

For comparison Figure elsewhere in this chapter also shows 830 nm absorption changes in samples which are deprived of their oxygen evolution capacity due to incubation with 3 mM NH_2OH. In this case μs-kinetics arise at the expense of complete disappearance of the ns-kinetics.

This phenomenon is indicative for a strong effect of the functional integrity of water oxidation on the $P680^+$ reduction kinetics. Therefore, it has been speculated that the extent of the ns-kinetics could be a measure of the oxygen evolution -capacity.

However, the latest detailed studies on the effects of *trifluoperazine, diisothiocyanostilbene-2. 2-disalfonic acid* (DIDS) and *lauroylcholinechloride* show this not to be the case. The data of Figure elsewhere in this chapter do not provide detailed information about the affect of temperature on $P680^+$ reduction as a function of the individual redox states S_i.

To check this point, dark adapted samples were illuminated with a laser flash train and the absorption changes caused by each flash were separately monitored. The results obtained are summarised in Figure elsewhere in this chapter.

An inspection of the data shows that there is almost no

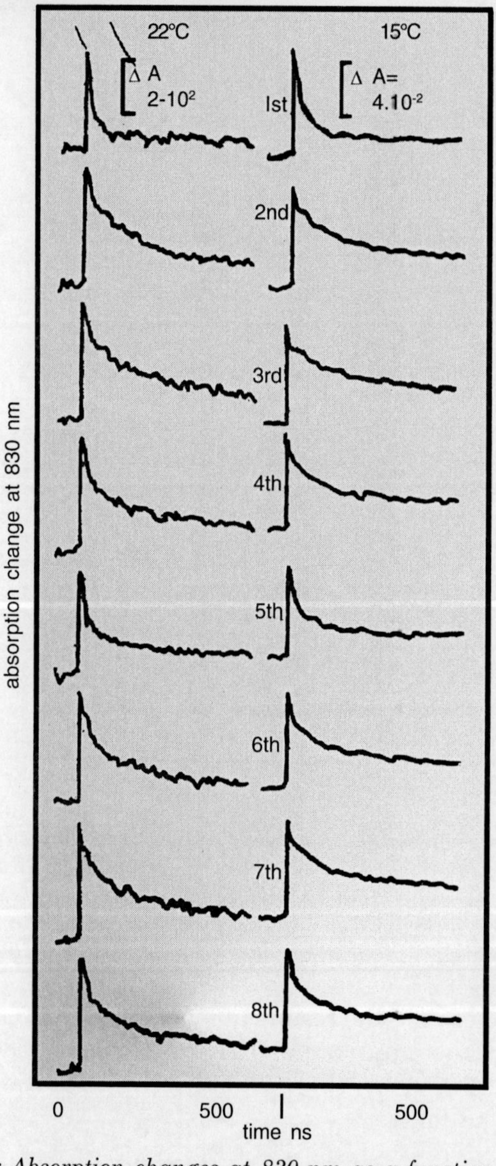

Figure 9.3: Absorption changes at 830 nm as a function of flash N° and time in dark adapted O_2 evolving PS II membrane fragments from spinach at –1.5°C (right side) and +22°C (left side). The measurement at –1.5°C were performed with suspensions of doubled chlorophyll concentrations compared with those used at +22°C.

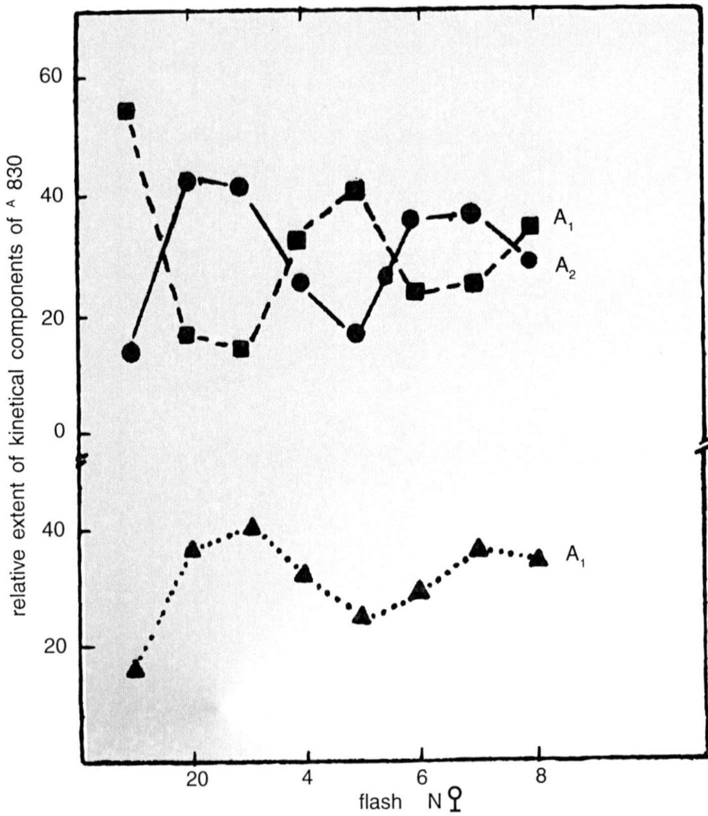

Figure 9.4: Amplitudes of the decay kinetics in the as-range as a function of flash N° in dark-adapted O_2-evolving PS II membrane fragments at –1.5°C. The values were obtained by a triexponential fit of the data depicted in Figure elsewhere in this chapter (right side) with fixed into constants of k_1=1.7.10^7 s^{-1}, k_2 = 3.10^4 s^{-1}, and k_2 < 7.10^5 s^{-1}.

difference between the results at –1.5°C and +20°C. A kinetic analysis of the data reveals that a satisfactory description can be achieved by the assumption of a *triexpon-ential decay* of the form

$$\Delta A_{830}(i)\sum_{\mu=1}^{3} a_{\mu}(S_i)e^{-k}\mu^{-1} \tag{1}$$

The amplitudes a_{μ} (S_i) depend on the redox state of the *catalytic* site as is clearly shown in Figure elsewhere in this chapter for the data obtained at –1.5°C. This depende-nce can be described by:

$a_\mu(S_i) = \sum_{i=0}^{3} c_{\mu.i}[S_i]$, where $[S_i]$ is the probability of a catalytic site being in redox state S_i. A reasonable fit can be achieved with the following approximations:

$$c_{1,0} \approx c_{1,1} \text{ and } c_{1,2} \approx c_{1,3};\ c_{2,0} \approx c_{2,1} \approx 0 \text{ and } c_{2,2} \approx c_{2,2},$$

$$c_{3,0} \approx c_{3,1} \approx 0 \text{ and } c_{3,2} \approx c_{3,3}$$

These relations are not exactly the same for a_2=(S_i) and $a_2(S_i)$ as reflected by small differences of the corresponding oscillation patterns depicted in Figure elsewhere in this chapter. The origin of this phenomonon will be analyzed in a forthcoming study.

The above mentioned relations tacitly imply that the small contribution, of µs-kinetics to the overall relaxation after the first flash is, caused by a minor fraction of systems II which contain a damaged catalytic site of water oxidation.

The oscillation at -1.5°C closely resembles the pattern at +20°C. The relaxation kinetics at -1.5'C are satisfactorily described by k_1=1.7.10^7 s^{-1}, k_2 = 3.10^4 s^{-1}, and k_2 < 7.10^5 s^{-1}. The same rate constants can be also used for the fit of the data obtained at +20°C, but in this case two different k_1-values of 5.10^7 s^{-1} (relaxation after the first and 5th flash) and of 1.7.10^7 s^{-1} have to be used.

Except for this specific effect which will be analysed else where, the present study shows that neither the kinetics nor the influence of the redox states of the catalytic site exhibit a significant temperature dependence.

The former phenomenon can be explained by a comparatively small activation energy of the electron transfer from Z to $P680^+$. Then oscillation pattern of the P680+ reduction kinetics could be interpreted either by the assumption that the structure of the catalytic site in S_0 and S_1 differs from that in S_2 and S_3, giving rise to markedly different coupling between P680$^+$ and Z, or that redox equilibria between electron transfer components responsible for the S, state dependence of P680$^+$ reduction are only slightly enhanced in the range of –1.5°C and +20°C.

Direct experimental evidence is lacking for these types of equilibria. On the other hand, structural differences of S_2 and S_3 versus S_0 and S_1, respectively, are very likely as reflected. by different Cl^- binding properties. Likewise, water substrate entry into the redox cycle is also discussed to occur at the level of S_2.

Therefore, regulation of P680$^+$ reduction via: structural changes caused by the redox transition $S_1 \rightarrow S_2$ seems to be more attractive than a simple electrostatic point-charge effect.

As a consequence of this idea, the temperature dependence of the oscillation pattern depicted in Figure elsewhere in this chapter indicates that the presumed conformational states regulating P680$^+$ reduction are practically the same at –1.5°C and –1-20°C.

(B) *Temperature dependence of the univalent redox steps at the catalytic site of water oxidation*

The kinetics of the univalent oxidation steps $S_i \rightarrow S_{i+1}$ cam be monitored by measurements of the rise-time of UV absorption changes. The oxidation rate depending on the redox level of the catalytic site of water oxidation kinetically coincides with the reduction of Z^{ox}. As these comprise protolytic reactions and structural modifications, the reaction coordinate of each individual process, $Z^{ox}\ S_i \rightarrow ZS_{i+1} + m_i H^+ + \delta_3 . O_2$ (where $i = 0, ..3$, with $i + 1 = 0$ for $i = 3$), is anticipated to depend on state S_i.

In order to resolve this problem, experiments were performed with PS II fragments from the *thermophilic cyanobacterium Synecho-coccus vulcanus* Copeland which permit covering a broader temperature region. The results obtained are depicted in Figure elsewhere in this chapter.

The data at the left side presenting 330 nm absorption changes induced by repetitive flash excitation at 0°C and

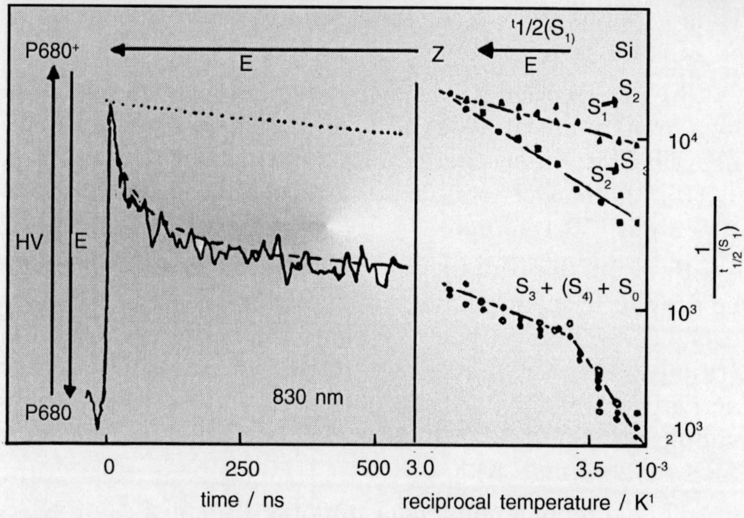

Figure 9.5: Absorption changes at 830 nm (left side) as a function of time and reciprocal half-rise times of S_i oxidation (measured at 350 nm) as a function of reciprocal temperature (right side) in PS II fragments from Synechococcus vulcanus *Copeland. The signal on the left side represents a trace monitored at +33°C, the dashed curve symbolises the data at 0°C. The dotted curve was obtained in the presence of 3 mM N H_2OH. Repetitive excitation (1 Hz) with laser flashes.*

33°C respectively, indicate that in PS II fragments from thermophilic cyanobacteria also the electron transport from Z to $P680^+$ is almost temperature independent. A markedly different behaviour is observed for the reactions $Z^{ox}\ S_i \rightarrow ZS_{i+1} + m_i H^+ + \delta_3.O_2$.

The right side of Figure elsewhere in this chapter shows the reciprocal half-rise times of absorption changes at 350 nm As a function of the reciprocal temperature. As the kinetics of the transition $Z^{ox}\ S_0 \rightarrow ZS_1 + H^+$ could not be resolved with Sufficient precision, the temperature dependence of this reaction is omitted.

The other three transitions exhibit remarkable differences of the corresponding reaction coordinates. Two 'findings are of special relevance:

(a) the activation energy of to reaction $Z^{ox}\ S_2 \rightarrow ZS_3 +$

H^+ is significantly higher (26.8 kJ/mol) than that of Z^{ox} S_1 $\rightarrow$ ZS_2 (9.6 kJ/mol), and

(b) the reaction Z^{ox} $S_3 \rightarrow ZS_0 + O_2 + 2H^+$ is characterized by a break point at about 16°C of its temperature dependence. The activation energy above the critical temperature, T_c (15.5 kJ/mol), is only about 25% of that observed below this point (59.4 kJ/mol).

Bred on these data, some interesting conclusions can be drawn. If one assumes that the transmission coefficient σ of be reaction path is the same for both reactions, the transition state of $S_1 \rightarrow S_2$ requires a markedly higher activation entropy ΔS^* than that of $S_2 \rightarrow S_3$ (in the most simple case of $\sigma = 1$ one obtains $\Delta S^*_{2.1} = -140$ J/mol K versus $\Delta S^*_{2.2} = -80$ J/mol. K).

This phenomenon also supports the idea that S_1 is structrally distinctly different from S_1 although on the basis of EXAFS studies the microenvironment of the catalytic site itself was recently inferred to exhibit almost the same structure in S_1 and S_2.

The latter conclusion is also hardly reconcilable with the assumption that substrate water enters the redox cycle at state S_2 rather than at S_0. Further studies are required to clarify this mechanistically crucial point.

The break point in the temperature dependence of S_3 oxidation leading to dioxygen release probably reflects significant structural changes of S_2 around the critical temperature of 16°C in PS II fragment from thermophilic cyanobacteria. This idea raises questions .about the nature of these changes.

One possible explanation is based on the previous postulation that S_3 already satisfies the energy requirements of dioxygen bond formation at the redox level of a peroxide.

Therefore, the break point could reflect a dramatic shift of the equilibrium between water substrate ligands and the oxidised manganese centre, *i.e.* above T_c the oxidation

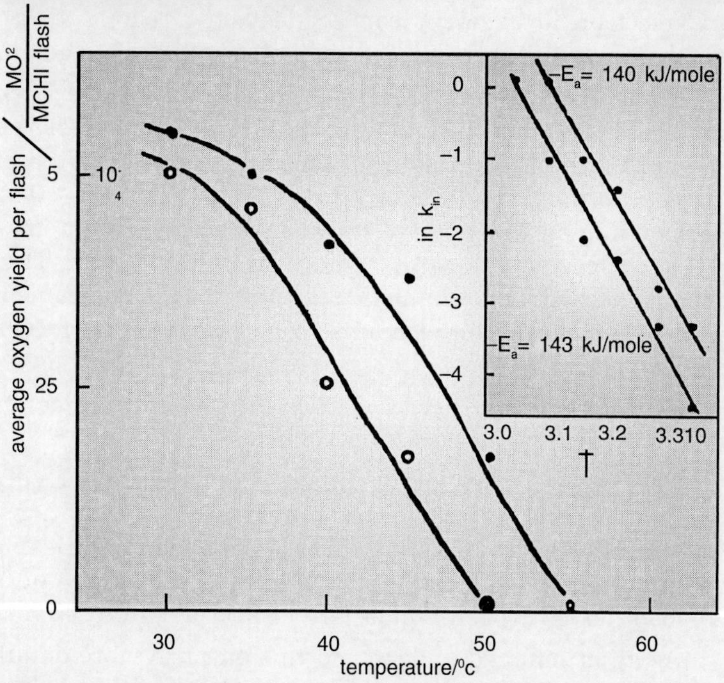

Figure 9.6: Average oxygen yield per flash as a function of the temperature at a 3 min dark incubation.

of S_3 could start at a peroxide-type level with a preformed 0-0 bond, whereas below T_c additional activation energy is required for peroxide formation.

Alternatively, changes of the protolytic reactions should also be considered. The break point phenomenon at T_c implies a rather sharp and simultaneous change of ΔS^* and ΔH^* in the reaction path of S_2 oxidation.

The origin of this "phase transition type" effect (structural changes of the whole membrane or "all or none" transition in the PS II polypeptide complexes) remains to be" clarified.

The latest thermoluminescence data provide additional (interesting information about the reactivity of S_3 as a functions of temperature. It was shown that in spinach thylakoids at subzero temperatures (between-50°C and –

5°C) electron. abstraction from ZS_2 leads to a redox state S* which cannot be further oxidised into S_0 and dioxygen.

If one excludes the trivial possibility of S^*_3 being $Z^{ox}S_2$ one could consider this. finding as further support of the idea that 0—0 bond preformation in S_3 is the key step of the reaction n.H_2O + $Z^{ox}S_3$→ ZSo+ O_2 + $2H^+$ (here n = 0 or 2 depending on the stage of water substrate entry into the redox cycle, see figure elsewhere in this chapter. This question of central mechanistic relevance for the mechanism of dioxygen, formation remains to be answered by future studies.

(C) *Effects of hydrogen bonds on the structural integrity of the oxygen evolution capacity*

The oxygen evolution capacity can be selectively eliminate& by a number of protein denaturing conditions. Among different_ interactions of charged and/or polarisable groups responsible for the structural integrity of a polypeptide, hydrogen bonds. are of special interest.

As an attempt to understand this effect in more detail, comparative experiments were performed with spinach thylakoids suspended either in H_2O or D_2O under denaturing conditions. The oxygen evolution capacity of spinach thylakoids was shown to be rather sensitive to a thermal shock.

If this degradation process comprises the break of hydrogen bonds, then suspending of thylakoids in D_2O instead of H_2O is expected to provide some kind of protection. The number of systems II fully competent in oxygen evolution was determined by measurements of the average oxygen yield per flash. Y_{ss}, under repetitive excitation at sufficiently low frequencies (2 Hz) to exclude kinetical limitations.

In order to separate effects of DO on thermal degradation from those of a possible influence on the activity, thylakoids were suspended in either D_2O or HO and subjected to a 3 min incubation of the desired temperature.

After this treatment the samples were injected into a

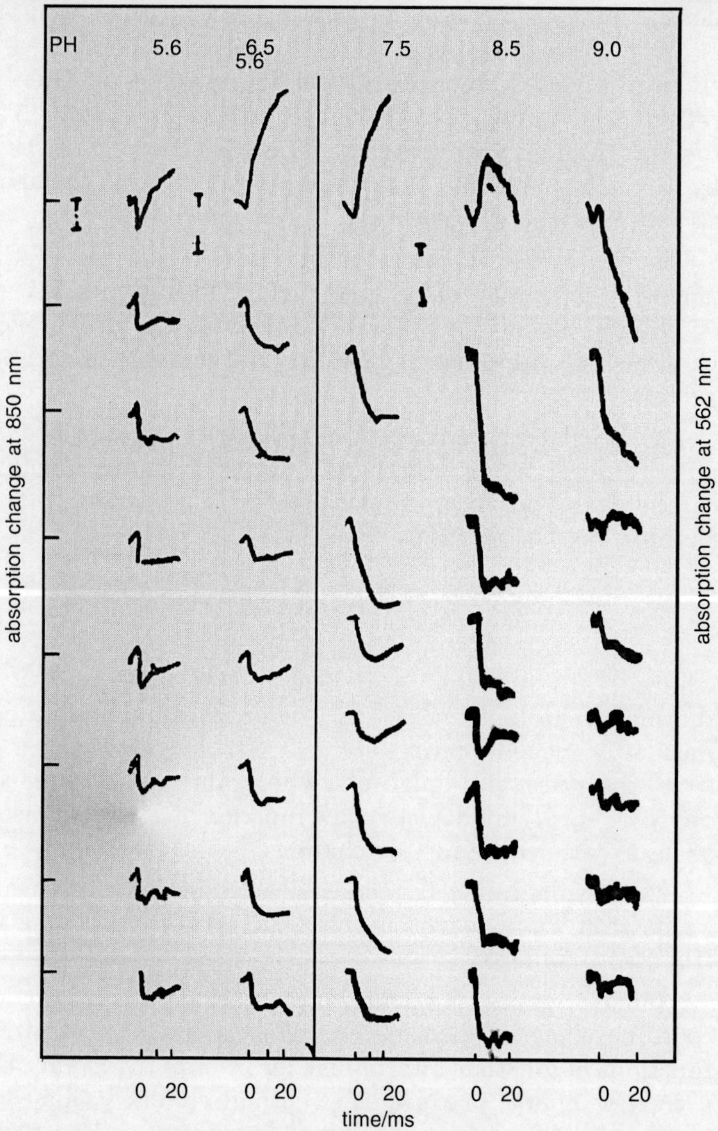

Figure 9.7: Δ pH-indicating absorption changes at 562 and 580 nm as a function of time in O_2 evolving PS II membrane fragments from spinach at room temperature. The traces at the left side were obtained with bromocresol purple, at the right side with phenol red.

normal aqueous (H_2O) buffer solution and Y_{ss} was measured at 20°C. The data depicted in figure elsewhere in this chapter reveal a significant stabilising effect of D_2O as reflected by the shift of thermal sensitivity by about 5 K towards higher temperatures. This result suggests that hydrogen bonds might: play an important role in the native structure of the oxygen evolving complex.

In the simplest case, the activation energies of the degradation process of samples incubated in either D_2O or or H_2O differ only in the zero point energies of hydrogen bonds which are essential for the native structure of the protein.

As the detrimental effect is satisfactorily described by a first order kinetics the apparent degradation rate constant can be evaluated from the data of figure elsewhere in this chapter by the equation

$$k_{in} = \frac{1}{t_{inc}} . \text{in} \frac{Y_{ss}(0)}{Y_{ss}(t_{inc})} \qquad (2)$$

where $Y_{ss}(0)$=average oxygen yield per flash at t=0 of thermal treatment and $Y_{ss}(t_{inc})$=average oxygen yield per flash after incubation time of 3 min. The k_{in} values obtained from the data of Figure elsewhere in this chapter by applying eq. (2) are depicted as a function of T^{-1} in the insert of figure elsewhere in this chapter.

The results can be fairly described by straight lines with activation energies of E_A (H_2O)=140 kJ/mole and E_A (D_2O)=143 kJ/mole.

If one assumes that deuteration affects only the reaction coordinate of the degradation process (i.e. the partition functions of all other internal modes remain invariant), the activation energy is expected to become changed solely due to the differences of the zero point energies of the hydrogen bonds –H...Y—and—D...Y—that are broken in the activated state.

To calculate the order of magnitude of this effect the

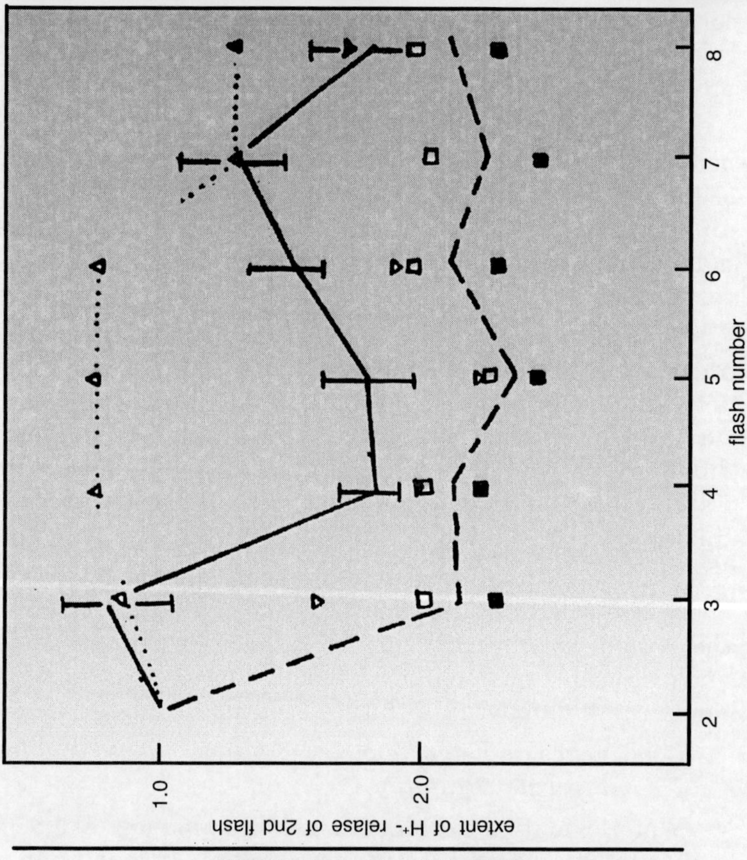

Figure 9.8: Extent of proton release due to the n-th flash normalised to the extent due to the 2nd flash as a function of flash No. (n) in dark-adapted PS II membrane fragments from spinach at different pH.

number of hydrogen bonds undergoing cleavage and their zero point energies are required. Using 20-25 kJ/mole as data taken from the literature for the average energy of hydrogen bonds in proteins, the experimental activation energy of 140-143 kJ/mole indicates a break of 6-7 hydrogen bonds in the activated state. Likewise, the activation entropy ΔS^* of denaturation is computed to be 190 J/K mole for thylakoids suspended in H_2O or D_2O. These values correspond with data reported for the denaturation of well-characterised isolated enzymes like trypsin or pancreatic proteinase.

The difference of the zero point energy per hydrogen bond is given by $\Delta_{\varepsilon D}$ =1/2h.υH (1—1√2), where υ_H=frequency of the normal hydrogen bond containing a proton and the difference in the reduced mass is about 2 due to the large mass of the protein compared with that of H and D. respectively.

Typical were numbers of hydrogen bonds are of the order of 200-300 cm^{-1} which gives rise to a difference of the activation energy of (5-10). 10^{-22} J per hydrogen bond. Accordingly, for the cleavage of 6-7 hydrogen bonds, a total difference of the activation energy of ΔE_A = 2—4 kJ/mole iss obtained, in close agreement with the experimental findings.

This supports the idea that some special hydrogen bonds are of crucial relevance for the native structure of the oxygen evolving complex. The localisation of these bonds and a possible functional involvement in protolytic reactions remain to be analysed in future studies.

(D) *Kinetics and stoichiometry of proton release coupled with, water oxidation*

Water oxidation to dioxygen by holes produced at $P680^+$ is inevitably coupled with the total release of four protons into the lumenal space of thylakoids. Therefore, the stoichiometry of H^+ ejection from the catalytic site in each univalent redox step. $S_1 \rightarrow S_{i+1}$, referred to as the *intrinsic* proton release pattern should provide direct information about the deprotonation sequence of substrate water during the redox cycle.

Results. obtained with special pH-sensitive indicators in thylakoids inside-out vesicles and PS II membrane fragments from spinach in the physiological range of 6.0<pH<7.5 can be satisfactorily explained by a stoichiometry of 1.0.1. 2 for the redox transitions $S_1 \rightarrow S_{i+1}$, with 1=0,1,2,3, respectively.

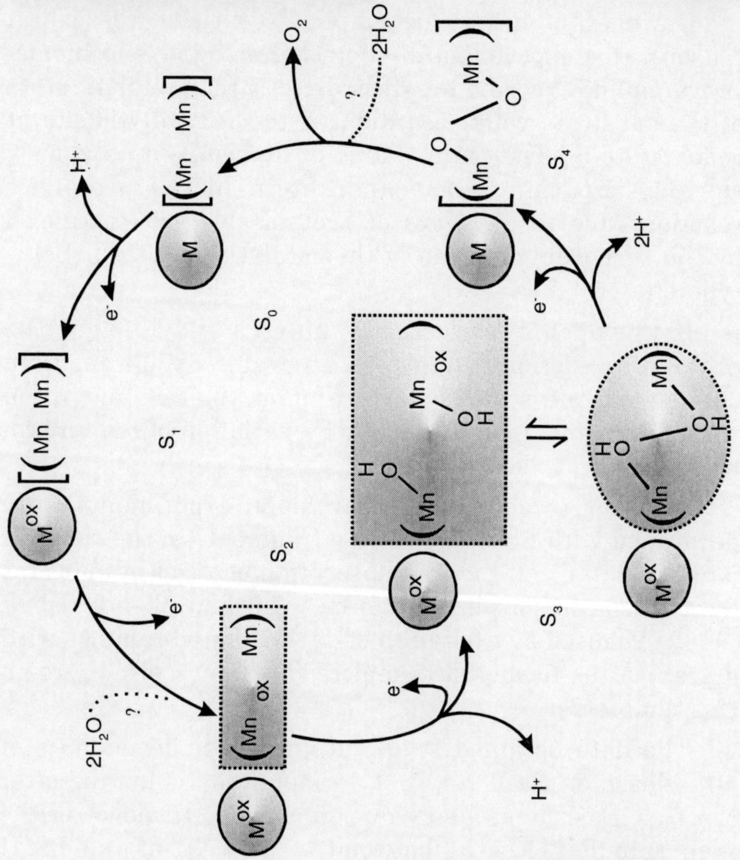

Figure 9.9: Mechanism of photosynthetic water oxidation to dioxygen. Only the manganeses of the binuclear catalytic core are presented, for the nature of M see text. As the stage of water entry into the cycle is not unambiguously clarified substrate ligation is only indicated for S_3 and S_4. The other ligands are symbolised by a half oval around Mn. Oxidised states are represented by grey areas. The possibility of a redox equilibrium between manganese and the water substrate ligands could lead to a peroxidic intermediate in S_3 as indicated in the scheme which tacitly implies that S_3 is oxidisable only in the peroxidic contiguration. For the sake of simplicity, redox equilibria are omitted, which can occur between the binuclear manganese site and redox centres other than the substrate. Likewise, each redox level (except that of S_3) is characterised by only one symbol.

However, it has to be emphasised that, for several reasons, this experimentally detected *extrinsic* stoichiometry cannot be expected to reflect directly the protolytic state of the substrate water coordinated to the catalytic site at redox state S_i. The main source of ambiguity is obviously the participation of the apoprotein in the protolytic reactions due to pK-shifts of protonisable groups caused by the turnovers of Z and of the catalytic site itself (Bohr-type effect).

If the apoprotein actually plays a key role for the protolytic reactions coupled with water oxidation, then changes of the stoichiometry and/or kinetics. of proton release are anticipated to occur by variation of the environmental pH.

In order to address this problem, experiments were performed with PS II membrane fragments in the range of $5.5<pH<9.0$. Flash-induced absorption changes of indicator dyes (bromocresol purple at $pH < 7.0$ and phenol red at $pH>7.0$) caused by excitation of dark-adapted samples with a train of μs-flashes are depicted in figure elsewhere in this chapter.

The data obtained reveal a significant dependence of H* release on Sash No. 0. A Pronounced H^+ uptake after the first Bash is probably due to a single turnover of the high spin Fe^{2+} located between Q_A and Q_S at the PS II acceptor side. This phenomenon will not be discussed here.

The amplitudes of H^+ release exhibit characteristic oscillation patterns that are dependent on the external pH as is shown in figure elsewhere in this chapter. No significant changes (within the limit of experimental error) are observed in the physiological range of $6.0<pH<8.0$, but marked deviations arise outside this region.

The results at alkaline pH are -seriously affected by a decline of the oxygen evolution capacity in PS II membrane fragments and therefore do not permit unequivocal conclusions. The interpretation of the other data within the framework of Kok's model depends significantly on precise knowledge of the probability of misses (a) ands double hits (b) and the apparent dark-state population $\{S_i\}o$.

A detailed analysis however indicates that a 1.0, 1,2 stoichiometry often does not provide the best fit. In many cases, stoichiometries of 0, 0, 2,2 and 0, 0, 1, 3 permit a better description of the data. Regardless of the details, these findings support the idea that the apoprotein seriously affects the extrinsic proton release pattern. This conclusion implies that the intrinsic proton release is still an unresolved problem.

An inspection of the proton release kinetics reveals a multiphasic pattern. Generally, at least a four-exponential kinetics with half-life times of ≤ 100 μs, 200-300 μs, 500-800μs and 1-5 ms is required for a satisfying fit.

We were not able to find an unequivocal correlation between the amplitudes of the different kinetics and individual redox. transitions $S_1 \rightarrow S_{i+1}$, even within the physiological pH range.

The most striking observation is the marked retardation of the proton release with increasing pH in the range of 5.5 up to 7.5. Preliminary studies did not show a clear kinetical correspondence of the rates of H+ release and the $S_1 \rightarrow S_{i+1}$, transitions in the above-mentioned pH range. Experiments. are in progress to analyse this point.

(E) *Mechanism of photosynthetic water oxidation*

The understanding of the molecular mechanism of photosynthetic water oxidation to dioxygen requires detailed knowledge of the electronic structure and the nuclear geometry of the catalytic site in the different redox states S_i for $i = 0...4$.

Different spectroscopic techniques (XANES, EXAFS, UV/VIS, IR, EPR, NMR) were used to resolve this problem but only few pieces of the huge puzzle were found. Despite lack of essential information (e.g. the ligands of the first coordination sphere at the catalytic manganese beyond substrate water, the existence and role of hydrogen bridges between substrate water and the apoprotein, dynamics of the apoenzyme and its effect on the reaction coordinate) an attempt will be made to discuss the mechanism of water oxidation within the framework of our current stage of limited knowledge.

This discussion is. based on two crucial postulates of our previous model (a) the central step of water oxidation, i.e. the 0—0 bond formation occurs at a binuclear manganese centre at the redox level of a peroxide in S_3 and (b) there exists a special state; or centre symbolised by M that undergoes a redox turnover at the steps $S_o \rightarrow S_1$, and $S_3 \rightarrow (S_4) \rightarrow S_o + O_2$ (protolytic reactions are omitted).

The former part of the first postulate is supported by the remarkable heterogeneity of the four manganeses which are present in each oxygen evolving complex.

Accordingly, twomanganeses are assumed to form the functional core of water oxidation whereas the other two manganeses could act asfurther redox centres (redox buffer or electronic coupling with Z) or as an essential structural element.

The second part of the first postulate appears to be mechanistically attractive because, in case of an intermediary peroxide formation, the electron abstraction from two water molecules takes place via two sequential 2-electron steps rather than by a more complex. single 4-electron step.

This idea has been accepted also for other models but, in contrast to our original postulate, the peroxide level is assumed to occur only as a transient S'_4 state.

However, it has to be emphasised that S_3 already satisfies the energy requirements for the formation of peroxidic state (based on experiments with $H^{18}{}_2O_2$ even S_2 might be considered as a candidate).

Recent mass spectroscopic studies were used as argument against the formation of a peroxidicstate prior to S_4. However, due to the very limited time resolution of this method, the data cannot be used as an unequivocal proof. Furthermore, a nonexchangeable metastable S_3 state does exist in strictly dark-adapted *oscillatoria chalybea.*

The latest results on the reactivity of S_3 as a function of temperature (see section B) might also support our postulate that 0-0 bond preformation occurs prior to S_4. The second postulate was primarily introduced in order to explain the extreme stability of S_1.

Actually, it was later found that, in sufficiently dark-adapted samples, almost all catalytic sites, attain the redox level S_1 M is not yet identified. It could be either a special valence state of the catalytic manganese or another redox-active component.

The latest and very elegant study confirms that the reaction $S_0 \rightarrow S_1$ does not cause significant absorption changes in the range of 290-570 nm, in contrast to the transitions $S_1 \rightarrow S_2$ and $S_2 \rightarrow S_3$. Based on this result, it was concluded that, most likely, no manganese oxidation takes place at the transition $S_0 \rightarrow S_1$.

With respect to the other redox steps, at least a 1-electron abstraction from manganese was inferred to occur for S_2 formation from S_1. On the other hand, it is not clear whether or not S, oxidation to S_3 is also mainly restricted to the manganese core.

The above-mentioned results neatly fit in with the basic conclusions of our previous model. Different lines of evidence support the idea that S_1 contains a [Mn (III) Mn (III)] and S_2 a [Mn (I11) Mn (IV)] core. As a summary of our fragmentary knowledge a molecular mechanism of water oxidation can be proposed which is depicted in figure elsewhere in this chapter.

Chapter 10

ALGAL PHOTOSYNTHESIS

Estimates of the rates of photosynthetic energy conversion on regional and global scales are required for predicting the energy available to food chains and for determining the role of algae in geochemical cycles.

As all organisms are ultimately dependent on energy input via photosynthesis, and limitations to global carbon dioxide assimilation may constrain the potential productivity of higher trophic levels. Riley (1944) provided the first estimate of global oceanic primary productivity of 860±560 mg $C.m^{-2}.d^{-1}$.

The large standard deviation associated with this estimate arose from uncertainty in extrapolating a small number of observations from a limited range of open and coastal ocean regions to the entire ocean.

Despite an additional 45 years of research involving the widespread incorporation of ^{14}Cassimiation measurements into biological oceanogra-phic sampling programs, there is continuing uncertainty about the magnitude of oceanic primary productivity.

Shipboard observers cannot adequately sample the ocean at all spatial and temporal scales necessary to adequately resolve variations in phytoplankton biomass and productivity. In contrast, satellite remote sensing offers the potential to provide a detailed assessment of phytoplankton spatial and temporal variations.

The remotely sensed signal is used to infer chlorophyll a concentration from measurements of light reflected from near surface waters. At present, remote sensors do not provide a direct measure of primary protivity; this must be inferred from the relationship between nary productivity and chlorophyll a concentration.

It has long been a challenge to estimate phytoplankton productivity from chlorophyll a concentration, because pigment concentration can be sampled much more rapidly than photosynthesis.

Introduction of in vivo fluorometry to continuously monitor chlorophyll concentration together with radiometric sensors for estimating chlorophyll a from aircraft or satellites and moored fluorometers to continuously measure chlorophyll a at fixed positions in continental shelf waters have greatly increased the spatial and temporal resolution with which phytoplankton abundance can be determined.

Unfortunately, there has not been a corresponding increase in the ability to measure phytoplankton photosynthesis, even though deployment of high-resolution O_2 sensors, pump and probe fluorometers and sensors to measure passive chlorophyll fluorescence may allow increases in the temporal and spatial coverage of phytoplankton primary production.

In lieu of more widespread application of these techniques, investigators have attempted to estimate primary production from chlorophyll a concentration and a range of environmental variables, using empirical and analytical algorithms.

This chapter considers (1) the methods for remote sensing of the chlorophyll a concentration in surface waters and (2) the ways in which chlorophyll a distributions can be used to estimate primary production.

Remote sensing of phytoplankton pigment concentration can be achieved by (1) passive measurements of water colour (2) passive measurement of solar-induced chlorophyll fluorescence and (3) active measurement of laserinduced fluorescence. Water colour is quantified by measuring the radiance upwelling from the surface waters using shipboard, aircraft, or satellite radiometers.

Satellite instruments currently employ radiometers with broad spectral bands (60-100 nm) in the visible region, limiting measurements to a single pigment (chlorophyll a) in clear waters, with a low diversity of optically active components.

However, in clear ocean waters, the ocean colour algorithms for remote sensing of chlorophyll a yield relatively, good precision over a wide range of chlorophyll a concentrations without the need for extensive, independent ground truth observations.

Much greater spectral resolution is possible with ship and aircraft borne radiometers with the potential for evaluating the concentrations of several major pigments even in turbid coastal waters with a large diversity of optically active components.

However, accurate remote sensing of the phytoplankton concentr-ation in a complex mixture first requires more detailed knowledge of the optical properties of phytoplankton as well as measurements of the other components of these assemblages, such as particulate material and coloured substances.

This information becomes more directly applicable to satellite remote sensing during the 1990s with the development and development of satellites that will carry moderate- and high-resolution spectrometers. Passive remote sensing of in vivo chlorophyll a fluorescence relies on high spectral resolution measurements of upwelling radiance at wavelengths around 680 nm.

The technique is based on the same principals as in vivo fluorometry but differs from the in vivo technique in two important respects. First, passive remote sensing of chlorophyll a fluorescence relies on a natural, variable light source (the sun) instead of an artificial source with a known spectral quality and irradiance.

Second, remote sensing of chlorophyll a fluorescence samples the upwelling irradiance that leaves the water surface rather than a known small volume.

The remotely sensed fluorescence emission is, however, superimposed on a backscatter signal of unknown magnitude which can complicate the interpretation of the fluorescence signal.

In addition, the approximately order-of-magnitude variability of in situ fluorescence yield. Active remote sensing of surface phytopla-nkton abundance relies on the use of lasers pulsed at short intervals to excite in vivo chlorophyll a fluorescence and a pbotomultiplier to measure the induced red (680 nm) fluorescence.

The primary fluorosc-ensor in use today is the Airborne Oceanographic Light Detection and Ranging Detector (AOL) developed at the NASA Goddard Wallops Island Flight Station.

In this system the excitation wavelength is 532 nm and the return signal to an airborne spectrometer includes contributions from back scattering at the excitation wavelength, Raman scattering by water, and fluorescenbe by chlorophyll a and phycoerythrin.

Laser systems for measuring pigment concentrations are limited to low-flying aircraft largely because of the power requirements for operating the laser, atmospheric attenuation of the signal, and bulky instrumentation.

The AOL allows simultaneous measurement of active laser-induced chlorophyll fluorescence, passive solar-induced chlorop-hyll fluorescence, and passive ocean colour and can be used to obtain simultaneous estimates of chlorophyll concentrations from passive and active techniques.

Good correlations between laser-induced chlorophyll *a* fluorescence and ground-truthed chlorophyll *a* concentrations suggest that variations in fluorescence yield are not significant during the approximately 1-2-hr flight time typically employed in experiments using the AOL.

Table 10.1: Summary of terms used in describing the relations between photosynthesis and phytoplankton concentration.

Symbol	Definition	Typical Units
C_a	Surface chlorophyll a concentration	g chla.m^{-3}
C_k	Mean chlorophyll a concentration within the top optical depth of the water column	g chla.m^{-8}
C_i	Integrated chlorophyll a content of the cuphotic **zone**	g chla.m^{-8}
E_o	Incident scalar irradiance	mol photons.$m^{-2}d^{-1}$
I_k	Light saturation parameter	mol photons.$m^{-2}d^{-1}$
K	Vertical attenuation coefficient (log, units)	m^{-1}
P_m^{chl}	Chlorophyll a-specific light-saturated photosynthesis rate	g C.g^{-1} chla.d^{-1}
D	Depth of the euphotic zone defined as the depth at which irradiance equals 1% of surface value	m^{-1}
π	Integrated euphotic zone primary productivity	g C.$m^{-1}A^{-1}$.
π_{chl}	Ratio of integrated primary productivity to integrated chlorophyll a ($\pi_{chl} = \pi/C_i$)	g C.g^{-1} chla.m^{-1}
ψ	Light utilization efficiency defined as π_{chl}/E_0	g C.mol^{-1} photons. $m^{-2}g^{-}$lchla

Table Contd.

Symbol	Definition	Typical Units
α_{chl}	Chlorophyll a-specific light absorption coefficient	$m^2.g^{-1}$.chla
a_{chl}	Chlorophyll a-specific initial slope of the photosynthesis light curve	g $C.mol^{-1}$ photons. m^2g^{-1} chla
η	Realized photon yield for integral photosynthesis	g $C.mol^{-1}$ photons
ψ_m	Maximum photon yield of photosynthesis	g $C.mol^{-1}$ photons

ESTIMATING SURFACE WATER CHLOROPHYLL *a*

Most phytoplankton abundance measurements to date have relied on ocean colour measurements using the now defunct Coastal Zone Colour Scanner (CZCS) on the Nimbus 7 satellite.

Estimating chlorophyll a from ocean colour measurements rests on the observation that dissolved or suspended, materials change the reflectance of water through the absorption and scattering of light.

Radiative transfer theory serves as the basis for examining the relations among reflectance, absorption, and scattering. A model developed by Gordon *et. al.* (1975) leads to the following equation relating subsurface reflectance to the absorption and back-scattering coefficients:

$$R_s(\lambda) = 0.33b_b(\lambda)/\left[a(\lambda) + b_b(\lambda)\right] \tag{1}$$

Where $R_s(\lambda)$ is the subsurface reflectance (dimensionless), a (λ) is the absorption coefficient (m^{-1}) and $b_b(\lambda)$ is the back scatter coefficient (m^{-1}). The absorption and back scatter coefficients with units of inverse length (i.e., m^{-1}) can in turn be expressed in terms of the concentrations and specific absorption or scattering coefficients of optically active material.

It is commonly assumed for open ocean waters that most of the back scattering is due to water itself and most of the variable absorption is due to phytoplankton pigments together with substances that covary with phytoplankton abundance, leading to the approximation.

$$R_s(\lambda) = 0.33b_{bw}(\lambda)/\left[a^*(\lambda)C + a_w(\lambda) + b_b(\lambda)\right] \tag{2}$$

where $a^*(\lambda)$ is the typical chlorophyll a-specific absorption coefficient for phytoplankton ($m^2.g^{-1}$ chla) and C is the chlorophyll a concentration ($g.m^{-3}$). More complicated expressions, including contributions of dissolved and suspended inorganic matter or dissolved organic substances, such as humic and fulvic acids, are required for near-shore waters and lakes. Changes in the concentration of chlorophyll a will markedly affect reflectance in those spectral regions in which phytoplankton absorb light most strongly (i.e., in the blue and red).

Algorithms for determining chlorophyll a concentration from CZCS images depend on an empirical relationship between the ratio of blue to yellow light upwelled through the ocean surface and chlorophyll a concentration.

This relationship depends on the observation that the "typical phytoplankton absorption spectrum has peaks centered in the blue (λ=440 nm) and red (λ=670 nm) regions but does not absorb strongly in the yellow (λ=550 nm). The algorithm has the form.

$$\log [C] = a + b \log [R(443)/R(550)] \tag{3}$$

where R(λ) is the reflectance centered at wavelength A and a and b are fitted coefficients obtained from a comparison of surface reflecta-nce derived from satellite measurements corrected for atmosp-heric effects and sea surface chlorophyll a concentrations determined from ship observations.

The approach (Eq. 3) is quasiempiric, resting on the observation that high absorption of blue light by phytoplankton reduces the reflectance in this spectral region relative to wavelengths in the yellow where pigment absorption is minimal.

The ratio of reflectances in the green (λ=520 nm) yellow (λ =550 nm) spectral bands of the CZCS have also een used to replace R(443)/R(550) in Eq. 3 with equally Dod precision. Estimates of remotely sensed chlorophyll a re within ±40% of surface observations over a range of pproximately 0.1-50 μg chla.dm^{-3}.

Limits on the precision re due to errors in making atmospheric corrections, variability in phytoplankton optical properties among diverse phytolankton assemblages, and variability in the optical properties if seawater due to the nonuniform distribution of dissolved organic matter and

10.2: Empirical relations between primary production and chloropnyll concentration in takes and selected marine environments.

Location	*Dependent Variable*	*Independent Variable*	*Slope*	*Intercept*	R^2
North Western Ontario Experimental Lakes District (2-50 mg $chla.m^{-2}$)	g $C\text{-}m^{-3}.Y^{-1}$	g $chla.m^{-3}$	1900	-0.5	—
North Western Ontaria Experimental Lakes District (1-6 mg chla.m)	g $C.m^{-3}.Y^{-1}$	g $chla.m^{-3}$	166	0.53	0.76
North American Lakes	g $C.m^{-2}.d^{-1}$	g $chla.m^{-3}$	22.9	-0.0426	0.81
Southern California Bight	g $C.m^{-2}.d^{-1}$	g chla.m	0.35	—	0.33
California Current	g $C.m^{-2}.h^{-1}$	g $chla\text{-}m^{-3}$	2.7	—	0.83
North Pacific Subtropical Gyre	g $C.m^{-2}.h^{-1}$	g $chla.m^{-2}$	2.3	—	0.50
MERL Microcosms	g $C.m^{-2}.h^{-1}$	g $chla.m^{-3}$	3.4(0.2)	0.478	0.51
MERL Microcosms	g $C.m^{-2}.d^{-1}$	g $chla.m^{-3}$	34.2(2.4)	0.437	0.47
MBRL Microcosm (Summer)[6]	g $C.m^{-3}.d^{-1}$	g $claa.m^{-3}$	125	0.25	0.76
MERL Microcosm (Nonsummer)	g $C.m^{-3}.d^{-1}$	g $chla.m^{-3}$	53	0.12	0.36

suspended sediments.

The reflectance ratio algorithms were developed for use in optically clear ocean waters in which chlorophyll and substances that covary with chlorophyll a are the major sources of optical variability.

Use of algorithms based on due to green reflectance ratios are unlikely to resolve phytolankton abundance in estuarine waters because of light absorption in the blue and green spectral regions by iron oxides and humic-acid-like material, which can be important s estuarine and fresh-waters.

To overcome this problem, the ratio of reflectances in the red to near infrared, where absorption by dissolved materials is minimal, can be employed. The principal is the same as that employed by Gordon et. al. (1983) for clear open ocean water measurements.

High phytoplankton absorption in the red reduces reflectance at this wavelength relative to a region of low pigment absorption in the near infrared. This approach has been used by Stumpf and Tyler (1988) to measure chlorophyll a concentrations in excess of 5 μg chla.dm^{-3} in turbid estuarine waters with a precision of ±60% or *5 μg* chla.dm^{-3}, whichever is the greater.

Although satellite remote sensing provides a means of greatly increasing spatial coverage, the technique is subject to a number of limitations including (1) restricted temporal coverage due to cloud cover, (2) inaccuracies in processing algorithms for making atmospheric corrections, particularly at large zenith angles Pan *et al.*, (3) poor vertical resolution that is limited to the upper 20°/$_0$ of the euphotic zone which includes a small and variable (1% to 8%) portion of chlorophyll a in ocean waters.

In addition, the depth interval that is included in a remotely sensed measurement will vary with wavelength (λ), being inversely proportional to the attenuation coefficient K(λ). For example, as the chlorobhyll concentration rises from 0.01 to 10 $mg.m^{-3}$, the depth zone that accounts for 90% of the upwelling irradiance decreases from 58 to 2 m at 443 nm and decreases from 15 to 4 m at 550 nm, while remaining virtually constant at 2 m for 670 nm light.

Thus, passive and active remote sensing of chlorophyll a fluorescence is limited to the very shallow depths near the surface, whereas observations of ocean colour depend on light that penetrates deeper into the water column.

Other variables, in addition to chlorophyll a concentration, that are important in determining photosynthesis rates, and that can be measured by aircraft and/or satellite sensors include temperature and downwelling irradiance at the earth's surface and the depth of the surface ocean mixed layer.

These measurements will not be discussed further, but the importance of including these variables in algorithms for the remote sensing of phytoplankton photosynthesis will become apparent in the remainder of this chapter.

Empirical Relationships Between Primary Production and Chlorophyll *a*

As a first approximation, primary productivity is expected to be proportional to plant biomass, all other factors being equal.

Both limnologists and oceanographers have observed linear relations between primary production and chlorophyll a concentration for data expressed on either a unit volume or unit area basis, with biomass accounting for 50% to 75% of the variance in primary production.

For remote sensing applications, it is desirable to relate integral primary production (with units of g $C.m^{-2}.d^{-1}$ and designated π) to near surface chlorophyll a concentrations (with units of mg. chl*a*.m^{-1}, and designated C_s).

Despite the linear relation that is sometimes observed between π and C_s, theoretical analyses suggest that the relationship between integral primary production and phytoplankton abundance should be nonlinear largely

Table 10.3: Empirical relations between integral primary productivity and surface chlorophyll a concentration.

Empiric relationship	*Primary productivity ($g\ C.m^{-4}.d^{-1}$)*	*Surface chlorophyll concentration ($mg\ chla\text{-}m^{-3}$)*	*Correlation coefficient*
$\pi = 1.53\ C_s^{0.457}$	0.06-11	0.04-28	0.539
$\pi = 1.00\ C_s^{0.500}$	0.10-10	0.05-100	—
$\pi = 1.88\ C_s^{0.579}$	0.3-2.3	0.05-1.4	0.759

because of the influence of other light-absorbing substances.

In fact, a logarithmic relation is often observed between areal primary production and surface phytoplankton abundance

$$\log_e(n)=\log,\ (a) \pm b \log_e (C_s) \quad (4)$$

or

$$\pi = aC_s^{\,b} \quad (5)$$

where *a* and *b* are empirically derived coefficients. Observations for various ocean regions are characterized by *b*=0.4—0.6. In contrast, Brylinsky found that annual phytoplankton production scaled as mean chlorophyll a concentration raised to the power 1.36 in lakes.

Whether this difference is due to the wide variation in the temporal scales over which data were averaged (one day for the oceanic data versus a growing season for the lake data), or because of a bias introduced by other uncontrolled variables, or to a fundamental difference in the relation between π and C_s in freshwater and marine systems remains to be evaluated.

Variations in primary production that cannot be accounted for by differences in surface biomass are presumably due to differences in other factors such as temperature, irradiance, nutrient availability, optical properties of the waterbody, vertical distribution and species composition of

Table 10.4: Vaviations in the slope (ψ) of the relationship between the areal productivity index (π_{chl}) and incident irradiance (E) abstracted from the summaries of Platt (1987) and Platt *et al.* (1988) with additional sources as indicated.

Location	*ψ g C.E^{-1} m^2.g^{-1} chla*	*Correlation coefficient*
New York Bight	0.43	0.86
Subtropical N. Atlantic	0.44	—
Baffin Bay	0.33	—
Jones Sound, Canadian Arctic	0.36	—
Bedford Basin, Canada	0.45	0.75
English Channel	0.43	—
Southern Ocean	0.37	0.29
Long Idand Sound	0.38	0.49
Petpeswick Inlet, Nova Scotia	0.43	0.84
Grand Banks of Newfoundland	0.30	0.02
Midsubartic Pacific	0.66	—
Southeastern United States	1.5	0.93
Chesapeake and Delaware Bays	0.47	—
Northeastern United States	0.52	—

the phytoplankton. Fee found that annual values of π/C_s for lakes in North-Western Ontario varied with the dominant phytoplankton taxta.

This ratio of π/C_s was greatest in lakes dominated by members of the Chlorophyceae, intermediate in akes dominated by members of the Chrysophyceae, and lowest π lakes dominated by cyanobacteria.

Two environmental Factors that are amenable to remote sensing and would be expected to influence the relationship between primary production and chlorophyll a concentration are irradiance and temperature.

Table 10.5: Dependence of integral primary productivity (π) on chlorophyll concentration (C_s), incident irradiance (E_0), and verti-cal attentuation coefficient (K).

Location	*Slope*	*Correlation Coefficient*
San Francisco Bay		
North Bay (1980)	0.15±0.026	0.72
South Bay (1980)	0.19±0.026	0.88
South Bay (1982)	0.22±0.034	0.78
idson River Plume	0.25±0.021	0.94
Puget Sound		
1966	0.16±0.026	0.60
1967	0.15±0.026	0.79
Lgansett Bay and MERL		
icrocosms	0.15±0.004	0.82

To examine the effects of these and other variables on the rate of phytoplankton photosynthesis, it is desirable to define an areal produc-tivity index (p_{chl}), as the ratio of integrated euphotic zone primary production (p) to integrated euphotic zone chlorophyll a content (C_l):

$$\pi^{chl} = \pi/C_l \qquad (6)$$

where $\pi = \int_0^D P(z)dz$ and $C_l = \int_0^D C(z)dz$, D is the depth of the eupho-tic zone, P(z) is the rate of primary production at depth z, and C(z) is the chlorophyll a concentration at depth z. A linear relation between the areal productivity index (π^{chl}) and incident irradiance (E_0) has been observed by several investigators. Platt (1986) suggested that the slope of this relation, designated (ψ), was related to the chlorophyll **a**-specific absorption coefficient a^*, the realized photon yield of photosynthesis in situ (η), the euphotic zone depth (D), and the vertical attenuation coefficient (K) for scalar irradiance as follows:

$$\pi = \pi^{chl}C_l = C_l\ \psi E_0 = C_l a^*\ \eta E_0\ DK \qquad (7)$$

From a review of published data, Platt and Platt concluded that ψ varied approximately by a factor of two and, based on theoretical grounds, argued for the relative stability of ψ. In contrast to Platt's (1986) conclusions, Campbell and O'Reilly (1988) found that ψ varied from 0.1 to 10, with a mean value approximately three times higher than obtained from Platt's summary.

Observations of Yoder for the Southeastern United States continental shelfalso yielded a value for ψ, which was about three times greater than the typical values given by Platt (1986) suggesting some regional variations. Variability in ψ may arise from a number of sources, including (1) variations in a,* (2) variations in η due to variations in the vertical distribution of phytoplankton abundance and in the relationship between phytoplankton biomass and vertical light attenuation, and (3) variations in η that arise from variations in the parameters of the Pl curve P_m^{chl} and a^{chl}.

It is necessary to consider the full equation for determining π from the depth-dependence of photosynthesis to examine the sources of variability in ψ. Recent theoretical treatments of this problem which explicitly consider the angular and spectral distributions of the underwater light fields, together with the vertical distribution of phytoplankton abundance, are beyond the scope of this review.

One variable that is particularly important in determining is the attenuation coefficient (K). Noting that the euphotic ne depth (D) and attenuation coefficient (K) are related by equality DK=log, (0.01) = 4.61 (i.e., K=D/4.61) allows equation 7 to be rewritten as

$$\psi = a^8\eta\ 4.61/K^2 \qquad (8)$$

Because of the K^2 dependence of ψ, explicit consideration of the vertical attenuation coefficient may improve models of integral primary production (π). Explicit consideration of the attenuation coefficient may be particularly important in estuaries where K can vary greatly because of changes in phytoplankton abundance, dissolved organic matter, and suspended sediments.

In fact, Cole and Cloern showed that π scaled with C_cE_0/K in five United States estuaries. A linear dependence of π on $C_s sE_0$/K has also been demonstrated in Delaware Bay and Narragansell Bay. Significantly, Pennock and Sharp found that the slope was three times greater in the summer than during the nonsummer months.

They attributed this difference to a change in species composition of he phytoplankton from predominantly microflagellates in summer to diatoms for the rest of the year.

Mechanistic Descriptions of the Relationship between Primary Production and Chlorophyll a

For remote sensing application, is is desirable to relate rv to the near-surface chlorophyll *a* concentration (C_s), which is easily measurable, rather than to the integral chlorophyll a concentration (C_l), which is not.

Strictly, the chlorophyll a concentration seen by an airborne or satellite sensor corresponds to a weighted average value of chlorophyll a within the first attenuation depth (equal to 1/4.6=0.22 times the euphotic zone depth) and designated C_k. For most practical applications, it is reasonable to assume that C_s=C_k.

Note that under the assumption of a uniform vertical chlorophyll a distribution $C_k = C_s = C_l/D = C_l/4.6K$. Tailing (1957 *a, b)* provided the original formulation for the dependence of π on chlorophyll a concentration, incident irradiance, vertical attenuation of scalar irradiance (K) and the PI curve parameters P_m^{chl} and I_h:

$$C_s P_m^{chl} \log_e \; 2E_0 / I_k \; K \tag{9}$$

This formulation has been verified in a range of freshwater environments, and a similar equation has been developed by Bannister. Note the similarity of Tailing's model (Eq. 8) to a recent treatment of the same problem by Platt:

$$\pi = C_s P_m^{chl} \log_e \left[E/I_k + \sqrt{1 + (E/I_k)^2} \right] / K \qquad (10)$$

The difference between the equations of Tailing and Platt arise from different assumptions about the shape of the P1 curve.

It can be easily demonstrated that Platt's model and Tailing's model converge for large values of E_0/I_k. The depth of the euphotic zone is not explicit in equations relating π to C_s and the surface irradiance does not enter as a linear multiplicative terms in Eqs. 9 and 10, but rather appears within the logarithmic term at the extreme right-hand side of these equations.

How can the different formulations of the dependence of π on E_0 given in Eqs. 9 and 10 be reconciled with the linear dependence implied in Eq. 7? Noting that $P_m^{chl} = \alpha^{chl} I_k = \phi_m a^* I_k$, and multiplying Eq. 9 by E/E(=unity) leads to

$$\pi \setminus \left[C_s a^* / K \right] \left[\phi_m I_k \log_e (2E_0 / I_k) \right] E_0 \qquad (11)$$

The terms within the first set of square brackets give the proportion of incident irradiance absorbed by phytopla-nkton, whereas the terms within the second set of square brackets give a measure of the efficiency with which absorbed light is used for photosynthetic carbon fixation, which is equivalent to h in Eq. 7.

The last term on the right-hand side of Eq. 10 is the incident irradiance (E_0). Thus, a logarithmic dependence on E_0 is implicit in Eq. 7. Several recent theoretical models treat phytoplankton growth rate as a function of irradiance, photon yield, and the absorption coefficient.

Models of primary production that are conceptually adentical to Eq. 11 can be derived from these models of phytoplankton growth. Estimates of primary production from chlorophyll *a* and incident irra-diance are dependent on a number of environmental and physiological factors.

The environmental factors involve the partitioning of absorbed photons between phytoplankton and other substances and can be para-meterised as the ratio of light absorbed by phytoplankton to total light attenuation. This has two components, the total pigment content within the photic zone and the vertical distribution of pigments. The physiological factors involved include genotypic and phenotypic modifications of the photosynthesis-light response curve and can be parameterized by $P_m^{chl}, \alpha^{chl} = a^* \phi_m$, and $I_k = P_m^{chl} / \alpha^{chl}$. The ability to estimate primary production from chlorophyll a will ultimately be limited by the variability of these parameters.

Chapter 11

GENETIC CONTROL OF PHOTOSYNTHESIS

The chloroplast, a miniature green laboratory of a plant cell, possesses a number of surprising properties. A unique one is its capacity to convert light energy into chemical energy to accomplish the most important biological process of primary solar energy storage on the earth. Photophysical, photochemical, and biochemical aspects of photosynthesis have been elucidated well enough in several reviews.

At present, genetic aspects of photosynthesis attract the attention of many scientists-plant physiologists and biochemists, molecular biologists and biophysicists, geneticists and plant breeders.

This interest is natural because the problem is very important and complex and its solution 'requires a combined physiological and genetic approach. The subject involves two basic biological processes:

(a) expression of genetic information, and

(b) regulation of photosynthesis.

Investigation of the genetic nature of photosynthesis will' enable us to understand the molecular mechanisms of selforganization and autoreproduction of chloroplasts, their inheritance and variability, the processes of plastid biogenesis, and the formation of its functional activity.

On the other hand, the study of genetic determination of chloroplast structure and function will make it possible to enrich breeding search with new methods and tests and to improve photosynthetic plant productivity.

Regulation of photosynthetic efficiency through inheritance is an important means of enhancing crop yield.

GENETICS OF PHOTOSYNTHESIS

The genetic material of eukaryotic organisms is localized not only in the nucleus, which is the main store of hereditary information, but it is dispersed throughout the cell in subcellular structures: mitochondria, kinetosomes, chloroplasts.

The plant genotype as a complex of all cell genetic factors is subdivided into chromosomal-nuclear genome-and extrachromosomal plasmone, comprising the cytoplasmic determinants, mitochondria and chloroplasts.

Interaction of nuclear and cytoplasmic genetic systems with one another and with the environment determines both the course and the dynamics of cell differentiation, plant growth, and development. Interaction of plant cell genetic factors has a very complex but rigid character.

The nucleus as an integrating center of genetic information is responsible for the strategy of formation of constant organism-specific properties. Cytoplasmic genes and organelles determine the cell life tactics, providing its greater flexibility and adaptation to environmental conditions. Cell organelles are closely interrelated in their development and functional activity.

Their cooperative interaction provides the integration of inform-ation, energy, and substance flow in cell activity. A living cell is not a sum of autonomous or semiautonomous organelles, but a unique and highly organized dynamic system attaining new properties differing from those of single organoids due to "concert" interaction of subcellular structures.

Regulation of photosynthesis requires close cooperation of the discrete genetic systems of a plant cell. The chloroplast genome is not large enough to provide all the diverse reactions of this complex process, so a considerable part of the genetic information necessary for chloroplast development and activity is localized in the nucleus.

In order to integrate photosynthetic activity in cell metabolism, it is possible that in the course of evolution chloroplasts acquired a double genetic subordination to the nuclear genome and to their own semiautonomous one.

Hereditary properties of chloroplasts were discovered long ago, whereas the study of the genetic nature of photosynthesis as a whole began only recently. We would say that genetics of photosynthesis is a new trend in plant physiological genetics.

It can be defined as an interaction between the balanced plant cell genomes which control self-organization and reproduction of chloroplasts, their hereditary continuity, and variability, carbon pathways, and photosynthetic potential.

History

Non-Mendelian plastid inheritance was discovered by Correns in spontaneous variegated mutants of *Mirabilis jalapa*. Crossing normal and variegated forms, he showed that, independently of the pollen type, the pigmentation of progeny is determined exclusively by the egg cell.

Proceeding from this fact, Correns postulated the principle of maternal or cytoplasmic inheritance which he called *Status albamaculatus*. Baur made an important contribution to the understanding of the nature of cytoplasmic inheritance and attempted to give it a scientific explanation.

He showed that *in Pelargonium zonale* both parents contributed to plastid inheritance. This principle was called a biparental cytoplasmic inheritance, *Status Paraalbomaculatus*. Baur was the first to assume that chloroplasts possess their own hereditary apparatus responsible for their inheritance and genetic continuity.

It is plastid genome mutation that causes the appearance of variegated plants. The intensive study of the mechanism of cytoplasmic inheritance is connected with the development of ideas and methods of molecular biology and molecular genetics.

At the beginning of the 1960s a specific DNA was found in chloroplasts. Its molecule differed significantly from that of nuclear DNA in size, nucleotide content, and other physicochemical properties.

At the same time, plastid ribosomes of the prokaryotic type were found which differed from the cytoplasmic ones in their sedimentation properties. These findings spurred the rapid development of investi-gations into genetics of chloroplasts and their transcription translation system (TTS).

Using gradient ultracentrifugation techniques in the presence of acridine dyes, as well as electron microscopy, autoradiography, and molecular hybridization, many advances have been made in the study of the structure and information capacity of the chloroplast, the mechanis-ms, of its self-replication and transcription. It has been established that chloroplast DNA is associated with the lamellar system and has different configurations: linear, circular, loop shaped, and superhelical.

Plastid genome replication has a semiconservative character. Optical registration of DNA renaturation made possible. determination of the chloroplast genome size in different plants.

An organelle DNA ranges from 1 to 2×10^8 daltons, which corresponds to 10^6 pairs of nucleotides. The DNA content in one chloroplast is 0.1 to 1.2×14^{-14}g, depending on, plant species.

These data make it possible to calculate the size of the chloroplast genome. The number of DNA copies in an individual chloroplast is 20 to 60. Chloroplasts contain all the components of the protein synthesizing system (PSS): ribosomes, RNA-polymerase, mRNA, tRNA, aminoacyl-tRNA synthetases, and other translation factors.

Etioplasts and chloroplasts isolated from green: leaves

are able to synthesize nucleic acids and structural and functional proteins. These data served as the basis for development of the concept of genetic and biochemical autonomy of chloroplasts.

An opinion was even expressed that chloroplasts have an independent genetic apparatus and resemble "a cell within a: cell." This was an additional argument in favour of the symbiogenetic hypothesis of its origin.

Division of chloroplasts in vitro found by Ridley and Leech speaks in favour of their genetic and biochemical autonomy and confirms the possibility of obtaining self-reproducing cultures of isolate& chloroplasts. However, despite numerous attempts, nobody has yet succeeded in obtaining a self-reproducing and functionally active chloroplast culture.

In experiments by Wellburn and+ Wellburn with etioplasts isolated *from* oats, disorganization of outer and inner membranes was observed even after 2 hr of illumination, and after 9 hr the internal structures were completely destroyed and eliminated.

Studying biogenesis of isolated maize etioplasts, Leech came to the conclusion that, chloroplast development is the result of collaboration of the whole cell, and "*longliving*" cultures of etioplasts and proplastids can be obtained by addition of a great number of cofactors and even other organelles to the suspension.

Differentiation of plastids depends on interaction of both chloroplast and nuclear genome. Indeed, possessing unique genetic information and TTS, the chloroplast is not an autonomous organelle, "a cell within a cell," because its genetic and biochemical function is semiautonomous.

The size of the plastid genome is not sufficient to code for the formation of the great amount of structural and functional proteins which are necessary for proliferation of membrane systems and for carrying out diverse light and dark reactions of photosynthesis.

Numerous available experimental data testify to the

essential role of the nucleus in chloroplast biogenesis. Using different physiological and chemical agents, we, induced a wide spectrum of higher plant mutations blocking different stages of biosynthesis of chlorophyll, components of the photosynthetic electron transport chain (ETC), and Calvin cycle enzymes.

Sixty nonallelic genes affecting biogenesis of plastid pigments were found in the model object *Arabidopsis thaliana* Heynh. Experimental mutagenesis combined with investigations using specific inhibitors of TTS enabled us to dissect the genetic regulation of synthesis of lamellar proteins, plastid enzymes, pigments, and formation of chloroplast photosystems.

With investigations as a basis, we have suggested a conception nuclear-plastid cooperative interaction in the development of chloroplast structure and function.

Structure and Organisation of Genes for Proteins of the Photosynthetic Membranes

As shown in Table elsewhere in this chapter, genes for the photosynthetic apparatus proteins are located both in the chloroplast and nuclear genomes.

The first indication of the distribution of these genes in two compartments came from early experiments on hybridization with various genotypes and mutants which indicated that whereas with respect to certain characters inheritance followed the Mendelian pattern in respect of others it did, not.

In the early seventies, experiments began employing compartment-specific inhibitors of protein synthesis. These experiments were followed by in vitro protein synthesis from mRNA isolated from cells-by separating poly A mRNA from other RNAs, one could further confirm whether the nucleus or the chloroplast DNA coded for a particular product.

In the late seventies, chloroplast genomes (cpDNAs) were characte-rised from several plants, e.g., spinach and maize. Although some variations do exist, most cpDNAs have turned out to be circular molecules of 120-180 kbp

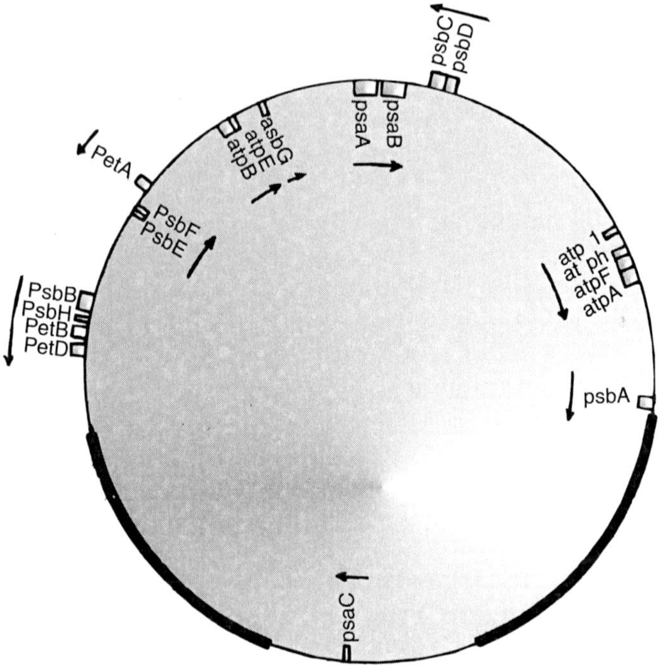

Figure 11.1: Lolation of genes, encoding photosynthetic membrane proteins on a typical plastid chromosome, e.g., from spinach or tobacco. Thick regions of the circle represent inverted repeats.

and containing a pair of 10-25 kbp inverted repeats, as illustrated in Figure elsewhere in this chapter which divide the remaining cpDNA into one large and one small single copy region.

Finally, with pure cpDNA available from several plants as also various restriction endonucleases and recombinant DNA technology,' the stage was set for detailed -characterisation of the chloroplast genome and for localisation of the genes encoded by the plastome on cloned cpDNA fragmerits.

Genes were assigned to various proteins by using the immunolo-gical approach, following one of the two preparative strategies for obtaining the proteins:

(*i*) the DNA fragments were cloned and transcription

coupled with translation employing cell-free extracts of *E. coli* itself,

(*ii*) cpDNA fragments were used to hybrid select specific mRNAs which were then translated. *In vitro* using the reticulocyte system. Many cloned -cpDNA fragments have now been sequenced and open reading frames (ORFs) for various polypeptides identified.

The deduced sequences have also been compared to partially or completely sequenced polypeptides. In 1966, the complete nucleotide sequences of cpDNAs from a higher plant, tobacco (*Nieotlana tabacum*,) and a liverwort *(Marchantia polymor-pha)* were reported.

Several ORFs have already been identified and— efforts are being made to find products for those ORFs whose function is not yet known.

Rapid progress has similarly been made in respect of genes residing in the nucleus. In the early eighties, cDNA libraries from a number of plants were made and clones encoding chlorophyll a/b binding polypeptides of PSII were identified.

The cDNA clones were then used to isolate genomic clones. More recently, a cDNA library of spinach has been made in expression vectors and clones, specific to several proteins of the photosynthetic membranes, have been isolated by using antisera.

The cDNA clones have been employed to isolate and characterise genomic clones. Interestingly, all these genes encode precursor polypeptides with amino-terminal transit peptides which help to target these polypetides into the chloroplast and which are removed during the transport across the chloroplast or thylakoid membranes.

Some details about the organisation and characteristics of the genes encoding polypeptides of various supramolecular complexes and other associated proteins of the photosynthetic membranes are given in Table elsewhere in this chapter. A general summary follow.

Photosystem II

Photosystem II of the Photosynthetic apparatus of higher plants is. made up of three smaller complexes, *viz.* the core complex, the light harvesting complex, and the water-splitting or oxygen evolving complex.

CORE COMPLEX

The core complex is made up of a dozen polypeptides. Genes for eight of these have been localised in the large single copy region of the chloropl$_a$st genome. Recently, Nanba and Satoh have made preparations showing P680 reaction centre activity containing three Polypeptides, namely, D1, D2 and cyt b559. Dl and D2 proteins show homology and conservation of residues with those of bacterial reaction centre proteins and might be responsible for binding P680, QA, QB, pheophytin and other electron transfer intermediates such as Z.

Dl, the herbicide-binding polypeptide, is encoded by the gene psbA and is one of the first to be localised on chloroplast genome. The gene encodes a polypeptide of 353 amino acids; but the latter is known to get post.translationally modified possibly by Tremoval of a stretch of 12-16 amino acids at the carboxyt anal end.

Sequencing of this gene from atrazine herbicide-herbicide-resistant plant species has shown a change from A to Gresulting in replacement of the amino acid serine by glycine at position 264.

The gene psbD encodes the poly peptide, D2, of 353 amino acids and, like D1, it is highly hydrophobic with several membrane traversing spans. As is well known, a cytochrome, cyt b559, is associatedd with PS II. This is now known to be made up of two polypeptides of 9 and 4 kDa encoded by genes psbE and psbF.

That cytochrome b559 is a product of psbE and psbF genes was predicted after sequencing a fragment containing the gene for psbE which revealed the presence of an ORF for psbF. Later research proved that this was indeed true.

Although the genes for psbE and psbF are highly conserved in *spinach*, *tobacco*, *Oenothera*, and *wheat*, the exact role of cyt b559 remains an enigma. Two genes, psbB and psbC, encode for 508 and 473 amino acid long polypeptides, commonly known as the 51 and 44 kDa polypeptides, which bind chlorophyll a and are possibly part of the antenna pigment system involved in transferring the light energy to P680.

Both polypeptides show homology and are predicted to have several spans traversing the membrane. The gene psbC at its 5'-end overlaps the 3'-end of another gene, psbD, by 50 bp. The genes, psbG and psbH, for two other proteins associated with PSII have also been identified and characterised recently.

These two genes encode polypeptides of 248 and 73 amino acid residues, respectively. The product of psbH is a phosphorylated protein.

LIGHT HARVESTING COMPLEX

At least four polypeptides of the light-harvesting complex of photosystem II are encoded in the nuclear genome by a. family of 3.20 cab genes which can be divided into sub-families on the basis of sequence homology. Furthermore, these genes have also been localised on individual chromosomes.

In pea, chromosome two contains a locus for the cab genes whereas in tomato the genes are distributed on at least 5 chromosomes at 5 different loci : cab-1 (chromosome 2), cab-2 (chromosome 8), cab-3 (chromosome 3), cab-4 (chromosome 7) and cab-5 (chromosome 12).

The locus cab-1 contains four genes, arranged in tandem, whereas locus cab-3 contains three genes and a truncated gene. The nucleotide sequences of these genes show an open reading frame with a coding capacity of 264-269 amino acids for the precursor proteins.

Of these, the first 33-36 amino acids represent the transit peptides which help in intracellular and possibly also intraorganellar targeting of the mature proteins and which get cleaved off by processing protease(s). Most of these gene(s) contain no intron.

But, one gene from *Lemna* has been found to contain an 84 by intron with certain features of a *transposable element*. Possibly, the intron is mot an ancestral feature of the *cab genes* and has got introduced into the gene later during evolution.

Recently, introducing cab genes have also been localised in *Petunia* and tomato. Their *encode* slightly divergent, type II, polypeptides which are also incorporated into the light-harvesting complex of PSII.

WATER-SPLITTING COMPLEX

At least five *polypeptides* have been found of be associated with the water-splitting complex of PSII. Genes for some of these proteins have been localised in the nucleus. Recently. cDNAs encoding the complete precursors for 33, 23, 16 and 10 KDa proteins have been sequenced and found to encode 331, 267, 232 and 140 amino acids which contain aminoterminal transit sequences of 84, 81, 83 and 41 amino acids, respectively.

Of the four polypeptides, three (33, 23, 16 kDa) are located inside the thylakoid lumen ; hydropathy plots show their hydrophilic nature. Nonetheless, the transit peptides do knot show any similarity with those of others at the primary amino acid sequence level.

However, they do share among themselves and with the transit peptide of plastocyanin—which is also located towards the thylakoid lumen—a unique hydrophobic domain, just before the final processing site, and a region which can form an amphipathic β-sheet and possibly includes the site for primary processing.

Secondary structure predictions for the 10 kDa protein suggest one transmembrane segment with the N-terminus in the thylakoid lumen and a 17 amino acid C-terminal segment outside. The transit sequence -does not show similarity at the primary sequence level with those of the three extrinsic, luminal proteins of PSII.

Cytochrome b-f Complex

This is the simplest of the supra-molecular complexes associated with; photosynthesis and consists of at least four components which are involved in electron flow from PSII to PSI and in cyolic-photophosphorylation. Polypeptides for three of its components, viz. cyt f, cyt b6 and subunit IV are encoded by the genes pet A, petB and petD, respectively, located in the large single copy region.

Gene petA, for cytochrome f has been shown to code for a pre-apoprotein of 320 amino acids in several species except for *Oenothera* where the pre-apoprotein is smaller by two amino acids. Comparison of the deduced amino acid sequence with that of the N-terminal sequence of the mature protein has revealed the presence of an N-terminal presequence of 35 amino acids, which gets cleaved off, possibly during transport of the protein across the thylakoid membranes.

A topological model for the arrangement of this polypeptide has been proposed on the basis of hydropathy analysis and partial proteolytic cleavage data: it appears that there is only a single span of alpha helix traversing the membrane and the bulk of the amino-terminus polypeptide lies in the intrathylakoid space.

Cytochrome b6 and subunit IV are encoded by two closely placed genes, petB and petD. Recently, Northern blot, reverse transcription, and St nuclease analysis have shown that both petB and petD contain introns (of 753 and 742 bp, respectively) and produce polypeptides of 215 and 160 amino acids, the smaller exons code only two and three residues of the amino terminus.

Earlier, cytochrome b6 and subunit IV polypeptides have been shown to have homology with the amino and -carboxy-terminal ends of mitochondrial cytochrome b, respectively. They have several histidine residues which have been implicated in haem binding.

The hydropathy plots show five and three membrane spanning regions for cyt b6 and subunit IV, respectively. The Rieske-FeS protein has been found to be encoded in the nucleus and a cDNA has been sequenced recently which encodes a complete precursor polypeptide of 247 amino acids, including also a putative N-terminal transit sequence of 68 amino acids.

Comparison of the deduced sequence of the mature polypeptide with sequences of the Rieske-FeS proteins of the respiratory electron transport chains of bacterial and mitochondrial origins shows remarkable similarities in secondary structure and the region involved in binding of the Fe_2S_2-cluster.

The transit sequence shows some similarity to that of 10 kDa polypeptide of the water-splitting system and delta subunit of ATP synthase complex.

Photosystem I

The core complex of PSI is constituted of at least eight polypeptides. So far, genes for only three of these have been characterised and these are located on the chloroplast genome : four others are located in the nucleus and the location of the remaining one is still unknown.

Of the three genes located on chloroplasts two psaA and psaB encoding 750 and 734 amino acid polypeptides (and which are substantially homologous) are located in the large single-copy region of the chloroplast genome.

These genes possibly arose by duplication. Their products constitute the photosystem I reaction centre and hydropathy analysis shows several regions which may traverse the membrane. More recently, a third gene psaC, encoding a 9 kDa polypeptide, has been identified in the small single-copy region of the tobacco plastome.

The polypeptide possibly functions as the apoprotein for the ironsulphur centres A and B and shows three regions, rich in cysteine residues, with a potential of traversing the membrane. The light-harvesting complex of photosystem I contains several polypeptides of 22-25 kDa.

Recently, one cDNA and one genomic clone (representing however another gene of the family) have been obtained from tomato these genes have been located on chromosome 5 at a distance of about 7 kbp.

The gene represented in the genomic clone contains three small introns of 107.87 and 89 nucleotides and the encoded poly-peptide has 246 amino acid residues. There is more than 55% divergence in the gene for PSI with members of PSII from. tomato.

Proteins Associated with Electron Transport

Plastocyanin, a soluble type I copper protein, is a component of the photosynthetic apparatus that transfers electrons from cyt b/f complex to PSI and is located towards the luminal face of the thylakoid membranes. Recently, cDNA and genomic clones for this have been isolated and characterised in *spinach* and *Stlene*. The gene, petE, encodes a precursor of 168 amino acids with a transit peptide of 69 residues.

The mature polypeptide is hydrophilic. The transit peptide shows structural similarity with corresponding regions of those members of the watersplitting complex which are located on 'the luminal face as discussed earlier.

Available data show that the protein derives from a single copy gene which does not contain any intron. Two other proteins associated with photosynthetic electron transport are ferredoxin-NADP+-oxido-reductase (FNR) and the stromal protein, ferredoxin. Genes for these are located in the nucleus and cDNAs, encoding complete precursor proteins, have been sequenced.

The ferredoxin cDNA encodes a polypeptide of 146 amino acids comprising 48 amino acids of the transit peptide whereas the eDNA for FNR encodes a Polypeptide comprising 55 amino acids of the transit peptide and 314 amino acids of the mature protein.

ATP-Synthase

The ATP-generating supra-molecular complex, ATP

synthase, is made up of nine subunits, of which four are part of the membrane-bound sub-complex CFo and five of the extrinsic sub-complex CFI. Subunits **a, A** and E of CFl and I, III, and IV, of CFo are encoded by the genes atpA (507 codons), atpB (498 codons), atpE (134 codons), atpF (184 codons), atpII (81 codonsT, and atpl (247 codons), respectively, which are located in two clusters (atpB, E ; atpl, H, F, A) about 40 kbp away in the large single-copy region of the plastome (63, 64 and references cited therein).

The atpF has been found to be split by a single intron in wheat spinach tobacco and pea. A comparison of the sequence of the actual protein product of atpF with that deduced from the gene sequence reveals that a 17 amino acid peptide from the N-terminal end gets cleaved off before integration.

The genes, atpB and atpE, overlap by 4 by in several species though not in pea. The genes for two subunits γ and δ of CFI and subunit II of CFo are designated as atpC, atpD and atpG, respectively, sand these have been found to be located in the nucleus.

A cDNA encoding the complete precursor (257 amino acids)· containing a 70-residue long transit peptide for the δ subunit, hal been sequenced recently. The transit peptide shows some similarity to that of the Rieske-FeS protein, but differs from those of the luminal proteins. A remarkable feature of the amino acid sequences deduced from those genes is the high degree of conservation not only among different plant species, but also with corresponding genes from bacterial sources.

Nuclear-Plastid Genetic Complementation

The presence of different genomes in a plant cell raises the question: where is the information for biosynthesis of structural and functional chloroplast-specific proteins encoded?

What are the contributions of plastid and nuclear genomes to chloroplast biogenesis and to realization of diverse pbotosynthetic reactions? It is clear that chloroplast

DNA is of utmost importance for plastid self-organization, replication, and genetic continuity.

This is well illustrated by Schiff's experiments on the elimination of *Euglena gracills* chloroplast DNA by streptomycin treatment. This antibiotic specifically blocks cbloroplast DNA replication and damages the normal cycle of algal development.

As a result of cell multiplication, in subsequent generations the strains formed are devoid of chloroplasts and plastid DNA.

Some *Euglena* forms, such as the mutant W_3, *bul* **co**mpletely lose their greening capability and are converted from phytoflagellates to zoofagellates. This experiment confirms that plastid DNA is essential as a master molecule for chloroplast formation and development.

Plastid genome mutations cause different kinds of hereditary abnormalities in chloroplast structure and function. Phenotypically, plastome mutants are manifested by the appearance of variegated chimeras with sectorial and periclinal localization of green tissues.

Unlike virus mosaic, which causes the boundaries between pale and pigmented parts of a leaf to be smeared, the plastome variegation is characterized by a regular distribution of pale and green sectors or by white edging of the dull green center of a leaf.

Such a picture of variegation is caused by a sorting out of normal and mutated plastids in the process of cell mitosis and tissue different-iation. "*Mixed*" heteroplastid cells with normal and mutated chloroplasts are found at the boundaries of green and white parts of variegated leaves. Plastome mutants are extremely interesting for evaluation of the amount of information and for mapping the chloroplast genome.

In nature they appear spontaneously with a low frequency of 0.02—0.06%. Plastome mutations can be induced, by different physico-chemical mutagens. Considerable progress in the investigation of genetic control of chloroplast biogenesis has been made with the model object *Chlamydomonas reinhardi.*

Levine and Goodenough Sager and Kvitko *et al* have induced a wide spectrum of mutations in *C. reinhardi* affecting chloroplast properties. Unlike higher plants in which the mutation blocking plastid function is lethal in *C. reinhardi* the cells with. inactive chloroplasts can be kept viable by growing the culture in heterotrophic conditions.

Genetic analysis of acetate-requiring, antibiotic resistant *C. reinhardi* mutants led Sager and Rammanis to the discovery of *cytoplasmic* gene recombination and segregation. They have concluded that in haploid vegetative cells of *C. reinhardi* the plastome is represented by a "*diploid*" system.

Studying the recombination frequency and cytoplasmic gene segregation in repeatedly marked *C. reinhardi* clones. Sager tried to define the linkage group of genophores associated with chloroplasts. This made it possible to start cytoplas mic gene mapping.

It turned out that the sequence of linkage groups in cytoplasmic genes represents a ring, which is in agreement with the circular configuration of the chloroplast DNA.

Analyzing the sequence of Mendelian genes affecting chloroplast properties in *C. reinhardi,* Levine and Good enough suggested that 8 from 16 linkage groups of genes are localized in chloroplast genoph-ores. However, the cytological data of McVittie and Davies do not support this point of view.

These anchors found 16 chromosomes in the metaphase and related them to 16 linkage groups of nuclear genes. According to Kvitko 16 from 18 linkage groups of genes are localized in the nucleus, 2 in cellular organelles, with one of these two being inherited uniparentally.

It is very probable that in meiotic division of *C. reinhardi* cells the transmission function is ful-filled not by all genophores but by single molecules. It should be noted that the task of mapping chloroplast genophores is very complex.

Efforts will be required to elucidate quantitative localization and identification of plastogene properties and functions. At present attempts are being made for restriction analysis std mapping of chloroplast DNA fragments.

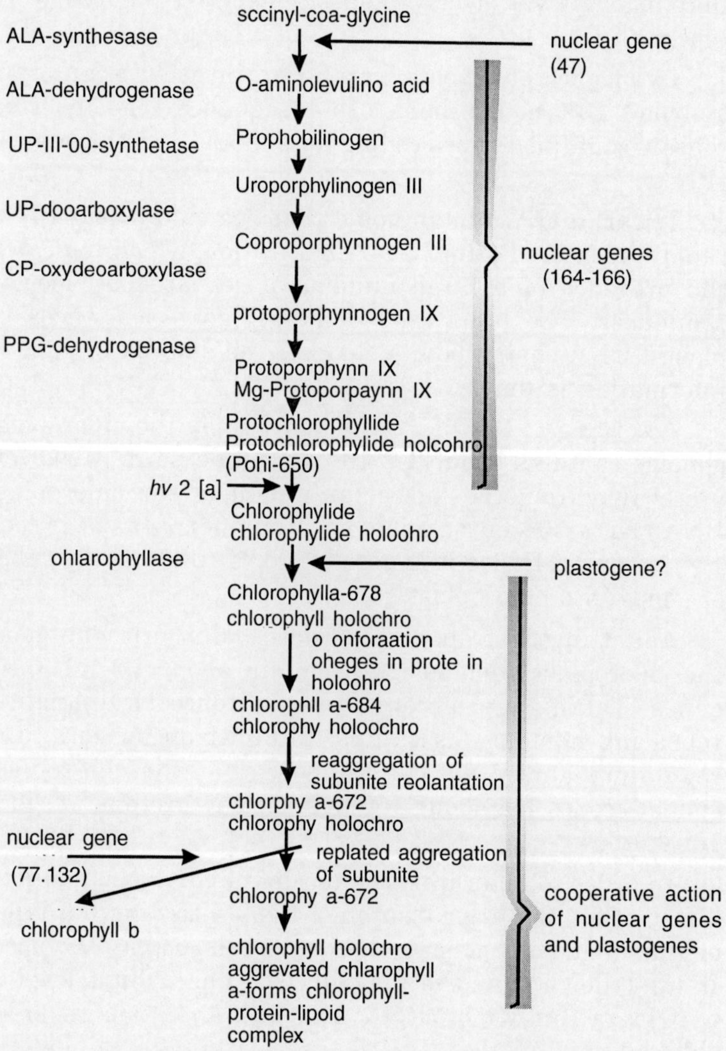

Figure 11.2: Scheme of genetic regulation of chlorophyll biosynthesis and the initial stages of formation of its native forms.

Using ends-nuclease-restrictase, Bedbrosk and Bsgsrad succeeded in splitting a circular DNA molecule of 85×10^6 daltons isolated from *Zea mays* chloroplasts. The analysis of DNA fragments by transcription of RNA copies showed that nearly 15% of chloroplast gensme sequences were repeated.

Two copies of repeats were in an inverted orientation and had 10% of non-homologous sequence. The inverted repeats contained genes coding for 23S and 16S chloroplast rRNAs.

Tewari and Wildman noted that pea chloroplast DNA-rapidly reentered after heat denaturation, which indicated the presence of a large number of repeated nucleotide sequences. The high level of homologous sequences in plastid DNA chains points out that the amount of genetic information is limited.

According to Smillie, Scott and Bishop the chloroplast genome contains about 2×10^7 nucleotide pairs. However, proceeding from the molecular weight of the chloroplast DNA ($1\text{-}2 \times 10^8$ dalton), the base content must not exceed 1×10^6 pairs. Hence it is possible to calculate the number of genes in a chloroplast genome.

Admitting that about 1500 dase pairs form one gene, the chloroplast genome must contain about $1.3\text{-}1.5 \times 10^3$ genes. Taking into account the existence of frequently repeating homologous chains, intercistron spacers, and regulatory genes, we can suppose that the chloroplast genome codes for about 150-300 specific proteins of 50×10^3 daltons.

In order to determine the nature of chlsroplast genetic information, the hybridization of DNA with different types of plastid and cytoplasmic RNA has been successfully used. It was shown that the plastid DNA has a high level of hybridization with rRNA and tRNA extracted from chloroplasts.

In the chloroplast gensme, 30-40 cistrons were identified for each 23S and 16S rRNA. Probably each copy of the plastid DNA contains one gene for the 23S rRNA and one for the 16S rRNA. As for tRNA specific for different amino acids, they are coded for by different genophores.

Cistrons of rRNA and tRNA make up about 4% of chloroplast DNA. The transcription of mRNA onto chloroplast DNA was studied using ^{24}C and ^{3}H uridine. It was shown that the formation of chloroplast mRNA is light induced.

In our laboratory we have extracted a light-induced fraction of chloroplast RNA (cRNA) with 9-11 S which upon incubation with ribosomes in vitro makes a "*working*" polysome. In the presence of the specific inhibitor *rifampicin*, the light-induced synthesis of all three types of RNA was repressed.

It should be pointed out that not all the components of the PSS of chloroplasts are "*products*" of their own genes. Schweiger and co-workers transplanted the nucleus from *Acetabularia mediterranea* into an enucleated *A. cliftonii* cell, and showed that hybrid progeny was similar to donor species by the composition of chloroplast ribosomal proteins.

Nuclear control of the formation of some specific chloroplast ribosomal proteins was demonstrated by Bogored *et al.* in *C. reinhardi* mutants. In higher plants (hybrids of *Nicotiana*), Wildman *et al.* found that 50S subunits of chloroplast ribosomal proteins were not inherited by maternal line.

On this basis the authors concluded that the information on the composition of chloroplast ribosomal proteins resides in the nuclear genome. Chloroplast aminoacyl-tRNA-synthetases are also coded for by the nuclear genome, translated on cytoplasmic ribosomes and then compartmentalized within the chloroplasts.

All these data are evidence that the formation of the PSS of chloroplasts is controlled by complementary cooperation of nuclear and plastid genes. The two genetic systems closely interact in the processes of chloroplast biogenesis, i.e. in the formation of lamellar proteins, chlorophyll biosynthesis, photosystems, and synthesis of Calvin cycle enzymes.

Electrophoretic separation of chloroplast membrane polypeptides by SDS acrylamide gel electrophoresis enabled one to identify more than 40 protein bands In thylakoids. A substantial part of these lamellar proteins is coded for by the nuclear genome, as shown in recent experiments by Bingham and Schiff with light-grown *E. gracilis* wild type cells (possessing normal chloroplasts) and dark-grown cells with proplastids and the mutant W_3 *bul* devoid of detect table plastid DNA.

In greening cells, five new polypeptide bands were formed in the light. The authors suggested that they were products of plastid DNA genes. Vasconcelos has noted the appearance of nine labeled polype-ptides of the thylakoid membranes in isolated *Euglena* chloroplasts.

Despite the fact that the number of plastid lamellar proteins is not large, they play an essential role in membr-ane proliferation, aggreg-ation, and packing of the pigments in thylakoids. It is well known that chlorophyll biosynthesis is controlled mainly by the nuclear genome. Experimental mutagenesis and induction of the so-called chlorophyll mutations is widely used in investigations of genetic control systems of chloroplast biogenesis.

A wide spectrum of mutations which block different stages of synthesis of chlorophyll, yellow pigments, photos-ynthetic ETC compon-ents, *Calvin cycle* enzymes, and low-molecular weight compounds (*amino acids*, *vitamins*, etc.) modifying *chloroplast morphogenesis*, was induced by means of physical and chemical agents (X and γ rays, *protons*, α *particles*, *laser radiation*, *ethylme-thanesulfonate*, *nitrosoal-kylurea*, and *others*).

Phenotypic manifestation of chlorophyll mutants depe-nds. on the mutation nature, whether this is gene or chromosome aberration. It is possible to observe forms from completely bleached up to dark green which differ also in their viability. If the mutation blocks the formation of ETC components or key enzymes of CO_2 assimilation, then the mutants are incapable of autotropic life and they are lethal.

Another group of mutations affects only the pigment system of chloroplasts, so their cycle of photosynthetic reactions is not damaged. This group is used for genetic mapping of biosynthesis of chlorophyll and formation of its native forms.

According to Walles' classification nuclear-induced plastome - mutants are subdivided into three groups : (*a*) mutants of one colour-white, yellow, pale green ; (*b*) variegated plants of two or more *colours-alb xantha, xantha alba, alboviridis, viridoalbina, tigrina, maculata*, etc.; (*c*) mutants changing the leaf-colour during ontogenesis from pale green to a yellow or from white to green, which is connected with photobleaching or chlorophyll stabilization.

Gustafsson was the first to obtain a large collection of barley chlorophyll mutants. Later on, 240 nuclear genes from barley affecting plastid pigment biosynthesis were discribed. *Gottschalk* obtained 176 mutation types from pea with genetic blocks in *chlorophyll* and *carotenoid biosynthesis*.

Using *cytogenetic* analysis of pea mutants of *chlorina* type, Blixt identified 15 loci controlling the formation of plastid . pigments. Wettstein *et al.* induced 198 recessive lethal chloroplast mutations in barley. Genetic analysis revealed 86 nuclear genes controlling chloroplast development.

Five of them *(xantha—f*, g, h, l, u) were classed with structural genes controlling the conversion of uroporphyrinogen to protochlorophyllide; 3 genes (*tigrina* 12, *"infrared"* 5 and 6) were identified as regulatory ones. Among 33 *albina* mutants, allelism was found in only two cases.

Unlike structural genes, two regulatory genes exhibited a similar dominant effect in wild type and mutant alleles in heterozygotes. Using the model plant *A. thaliana*, we have found 60 nonallelic genes controlling chlorophyll biosynthesis and affecting chloroplast ultrastructnre and function. An essential problem in studying the biosynthesis of chlorophyll is the elucidation of regulatory mechanisms in the development of its native forms.

Accumulation of a definite amount of chlorophyll is not sufficient for normal functioning. of photosynthetic membranes. Specific structural organization of chlorophyll into pigmentprotein complexes (PPC) responsible for primary photochemical processes of light energy conversion in photosynthesis is required.

Even at the first hours of greening of etiolated seedlings when the total concentration of chlorophyll is far from being normal, its aggregated forms appear which differ in their spectral properties. The membrane lipoproteins carrying native chlorophyll forms also play an important role in the molecular organization of pigment systems.

Pigment aggregation and packing in photosynthetic membranes are determined by lamellar proteins, synthesis of which is under the dual nuclear and plastid control. Complementary cooperation of nuclear-plastid genetic systems ensures the development of *photosynth-etically* active membranes, formation of pigment-protein photosystem (PS) assembly, and ETC components.

Mutation of both nuclear and plastid genes causes, defects in PS I and PS II. Heber and Gottschalk have described a mutant of *Vicia faba* with a block in PS I. Chloroplasts of this nuclear mutant are incapable of NADP photoreduction. Bishop induced a mutation in *Scenedesmus obliquus* with a block in the synthesis of eytochrome *f-552,* which caused a suppression of cyclic photophosphorylation.

A defect in PS II caused by mutation of one nuclear gene was found by Voskresenskaya, Drozdova and Gostimskii in the pea lethal mutant. Yakubova *et al.* discovered a block in the formation of ETC components between PS I and PS II in the cotton nuclear mutant.

On the other hand, the mutation of chloroplast DNA also causes defects of photosynthetic ETC. Investigating photochemical activity of chloroplasts from *Oenothera* plastome mutants, Fork and Heber and Hallier found that some mutants had defects in PS I and others in PS II. Hagemann *el al.* studied chloroplast photochemical reactions in two plastome mutants with damaged photosynthesis.

It turned out that in *Antirrhinum majus eniviridis* the mutation of chloroplast DNA caused a defect in PS II. As a result, they lost ability for the reaction. PS I in this mutant was normal; it did not differ from the wild type by the character of light-induced ESR signals in leaves indicating the normal state of P 700.

On the contrary, a damage of PS I and normal functioning of PS II were observed in the mutants '*Mrs. Pollock*' of *P. zonale*. This defect correlates with the loss of specific proteins of PPC I. Dissection of genetic systems controlling chloroplast biosynthesis requires a combination of methods of mutational analysis with investigations using specific inhibitors of cell organelle transcription and translation.

Regulation of Expression

In this section, we shall briefly touch upon the regulatory aspects of expression of genes for the photosynthetic membranes. As mentioned earlier, these genes are located both in the chloroplast and nucleus-demanding a tight, coordinated, expression which is also evident from the *incompatibility* of *nuclear* and *plastid genomes* in certain intersp-ecific hybrids as studied in detail in the genus *Oenothera*.

Although the molecular basis of various malfunctions (e.g. yellowing of hybrids) is still unknown, it is possible that these may arise either from altered signals, and thus breakdown of communication between *chloroplasts* and nuclei, or the failure to reassemble functional *photosynthetic* complexes due to improper *juxtaposition*.

Quite apart from the problem of nuclear-organelle interaction expression of the various genes is also affected by developmental and *environmental stimulis particularly* light. A proper understanding of various control mechani-

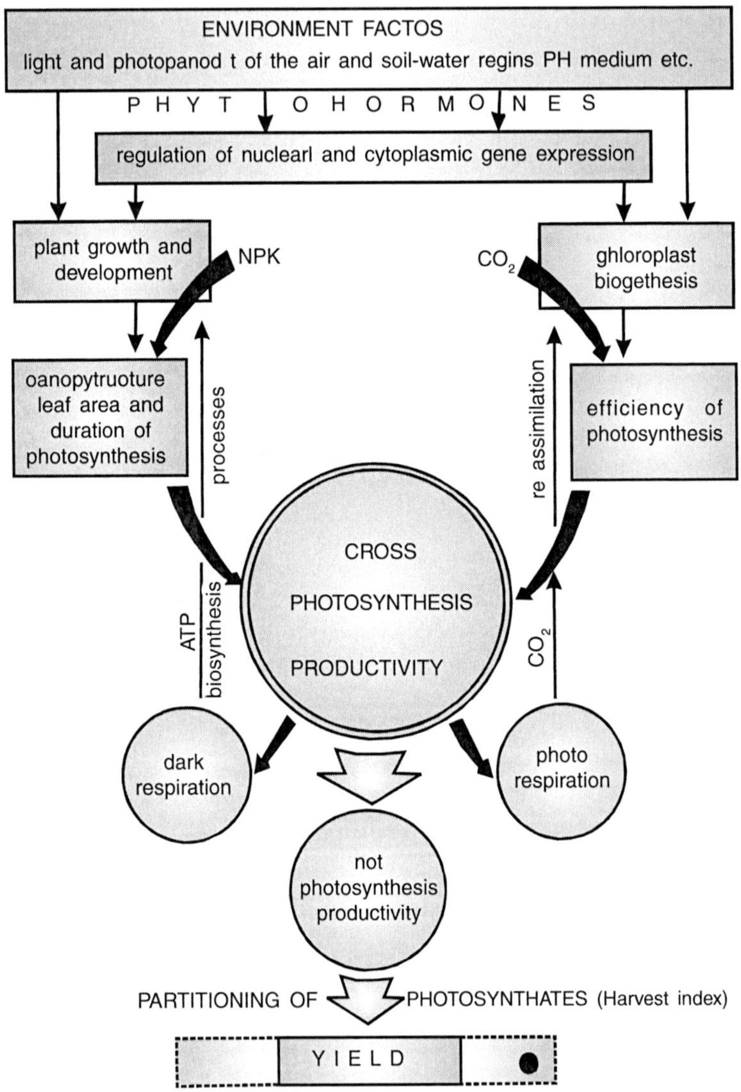

Figure 11.3: Scheme of phenotypic expression of plant productivity processes.

sms has not developed yet, although some insight has been gained by certain recent *investigations* as summarised below.

Regulation of Genes of Chloroplast DNA

One extremely important finding is that the cpDNA often codes for a large primary transcript having information for more than one gene which is then processed to smaller units. Such organisation of information is similar to that of operons in bacteria and is reflective of the prokaryotes ancestry of the chloroplast.

Structurally also upstream regulatory sequences of chloroplast genes resemble those from prokaryotes in having the 10 and the-35 canonical sequences. At the 3'-end, the precise location of the processing region (i.e., where termination of mRNA may occur) is not clear although several sequences in the non-conding 3' region show the capacity to form stem and loop structures as in *prokaryotes*.

No *polyadenylation* of transcripts takes place in *chloroplasts*. One reason for the very limited understanding of *mechanisms* of regulation of expression of chloroplast genes is the non availability of *chloroplast* transformation methods.

However, as an alternative, *in vitro transcription* systems have recently been developed for chloroplasts and are being employed to transcribe plastid genes and hopefully rapid progress will be made in the near future. We have remarked above that light strongly influences plastid development through stimulation of synthesis of certain proteins. This provides a special opportunity to investigate the control mechanism of gene expression.

Recent studies have shown, however, that mRNA for most of the chloroplastencoded genes are already present in the dark. Their levels are increased by light, but this increase is rather marginal and much less than of the several proteins which rapidly accumulate in light.

By run-on transcription assay, it has been demonstrated that light does not affect relative transcription activities of different plastid genes. Thus, light seems to exercise its effect mediated not so much at the transcriptional but at the post-transcriptional or translational levels.

The best opportunity for a study of events associated with the processing of the primary polycistronic transcripts is provided by the psaA: psaB, psbD: psbC, psbB: psbH: petB petD and atpl: atpH: atpF: atpA operons.

An understanding of such control is important since of the multiple polypeptides encoded by a single transcript (4 in case of psbB operon), one or more may accumulate even in the dark and others may need light.

An intensive investigation into the processing of the transcript of the psbB operon (containing also the psbH, petB and petD genes) has shown a highly complex mechanism.

Here, surprisingly, the processing takes, place even in the dark, indicating that further controls, including those mediated by light, must operate at the post-transcriptional, translational or post-translational levels. However, we know very little about such controls and unravelling them is a task for the future.

Regulation of Nuclear Genes

As mentioned earlier, genomic clones for only three polypeptides, viz. chlorophyll a/b binding polypeptides of PSI and. PS II and plastocyanin, have been characterised so far and they contain the typical eukaryotic expression signals in the5'-upstream and 3'-untranslated, downstream, regions.

Involvement of light in regulation of nuclear-encoded genes becameapparent with the studies of Apel and Kloppstech. Sub. sequently, with the availability of specific gene probes, it was found that both quantity as well as quality of light greatly influence the transcript levels for cab genes, also various. members of the gene family are expressed differentially in various organs and cells.

In an effort to identify the elements involved in such regulation, various 5'-upstream regions of the cab gene have been. tested by transforming a heterologous system with engineered genes in which either deletions have been made in the 5'-upstream region or various parts of this region have been fused to a marker gene containing its own constitutive type of promoter.

Simpson *et. al.* reported that in pea a 400 by fragment from the cab gene is responsible for light-regulated and organspecific expression as is evident from experiments involving fusion between this fragment and a modified bacterial kanamycin resistance gene-both engineered into a Ti plasmid; and subsequently employed for transformation of tobacco.

Out of this, a 247 by (-100 to -347 by upstream) stretch acts not only as a light-regulated enhancer element but also as tissuespecific silencer. Lamppa *et. al.* have reported that a wheat cab gone maintains its light-regulated characteristics even after transfer to the more distantly related tobacco and *Petunia* indicating that the controlling elements are ubiquitous in flowering plants.

A 5'-upstream region of this gene from +31 to -1816 by has been shown to confer light-regulated and organ-specific expression also on a bacterial chloramphenicol resistance gene. Expression of this gene is in fact, affected reversibly by red/ far-red light implying a role of phytocbrome in the regulation of its expression.

Further experiments have shown that only a 268 by fragments from -89 to -357 by in the 5'-upstream region, which acts as an enhancer, is sufficient to confer the typical regulatory characteristics.

The work mentioned above has set the stage for more detailed investigations on the mechanism of action of the enhancer elements. Such sequences from the rbcS gene have already been used to identify, by gelretardation and foot-printing methods, possible trans-acting factor(s) responsible for light-regulation as also organ-specific expression of the genes.

It is hoped that similar work with the cab gene in the

near future will further elucidate the pathway and mechanism of transfer of a stimulus to a gene. As in the case of cab and rbcS genes, mRNA levels of many other nuclear-encoded genes are greatly increased by illumination. However, the quantity by which mRNA levels increase is often greater than that of the increase in level of proteins for several components of the photosynthetic apparatus-e.g., mRNAs of the delta subunit of ATP synthase, the Rieske iron sulphur protein of the cytochrome b/f complex, and the 33, 23, and 16 kDa polypeptides of the water-splitting system.

This indicates again that there must exist novel post transcriptional control mechanisms for further regulation.. Such controls may lie at the translational level or even at the level of transport of precursor proteins into the chloroplast. (the latter may in turn depend on the availability of receptors) for final localisation in the supramolecular complexes. All, these putative mechanisms of control remain to be elucidated.

PHYSIOLOGICAL AND GENETIC BASIS OF IMPROVING PHOTOSYNTHETIC PRODUCTIVITY

Analysis of advances in modern agriculture when technical of husbandry has reached a high level shows that In increase in the productivity of the main crops has a tender to stabilization. Further elaboration of agricultural technology and considerable increase in mineral nutrition dosage does not cause corresponding yield enhance-ment.

Does it mean that all the productivity potential of modern plantgrowth has been exhausted and maximum yield for some crops achieved? Basic physiological and genetic investigations of plant productivity show that the yield potential is rather high and not yet fully exploited.

A rich gene pool in crop plants has not been fully utilized for the purposeful and efficient. enhancement of those processes which at present limit crop productivity.

Among the yield-limiting factors, we should mention first of all photosynthesis, the efficiency of which is extremely low.

Efficiency of solar energy utilization for many crops does not exceed 1%. Moreover, cultivated varieties of such, plants as s heat, cotton, and others have lower rates of photosynthesis that their initial wild types.

However, high productivitry of crops has been provided by leaf area increase, changes in the ratio of the biomass of reproductive organs to of vegetative ones, and by other morphophysiological prop properties. It is quite evident that plant breeding research has not not bee aimed at improvement of the photosynthetic apparatus.

Mass selective screening has been conducted according to the morphological properties and traits, of agronomic value with much attention being given to increasing the size of sink and Storage organs-the number and size of ears, bolls, tubers, etc.

Enhancement of the plant sink and storage capacity resulted in an increase of the agronomic yield as long as the photosynthetic potential permitted. At present an imbalance can be observed between the desirable number and the size of economically valuable plant organs and the possibility of providing them with the products of photosynthesis in the newly obtained promising varieties and hybrids.

This imbalance between the accumulation and partition of assimilates leads to puniness and immaturity of seeds, falling of ovaries and bolls, decrease of sugar content, and other disorders.

Besides, an excessive increase in the sink power can provoke, by the negative feedback mechanism, a decrease in the activity of the photosynthetic apparatus due to the withdrawal of nitrogen from leaves into other organs thereby causing their premature senescence. From the above we can conclude that low photosynthetic efficiency became a "bottleneck" for productivity enhancement.

Development of methods for photosynthesis regulation

and the increased efficiency in utilization of solar energy up to 3-5% are the most important means of obtaining high agri-cultural yield.

The world's experience in obtaining highly productive varieties and high yield on the basis of modern agricultural technology shows that the possibilities of crop yield enhancement by the best utilization of water, fertilizers, light energy, and other factors are related to the optimization of canopy structure and improvement of the photosynthetic apparatus on physiological and genetic bases.

It is calculated that an increase of photosynthetic utilization of photosynthetically give radiation (PAR) Up to 3-5% will permit the following crop yields : maize-15 tons of grain, winter wheat10 tons of grain, seed cotton-8 tons per hectare.

The relationship between photosynthesis and crop yield is very complex. In the literature there are contradictory data on the correlation between photosynthetic rate and crop yield.

The absence of a direct relation between them is probably explained by the dependence of crop yield on the net assimilation value which in turn is determined not only by photosynthetic rate but also by leaf surface, size, duration of vegetable period, canopy structure, dark and light respiration, translocation, and partitioning of assimilates. Figure elsewhere in this chapter represents an integral scheme of phenotypic expression of nuclear and cytoplasmic gene action in formation of the factors of photosynthetic productivity and crop yield.

It is seen from this scheme that crop yield is the result of complex diverse processes and reactions occuring at ontogenesis under the influence of external conditions. Thus, three ways to increase the productivity follow from those conceptions:

1. optimization of the canopy structure as all optical system;
2. improvement of efficiency of the photosynthesis

process itself; and

3. rational partition and usage of assimilates for formation of the agronomic yield (harvest index).

The first way, based on the morphophysiological and agroeco-logical data, is widely used in agronomy. The theory of this problem and the principle of canopy structure optimization with favorable leaf area index (LAI) allowing improvement of radiation and aerodynamic conditions for different crops were developed in detail by Nichiporovich and other investigators.

The second and the third ways to increase photosynthetic product-ivity concern the genetic balance of plant source and sink abilities. According to Evans, it is important to know when source or sink limit the crop yield.

In cereals, for example; grain filling is largely dependent on photosynthesis and environmental conditions after flowering, whereas the capacity for storage is determined by conditions before flowering. Nalborczyk and Gej showed that in different varieties of spring wheat the photosynthetic productivity during milk and mall maturity played an important role in obtaining high economic yield.

A remarkable peculiarity of the intensive varieties was a coincidence of net assimilation rate (NAR) maximum with that of LAI. The interrelation between source and sink has a pronounced feedback effect. For example, removal of the wheat ear or the cotton boll causes a considerable depression of photosynthesis.

On the contrary, increasing sink capacity can enhance to a certain extent the rate of photosynthesis. In.. experiments by Thorne and Evans grafting of spinach to sugar beet led to an increase in assimilating ability of the graft.

Analyzing the numerous data on the correlation between source and sink capacity, it should be noted that the one-sided approach to these processes does not give positive results.

For example, CO_2 feeding usually results in considerable

alteration of ehloroplast ultrastructure due to an excessive storage of starch. At the same time, a great attractive power can lead to chloroplast "wear" and pressure leaf senescence. Selection of plants on a physiological and genetic basis will make it possible to get varieties and hybrids with a balanced ratio between source and sink that will provide the maximum expression of yield· potential for each plant.

Analysis and Mobilization of the Germplasm

Evaluation of the diversity of photosynthetic functions and identification of the parameters of photosynthetic efficiency allow practicing breeders to manipulate the genotype for significant improvement of plant productivity.

Ecological and geographical populations of plant species have a large-geneticvariability of chloroplast photochemical and enzymic activity which provides their different photosy-nthetic ability. The genotypic determination of chloroplast structure and function is clearly manifested in photosynth-etic pathways of C_3 and C_4 plants.

The plants with Kranz anatomy of the leaf (maize, sorghum, sugar cane, etc) are known to possess an addition-al pathway of CO_2 fixation with the participation of phosph-oenolpyruvate (PEP) and the formation of C_4 dicarboxylic acids. Hatch and slack earlier proposed that the C_4 pathw-ays are an autocatalytic cycle of CO_2 assimilation through transcarboxylation of C_4 acids.

Later it became obvious that the C_4 pathway is an auxiliary channel of primary CO_2 fixation on the Calvin cycle. In all higher plants, irrespective of the type of primary fixation, CO_2 reduction to carbohydrates occurs in the pentosepbosphate cycle.

However, C_4 plants have the advantage of high resista-nce to extreme temperature and more efficient use of water, thus adapting better to arid climates. Besides, C_4 plants are characterized by a CO_2 compensation· point close to zero, the photosynthetic rate being independent of the concentration of oxygen since they practically do not have photo-respiration.

All this, together with high light requirement, provides a very high photosynthetic capacity which is about twice; as great as that of C_4 plants.

The highest rate of photosynthesis (85 mg CO_2 dm^{-3} hr^{-1}) is, observed in maize in natural conditions. Photosynthesis in C_4 plants in natural conditions is not light saturated. The moat important Lure of C, plants is the presence in their leaves of two types of chloroplasts which dyer by their ultrastructare and functions.

In palisade mesophyll cells the chloroplasts have a pronounced granal structure, while inn parenchyma bundle-sheath cells they are usually paucigranal. These chloroplasts differ greatly in their photochemical properties: PS II is active in mesophyll cells while PS I is active in bundle-sheath chloroplasts.

The key enzyme of the Calvin, cycle, RuDP carboxylase, is absent in mesophyll cells, According to Hatch, the primary CO_2 fixation in C_4 plants occurs by PEP carboxylation which leads to the formation of oxaloacetic acid (OAA).

The process proceeds in the cytoplasm since PEP-carboxylase is a purely cytoplasmic enzyme. Inn chloroplasts OAA is transformed into malate and aspartate.

Further, depending on species, malate or aspartame are traris ported to the bundle-sheath cells where due to decarboxylation of the acids CO_2 is released and refixed in the Calvin cycle. Cooperation of two types of plastids in C_4 plants leads to a concentration of CO_2 in the bundle-sheath cells where it decreases to a certain extent the limitation of photosynthesis by the diffusive CO_2 resistance and thus aids in increasing the efficiency of the process.

On the other hand, all this prevents the CO_2 burst due to photorespiration. Probably the primary function of the C_4 pathway is the reassimilation of CO_2 as a result of this wasteful process. How can the dimorphism of chloroplasts in C_4 plants be explained from the genetic point of view?

Is this a result of sorting out the genetically nonhomogeneous plastids originated from the parental pair, or are they formed under the control of the nuclear genome during cell differentiation?

We believe that the second assumption is more correct. For example, maize belongs to the group with the maternal type of plastid + inheritance therefore it has homogenous initial plastid material. In the process of differentiation of the cells and tissues under nuclear control, mesophyll control are spedlalizcd for the C_4 pathway.

This is Probably achieved by a repression of nuclear genes for the small subunit RuDF carboxylase which as mentioned above, plays a regulatory role in transcription of the chloroplast mRNA of the large subunit. It is quite possible that genes coding for the formation of ETC components of PS I (ferredoxin, NADP reductase, cytochrome b-563) are localized, namely on the small subunit chromosome.

As a result of this gene repression, the activity in PS I of mesophyll chloroplasts is three to four times lower than that of bundle-sheath cells. Thus the nucleus controls the division of labour between the chloroplasts of mesophyll and bundle sheath cells. However, this hypothesis requires further experimental confirmation.

The C_4 pathway is observed not only in tropical grasses, but it is also widespread among dicotyledons. Within one genus, C_3 and C_4 species and intermediate forms are encountered. It is possible by hybridization to impart to C_3 plants the C_3 pathway?

Bjorkman *et al.* successfully carried out the crossing and obtained a fertile hybrid between C_3 and C_4 *Atriplex* spp., but the efficiency of photosynthesis was lower than that of either parent in all F_1 and F_2 hybrids.

These experiments are currently being continued by Nobs but they have not yet led to desirable results. The C_4 pathway is connected with the leaf Kranz anatomy, and therefore it is impossible to impart properties of cooperative photosynthesis to C_3 plants.

However, we should not exclude the possibility of enhancement of the auxiliary CO_2 fixation through PEP carboxylase. As has already been mentioned, this enzyme operates in the cytoplasm and its formation is controlled by the nucleus. It has a higher affinity for HCO_3^- than for CO_2; therefore it can bind the hydrated CO_2 more efficiently and transfer it to the chloroplasts, thus decreasing the limitation of photosynthesis by carboxylation resistance.

The activity of PEP carboxylase in C_3 plants is 60 times lower than that in C_4 plants. Since the C_4 pathway originated in the course of evolution as a '*result*' of plant adaptation to and and hot climates, it might be assumed that the forms with high activity, of. PEP carboxylase can be obtained among C_3 plant mutants by genetic screen-ing in rigid condition.

An essential part of this assumption is that the cytoplasmic system of carboxylation and CO_2 transport to the chloroplast RuDP of C_4 plants should be provided with the mechanism of acceptor regeneration, i.e.. pyruvate conversion into PEP by pyruvate kinase.

Experimental mutagenesis is a powerful means of reconstructing the genome and breeding new promising forms which ado not occur in nature. Nuclear mutations produce considerable shifts in the structural and biochemical organization of -chloroplasts. As a result, -the overwhelming majority of viable mutants have a reduced *photosynthetic* capacity.

There are still a few mutants (1-2%) belonging to the "*plus*" class as measured by the increased photosynthetic efficiency. *Photosynthetically* positive mutants were obtained in *Chlorella,* pea and cotton. In research at our institute with γ radiation, 60 cotton mutants were obtained among which there was one promising *mutant-Duplex* with a compact type of branching, *high frequency* of double *sympodial bolls*, fast ripening, and high agronomic yield.

Its harvest index amounts to 50%, which points to rational partition and utilization of assimilates. The economic yield of this mutant is at the rate of 1 ton per hectare of seed cotton higher than that of the initial variety 108-F. Physiological and biochemical studies have shown that the mutant *Duplex* is characterized by a higher photochemical and enzymic chloroplast activity during the reproductive period.

In this mutant the endogenous delay of leaf senescence is observed, whereas in the initial variety, as well as in many other crops, a decrease in the specific activity of key *Calvin cycle* enzymes occurs on the 20th-30th day after the leaf expands, when there are no visible alterations of *chloroplast ultrastructure.*

Physiologic-genetic *prolongation* of the functionally active state of chloroplasts and prevention of premature leaf senescence are important factors in high photosynthetic productivity.

In the last few years the attention of many researchers has been attracted to the problem of photorespiration. According to the data obtained by Zelitch in C_3 plants (sunflower, soybean, sugar beet, etc), photosynthesis product losses upon photorespiration can reach 50% of the net assimilation.

Photorespiration is considered to be a waste of organic compounds which could be used in the productive process. This is evidenced by the data on photosynthetic efficiency of C_4 plants in which photo-respiration is practically absent.

This circumstance can serve as one of the arguments proving that photorespiration as a process of CO_2 release in the light has no great physiological importance. The main source of CO_2 release in the process of photorespiration is decarboxylation of intermediates of glyeolate metabolism.

The glycolate pathway is closely connected with. the Calvin cycle, particularly with oxygenation of RuDP resulting in the formation of the phosphoglycolic acid. It is generally accepted that the key enzyme of the Calvin cycle; RuDP carboxylase, plays a bifunctional role catalyzing. carboxylation and oxygenation reactions. Oxygen and CO_2

compete for the reaction substrate RuDP. In the enzyme oxygenase reaction, the sulphydryl groups take part; their total amount is 96, but the number of easily modified, "accessible" ones is 12.

It has been shown recently that the photore-spiration inhibitor glycidate irreversiblyinactivates oxygenation, the carboxylase activity of the enzyme not being affected, Apparently oxygenation-specific inhibition is connected with blocking of enzyme SH groups located in its active center.

In its native state the conformation of this aligomeric protein complex and its functional activity depend on conformation and dimensions of large and small subunits.

Analyzing the peptide composition of the enzyme in 60 tobacco species and 10 plants belonging to different phylogenetic groups-from blue-green algae to ginkgo—Kung has found that in all species studied the large subunit eontaifs only threw polypeptides, while the number of polypeptides in the small subunit varies from 1 to 4.

The latter may serve as a genetic marker in the investigations of nuclear cytoplasmic interaction. It may be assumed,; that depending on the polypeptideecomposition being coded for by the small subunit of the nucleus, the carboxylation or oxygenation activity of the enzyme may vary within plant species.

Indeed, varieties with low photorespiration have been found within populations of C_3 species. By means of genetic screening, Zelitch has distinguished tobacco population from the variety '*Havana Seed*' in which 25% of the progeny had low photorespiration.

It is essential to determine what methods can be used for mass screening for the desirable forms with low photorespiration. Growing the plants in a hermetic chamber at low CO_2 concentration prior to screening them for viability is one of the simplest methods of mass genetic screening for photorespiration.

However, this method has not been successful since plants in the closed chamber were not viable. In this relation the method of photorespiration estimation by CO_2, burst measurement after illumina-tion appears to be promising as do investigations of dependence of NAR on O_2 concentration fixation.

In conclusion it must be noted that estimation of photosynthetic efficiency, genetic screening of "plus" mutants, and the mobilization of the species germplasm for the improvement of plant productivity should be conducted, taking into account other physiological properties such as immunity and stress resistance.

In the near future, the possibility of genome mapping and genotype manipulation by means of somatic hybridization and gene engineering will allow practicing breeders to create new, synthetic plant varieties with. a desirable combination of the valuable traits, high photosynthetic efficiency and maximal expression of economic yield.

INDEX

A

B

C

D

P

Q

R

V

W

X

Y

Z